Understanding Catholic Christianity

Genuine recycled paper with 10% post-consumer waste. Printed with soy-based ink.

Nihil Obstat: Rev. William M. Becker, STD
Censor Librorum
1 July 1996

Imprimatur: †Most Rev. John G. Vlazny, DD
Bishop of Winona
1 July 1996

The nihil obstat and imprimatur are official declarations that a book or pamphlet is free of doctrinal or moral error. No implication is contained therein that those who have granted the nihil obstat or imprimatur agree with the contents, opinions, or statements expressed.

The publishing team included Michael Wilt, development editor; Shirley Kelter, Stephan Nagel, and Robert Smith, FSC, consulting editors; Peter C. Phan, consultant; Rebecca Fairbank, copy editor; Gary J. Boisvert, production editor, page designer, and typesetter; Maurine R. Twait, art director; Penny Koehler and Kent Linder, photo researchers; Michael O. McGrath, artist; and Alan M. Greenberg, Integrity Indexing, indexer.

The passage on the title page is from C. S. Lewis, *Mere Christianity,* anniversary edition (New York: Macmillan Publishing Company, 1981), pages 150–151, 191. Copyright © 1943, 1945, 1952 by Macmillan Publishing Company.

The acknowledgments continue on page 334.

Printed in the United States of America

Printing: 9 8 7 6 5 4 3 2

Year: 2005 04 03 02 01 00 99 98

ISBN 0-88489-372-3

Saint Mary's Press
Christian Brothers Publications
Winona, Minnesota

Understanding Catholic Christianity

If you want to get warm you must stand near the fire
if you want to be wet you must get into the water.
If you want joy, power, peace, eternal life,
you must get close to, or even into,
the thing that has them.

They are not a sort of prize which God could
if He chose, just hand out to anyone.
They are a great fountain of energy and beauty
spurting up at the very centre of reality. . . .

Look for Christ and you will find Him, and with Him
everything else thrown in.

Thomas Zanzig and Barbara Allaire

Contents

1

Identity and Development: Becoming Who You Are Called to Be

Unique in All the World

Fifteen years ago, about four and a half billion people lived on this global village we call earth. Men, women, boys, girls—four and a half billion human beings with dreams, fears, loves, hates, hang-ups, and hopes. Those billions of people do not include all the human beings who lived on this earth throughout human history and for the thousands of years before history was recorded.

More than fifteen years ago, two of those billions of people, each with her or his own special history, crossed paths on a particular day and at a particular place. Out of all the people in the world, they were drawn together. This man and this woman began a relationship and a history unique to them. Against the backdrop of their shared history, they celebrated their union of spirits by becoming one in body as well.

When that man and that woman joined in sexual intercourse, literally millions of possibilities were present. In one act of sexual intercourse, the man shared millions of sperm cells with the woman—any one of which might have united with one of her hundreds of eggs, or all of which might have died after a short time. Yet one of those sperm cells survived—one unique from all the others in its potential and its characteristics. That one sperm cell united with one of the woman's equally unique eggs, and the miracle of human creation began.

1

Have you been told about your origins—about how your parents met, the circumstances of your coming into the world, the day or night you were born? If you were adopted and do not know about your biological parents, have you been told about the day you came to live with your family? Write about any stories you have been told.

Nine months or so later, a new human being entered the world—a new human being that shared many of the characteristics of the billions who came before it. Yet this person was distinct, different, unique. Never before had the world seen anyone exactly like this human being. Never before had this special combination of genes and chromosomes, this combination of blood and bone, this wonderful potential of talent and gift, been born. Never again in the future of the world would that miracle be precisely repeated.

That indescribable mystery of some fourteen years ago, that nearly unimaginable wonder, that never-to-be-repeated moment, was the birth of someone very special—you.

The Journey of Your Life

Very possibly you have never thought of your own birth with a sense of drama or a sense of wonder and awe. Perhaps you have never reflected seriously on the miracle of birth as being only the beginning of an equally amazing story—the journey of your life. Since the moment when you burst into the world, you have continued the process of growth. And it has been a total process, during which not only your body has been changing but also your mind, your emotions, your attitudes, your values, and your relationships with others. You have continued, for example, the often difficult process of defining that relationship with your parents that began in your mother's womb. Included in this relationship is the conflict between wanting and needing protection and affection while, at the same time, kicking to be free of restrictions.

Each human being comes into the world distinct, different, unique. *Student art:* "Little Boy Blue," watercolor painting by David Christianson, Sacred Heart High School, Kingston, Massachusetts

Outside the family you have also been confronted through the years with new experiences, new challenges, new feelings. Many ideas you accepted unquestioningly before, you may now either reject or seriously challenge. Perhaps life has not been easy for you. And as you enter adulthood, life will not soon get easier. Yet like all the great journeys we learn of in history and literature, it is precisely the challenges, the dangers, and even the pain that make the journey of life such a grand adventure.

This Course and Your Journey

As you grow through adolescence, a significant part of your journey will be to look at the deeper meaning of life, to wrestle honestly with questions you probably never thought about or took for granted when you were younger.

Perhaps you were raised in a family that faithfully practiced Catholicism. You learned certain prayers and religious customs; you attended Mass with your family and made your first Communion. Maybe you went to a Catholic grade school or a parish religious education program, where you learned about the sacraments and beliefs of the church. You may not have had a lot of questions about religion because you just accepted what you were taught.

However, the understandings you had about God and your religion from childhood were likely quite limited—probably a mixed bag of some truth, some confused notions, some genuine understanding, and perhaps some humorous misunderstandings. Mixed-up religious ideas you might carry from childhood are not necessarily the fault of your parents or religious educators but simply the result of your

2
Find four photos of yourself, one taken recently and three from younger ages. For the "you" in each photo, describe in writing a memory you have (or have been told) that expresses what you were like at each age.

3
If you are Catholic and have celebrated your first Communion, try to locate a photo of yourself on that occasion. Recall what you felt on that day. Then write a paragraph comparing your attitude toward religion at the time of your first Communion with what you feel about it now.

4
Recall images of God or religious beliefs held by young children that now seem humorous to you. Draw upon your own childhood as well as that of other children you know. Briefly describe a couple of these humorous images in writing.

being too young then to understand the deeper issues of faith as adolescents and adults can.

Simple answers are all right for little kids, but they will not be accepted by teenagers, who need and deserve the chance to go deeper. Adolescence is the time in one's life journey when the old childhood notions of God and religion can be examined, and the questions and struggles about faith that never seemed to crop up in childhood can be wrestled with. If you have been brought up in the Catholic tradition, this course can serve that purpose for you, helping you gradually replace childhood knowledge with a more mature understanding of your faith.

Possibly you were baptized and raised Catholic, but you are at a point of uncertainty about this faith, and you question everything—the church's teachings and practices, or even the very existence of God. Know that your questions, offered in a spirit of openness and sincerity, are welcome in this course. A sincere search for truth, guided by God's grace, ultimately will lead to truth.

You may not have been raised Catholic, but because you are attending Catholic high school, you may be required to take this course. May this course be an opportunity for you to learn, in a mature and open way, about the faith tradition of the school you and your family have chosen for you. This course has been designed with awareness of, and respect for, other religious traditions. It is not the intent of this course to convert non-Catholic students to Catholicism, but to give everyone, Catholics and non-Catholics alike, the chance at least to understand what the Catholic heritage is all about.

A Question at the Heart of the Journey

A fundamental question related to the Catholic heritage you are about to study has to do with our very existence. Have you ever wondered, *"Why* am I here at all?" Why are you, in all your uniqueness, living on earth anyway? Let's look briefly at two distinct answers.

Just an Accident

One way to answer that question is to say, "Look, there's no mystery about it. I was just the product of a random series of events and co-incidences, including that this one particular sperm happened to get together with this one particular egg. So here I am. No big deal. It was sort of an accident that I happened at all."

Called into Being by God

The answer that life is merely an accident may not be very satisfying, but at one level, the purely physical level, it is correct. However, the Catholic Christian Tradition, which you will study in this course, offers a very different answer to the question of why you exist. It does not deny the physical explanation of things (how you got here), but it sees beyond that to a much deeper kind of why: *You were called into being by God.* You are not an accident (whether your parents planned to have you or not)! You have been in God's heart from all eternity, until God called you into existence some fifteen years ago when you were conceived in your mother's womb. God called you into existence out of love for you, and God longs for your love in return. You were created to live in union with God in this life and forever, even beyond death.

And that is the awesome, mysterious reason you are here.

5
In a one-page essay, answer this question: *Why are you taking this course, and how do you feel about it?*

[Handwritten:] I am taking this course because I have to. My school choose it for me.

6

What are the gifts and givens in your life? In a paragraph, summarize what has been given to you as part of your heritage or background.

Your "Gifts and Givens"

Yes, you were born with a unique set of chromosomes, which determines a lot about your body and even your intellect and emotions. And you were situated in a particular family, neighborhood, race, culture, religion, and economic class. You have certain talents and opportunities, as well as certain struggles and limitations, because of your background. These are the "gifts and givens" of your life—things you did not choose or do not have control over. They are the "raw materials" you have to work with, to become who God is calling you to be. Your **identity** is what you have become at any point in time as a result of choosing what to do with what you have been given. God created you knowing that you would have some special gifts to share with the world, something that no one else in all of history could offer because no other human being is just like you. Life is a journey of gradually discovering unique gifts one has to offer, embracing them, developing them, and sharing them with others.

Your life is God's gift to you. What you do with your life is your gift to God.

To begin our study of the Catholic faith and how you relate to it, let's look at where you are in your development. You are in the period of adolescence, the crucial years in a life's journey when a person moves from being a child to being an adult.

For Review

- What is the intent of this course?
- According to the Catholic Christian vision, why are you here on earth?
- What are the types of givens that are part of everyone's life? How do they relate to what God is calling each person to be?

The "If Only" Test

CONSIDER for a few minutes the many things in your life over which you have had little or no control. For example, you did not choose to be born. The initial choice of beginning your life was the decision of your parents, or in an even more profound sense, your life was a gift from God. Similarly, you could not control which historical period you were born in, or your country of birth, your ethnic background, your family, or your social and economic background.

This list could be longer, but the point is clear. Much of who we are is beyond our control. For better or worse, that is just the way life is. But the sad fact is that most of us spend a great deal of time and effort regretting this reality, denying it to ourselves, and trying to escape it. We would be much happier if we could accept the givens in our life.

Here is a simple test of our acceptance of the conditions we encounter as givens. Try to recall the last time you started a sentence with the words *if only*. Also try to remember when you heard friends, relatives, or others use that expression. A few examples might help to jog your memory.

- If only I could be better looking . . .
- If only I could have more money . . .
- If only he or she would like me . . .
- If only I were smarter . . .
- If only I had different parents . . .
- If only I had a nicer home . . .
- If only I had teachers that were more understanding . . .

Too often we live in a world of "if onlys." We look back at our past with regret or anger. Or we look ahead to our future with fear or lack of hope. The problem, of course, is that we overlook the possibilities of the present—the here and now. Unfortunately someday we will recall these moments we have wasted, these great opportunities for growth we have missed, and we will say, "If only I had done that differently."

One way to try to get control of our "if onlys" is to reflect on the Serenity Prayer. This popular prayer conveys a deep sense of peace and inspires us to be true to ourselves and all that we have been given in life.

God, grant me
serenity
to accept those things that I cannot change,
courage
to change those things that I can,
and wisdom
to know the difference.

Adolescence: Journeying from Childhood to Adulthood

If you have ever moved from one city, state, or country to another, you know how difficult and even depressing it can be to leave behind everything familiar and try to fit into what feels like a totally new world. Yet despite the trials of moving, you may often find great adventures and possibilities in the new place.

In adolescence, as with a geographical move, you are leaving the comfort and security of one stage of human life to venture into the unknown of another stage. This change can be frightening, confusing, and lonely. Yet, like moving from one city to another, it can also be exciting and hope filled.

At few other times in your life will things happen so quickly, yet so deeply; rarely will you need to adjust to so many changes in so short a time. This is one of the reasons most people look back on their high school years as among the most memorable in their life—even though not all the memories are pleasant.

Experts in human development disagree as to the exact definition of adolescence. For our purposes in this course, however, **adolescence** begins with the physical event of **puberty**, which results in our being capable of reproducing sexually. Adolescence ends with our gaining social status as an adult at about the age of twenty. The years in between are a fascinating journey.

In adolescence, you are venturing on a journey to adulthood.
Student art: "Passage to Beyond," color photo by Martin Rodriguez, Saint Anthony Catholic High School, San Antonio, Texas

Scenes from the Journey

Here are "scenes" from the lives of some ninth graders—people in the early stages of the journey from childhood to adulthood, which is adolescence. See if you can identify with any of these young people:

Josh

Josh spends a fair amount of time in front of the mirror, checking out his body and seeing how everything is developing. He is mostly concerned about the size of his body; he is one of those guys who hasn't hit his peak growth yet. He is four feet eleven, 110 pounds, and embarrassed to death about it. He flexes his muscles and makes up his mind—again—that he needs to get some bodybuilding equipment right away.

Shawn

Shawn is already six feet, 170 pounds, and has the varsity basketball coach dreaming of a trophy once he gets this kid on his team. Shawn, though, is quite self-conscious because he is often clumsy and hasn't learned to coordinate his rapidly growing body.

Jenny

Jenny is attracted to older guys—eleventh graders. She figures they'll like her if she looks good to them, so she also goes to the mirror often to check things out. She's likely to say "Yuck!" when she sees herself, though, because she knows she'll never look like those incredibly thin, beautiful models on TV and in magazines, who have perfect figures, fantastic clothes, flawless skin and hair.

Angela

Angela finds life a lot harder than it used to be. She feels sad more often. She loves being with her friends, laughing and talking for hours at a time, yet at times she feels lonely, close to tears, and wonders why. She gets depressed about how messed up the world is and how nobody seems to care. She just can't see why terrible things go on, like that little boy getting killed in a shooting two blocks from her house. How can there be a God if such awful stuff happens?

Anthony

Anthony hears a lot about sex from older guys who brag about all the girls they've had. Their bragging just seems funny and kind of weird. Now Anthony's feeling really attracted to one particular girl, and he wonders, "What's supposed to happen? Do I just go out with this girl and we suddenly have sex, or what?" Anthony is nervous and shy about even talking to her, let alone thinking about whether they're supposed to end up in bed.

Carlos

Carlos remembers when his family was real close, about four years ago, before they came to the States. In Mexico, they were poor and had a hard time getting by. But, at least they laughed a lot, hugged one another, and talked to one another freely. Now things are different; Carlos's parents don't like anything he's into—his friends, how he dresses, the music he listens to, where he hangs out, what time he comes in. They're so afraid he's getting into trouble. And lately he finds himself disagreeing with all their ideas about life, religion, God—everything important. To keep things peaceful, Carlos decides to be quiet about his life and his

7
Do boys experience the same social pressure as girls to measure up to certain physical standards of attractiveness? Explain briefly in writing.

8
Based on current magazine and TV ads, describe in writing what is considered attractive nowadays in women's looks. Then answer this question: *How are most teenage girls likely to feel about themselves when compared with this standard?*

9

Write down five suggestions for parents on how they might respond positively to the growing independent thinking, or intellectual independence, of their adolescent children.

10

Explain, in writing, whether you agree or disagree with the following statement: *Boys tend to treat girls as sex objects, but girls do not tend to treat boys as sex objects.*

thoughts around his parents; it's better to withdraw from them than have a big scene over every little thing. But of course then his parents get more suspicious!

Lisa

Lisa is physically mature for her age, and very attractive. Lots of older guys are calling her. She's mad because her mother says she can't date until she is seventeen. The guys keep calling anyway, and she feels silly having to tell them she can't go out with them for two more years! Once in a while, though, she wonders what these guys are really looking for. Do they really like *her*, do they even care what she's like as a *person?* Or do they just see her as a great body and nothing more?

Dianna

Dianna has always been smart, but it never seemed to be a problem until this year. Now when she aces a test or knows how to solve a really hard problem in algebra class, she figures she'd better not let anyone know. The guys will be threatened, the girls will be jealous, and nobody will want to talk to her. If she acts dumb, they'll like her. But it bothers Dianna to have to disguise her own abilities.

Adolescence can be an anxious but also an exciting time.
Student art: "Cora," watercolor painting by Emmy Murray, Sacred Heart High School, Kingston, Massachusetts

Dramatic Changes at Every Level of Life

Most ninth graders, like those just described, are changing dramatically on all levels of life—**physically, emotionally, intellectually, socially,** and **spiritually.** But even though we can talk about these levels separately, we do not experience them that way. They are all mixed up together in a person's life, and in adolescence they make a pretty powerful combination!

For example, many of the emotional changes you may be encountering are directly related to physical changes you are undergoing. Likewise, your attitudes toward faith and religion may be changing as a result of your increasing intellectual ability—your power to think about difficult concepts and philosophical issues. You are a whole person, not a bunch of separate pieces glued together.

You may have been able to identify with certain of the eight young people introduced above—or maybe not. Perhaps none of them fits your life and the dilemmas you face. That is because no small group of people could ever represent the variety of struggles that people your age have. For one thing, puberty begins at different ages for people. Traditionally it has been considered to begin about age twelve for girls and age fourteen for boys. Actually it starts as early as age nine or ten for some people and as late as fifteen or sixteen for others. Any group of ninth graders will vary enormously just because they begin puberty at different times. But even for those on the same "time schedule," their individual journeys are unique.

We Are More Than Our Body

Because the physical changes of puberty are so noticeable and dramatic, we may not be as aware of the changes we are going through at all the other levels—emotional, intellectual, social, and spiritual. In early adolescence it sometimes seems that our body is *everything* about us. But we need to get a sense of perspective about how central our body is, with its particular traits, to who we really are as a person.

Media advertising tries to convince teenagers that having a fabulous body is *everything*—the most important thing about who a person is.

Overcoming Obstacles

JOHN Hockenberry, then age nineteen, and a friend were hitchhiking home from college in 1976. They were picked up by two young women on a similar trip. Fatigued, the driver fell asleep at the wheel. In the ensuing crash, she was killed, and Hockenberry was seriously injured. He became paralyzed from the middle of the chest down. Nearly twenty years later, he wrote:

> Sometimes in my wheelchair I achieve a moment of unity between the chair, the arms that push it, and the mind that observes it all, when I feel like a character on horseback in an elaborately constructed Tolstoy or Dickens novel. Riding over a landscape that seems to be endless and always arriving somewhere new and wonderful, I can't help but believe that if I had not insisted on hitchhiking along a road in Pennsylvania back in February 1976, I would have missed the moment of my accident. The thought always produces a harrowing twinge, as though it was a close call, a cliffhanger rather than a fact. I might have missed what my life has become, each subsequent event locked to the preceding one like the sequential rhythm of a horse's hooves. (*Moving Violations*, page 69)

What did Hockenberry's life become? He is a popular, respected, and award-winning radio and TV reporter, covering news from Washington, D.C., to Iraqi war zones. Hockenberry's damaged body limited him in some ways, but it also gave rise to his determination to overcome whatever obstacles he encountered. His rich and satisfying life demonstrates the principle that although our body defines us in some ways, we are much more than our body. Every one of us has physical limitations; it is up to us to allow our true skills, talents, and beauties to thrive regardless of those limits, and sometimes even because of them.

More or Less Body Equals More or Less Me?

Buckminster Fuller, one of the creative geniuses of modern times, once reflected on his body and his attitude toward it. He remembered that he had come into the world weighing only 7 pounds, the sum total of all he was. Eventually he grew to be 70 pounds, then 170, then over 200. During that time he ate literally tons of food, some of which became hair that was cut off in regular trips to the barber.

Then he dieted and lost 70 pounds. After all that, he asked himself: "Just who am I anyway? Who was the 70 pounds lost through dieting? Am I less myself after that? Was I more or less myself before or after the haircut?" Fuller realized that his body could weigh 70 pounds less, yet he could feel more fully himself at the lighter weight.

Finally Fuller not only knew but understood in a deep sense a fact we so often miss in our society: We are more than our body. Besides a body, we have intelligence—the incredible ability to seek out and grasp truth. We also have emotions—the tremendous gift of our feelings and the ability to identify with the feelings of others. We dream. We interact socially. We reach out to one another in love. We create. And we can do all these things regardless of the shape of our body. In fact, the traits that make us truly human—creatures unique among all forms of life—are not dependent on our physical appearance.

Caring for Our Body, with All Its Limits

We must judge our own lovableness by more than what we see in the mirror. We must measure our value as human beings by more than the strength or shape of our body. Obviously our body is important. It affects what we physically can and cannot do. We must exercise, keep in shape, and avoid faddish diets and bad habits that can harm us. Our body is our primary contact with the rest of the world, the vehicle through which all our values and talents are expressed. So we should take care of ourselves but not lose sight of what is most important—that our true beauty will show through our body regardless of its limitations. And indeed our physical limitations often help us discover and reveal our true beauty.

Made in the Image of God

The Bible's Book of Genesis, which contains stories about our origins that are sacred to Christians and Jews, tells us that we are **made in the image and likeness of God:**

> Then God said, "Let us make humankind in our image. . . ."
>
> So God created humankind in his image,
> in the image of God he created them;
> male and female he created them.
>
> (1:26–27)

What makes us human is something more than our body. We are images, or reflections, of God, who is pure spirit. Yes, we are our body, but also so much more than that.

11
Write about some change each of the young people described in the text is going through at either the physical, intellectual, emotional, social, or spiritual level. Then compare those changes with what you are going through at each of those levels.

12
List five improvements you could make in the way you care for your body.

13
Before reading ahead, make a list of the important characteristics of a good friendship, especially those you have learned from personal experience. Then compare your list with the one on page 23, and see if you want to add to your list. Rank each item on your list, with 1 being the most important characteristic.

Are We Related?

Being made in God's image, we are also relational. God is a community of three Persons—Father, Son, and Holy Spirit—commonly referred to as the Trinity. Similarly, we exist in community with others. We will learn more about the Trinity later in this course. At this point it is enough to emphasize that just as it is God's nature to be in relationship, in community, so it is our nature to be related to others in community—other human beings and all of creation! Our social nature is a reflection of God.

Crucial Tasks of Adolescence

This course cannot deal with *all* the changes that happen as a natural part of adolescence. However, some changes in this period do not simply happen automatically; they must be accomplished. Psychologists call these the **developmental tasks of adolescence**—tasks that are required of young people if they are to move effectively from adolescence to mature adulthood. Among these tasks three stand out as most important:

1. The development of a capacity for friendship. One of the most significant tasks of adolescence is the development of a capacity for friendship. In studies about the needs and concerns of young people, one of the most consistent and highly rated desires of young people is to learn how to make friends and how to be a good friend.

Adolescents' deepening capacity for friendship is at the heart of their growth to adulthood. Two other tasks of adolescence, described below—forming a healthy sexual identity and developing a mature relationship with parents—are related to friendship. A good, healthy sexual relationship, the kind that characterizes a marriage, is above all a deep friendship. And the parent-child relationship needs to develop from total dependency of the child on the parents to a more equal, sharing style of relating as adults—a friendship. Now, during this pivotal period in your development, is a good time to consider the qualities and skills of friendship, so as to discover ways to grow in your own ability to nurture friendships in your life.

2. The development of a healthy sexual identity. A person must develop a strong enough sense of self to be able to relate sexually with others in ways that are positive, life affirming, caring, and responsible. This will involve acceptance of one's own body as well as respect for the bodies of others. Sexual maturity involves far more than our body, however. Also involved are emotional maturity, communication skills, a capacity for developing trust in one's relationships, the ability to care deeply without trying to possess or control the other, and much more.

3. The development of a more mature parent-child relationship. Young children depend on their parents for virtually everything required for survival—food, clothing, shelter, affection, and so on. As children grow older, this dependent relationship tends to change, as they assume more and more personal responsibility for their life. Unfortunately parents and their children are often very clumsy in the way they handle this transition. They frequently step on one another's emotional toes as they work toward a new adult relationship. Young people value freedom; parents value security for their children. Far too often parents and children who care deeply for one another go through a painful wounding break in their relationship. A little understanding of what is taking place could reduce, if not eliminate, much of the tension involved.

Our childhood relationship of dependence on home and parents changes as we grow into more personal responsibility for our own life.
Student art: "Family Home," ceramic sculpture by Lane Barham, Mother McAuley High School, Chicago, Illinois

Full of Longings

Adolescence is full of excitement and promise—for friendship at a deeper level, for growing independence, for discovering oneself as a sexual person. Those same possibilities contain hazards, but for most young people the sense of promise outweighs the sense of danger.

With all those good, exciting developments happening or soon to happen in your life, though, the truth is (and you have no doubt already felt this) that this time is also full of longings and downright pain. Such longings are brought on by losses of all kinds—a friendship that ends, the divorce of one's parents, an unmet goal. We experience loss and longing when friends or relatives are damaged by alcoholism, drug addiction, or disease. When we lose our innocence about the way the world works, and find that all is not as pure and simple as we imagined in childhood, we often long for a "simpler time." All these events can make life seem empty, hollow, disappointing.

Maybe you put all your hopes in going out with someone you are attracted to, and then the whole thing fizzles. You are crushed. Or you feel your independence from your parents rising, and you long for them to treat you like an

14
Interview one or both of your parents about what their adolescence was like. Write up the interview and give it to them to read. Then ask them to interview you about what *your* adolescence is like.

Create a piece of art or an artistic symbol that represents some loss or pain you have gone through. Then write about the ache or longing you felt, or still feel, as a result of that difficulty.

adult, respecting your viewpoints and letting you be. But instead what you get are clashes with them—sharp words and ugly scenes. Or you see yourself as part of a stable family, but one day your parents announce that they are separating. Perhaps you long to be comforted by a friend when things are going bad for you, but that person just doesn't understand, even though he or she claims to. Sometimes you just ache, you feel so lonely—even when you're in a crowd of people you know, or maybe especially then. Maybe you are bored most of the time; you cannot seem to find anything worth pouring your energy into.

Another form of longing may be the endless questions you have—about life, about God or religion, about why things have to be as they are. These are questions without ready answers, and at times they may consume you with uncertainty. You long to have answers, but instead you get only more questions.

The aches and the longings for *more* that are so much a part of adolescence do not really go away as human beings get older. The longing takes different forms, but it is still there, like a huge gap in us that is waiting to be filled. We are so incomplete. That is part of the pain of human existence. We are constantly searching for happiness, looking to fill up our emptiness.

For Review

- Using the stories of the young people described in this section, give an example of a change at each level of existence: physical, intellectual, emotional, social, and spiritual.
- According to the Christian tradition, in what ways are human beings made in the image of God?
- Name the three crucial tasks of adolescence. How does the deepening capacity for friendship relate to all of them?

The Qualities and Skills of Friendship

*T*HESE brief descriptions of the qualities and skills of friendship can serve as the starting point for conversation. You may want to discuss each of these points and add others that come to mind.

- *Your best friend is yourself.* The more I like and accept who I am as a person, the more likely I am to have the courage and desire to give myself to others in friendship.

- *A friend wants the best for the other.* Although we obviously gain personally from all our friendships, our goal is to promote the happiness of others, not to use others for our own fulfillment or satisfaction.

- *Friendship takes work.* Friendship requires a commitment by the friends to nurture their relationship through both the happy times and the inevitable tough times.

- *Friends talk with their heart.* Friends share their feelings and thoughts honestly and openly. They also listen with their head and their heart to what the other person is communicating.

- *Friendship grows in the soil of trust.* Building trust takes a lot of time. We learn to trust others gradually, based on our day-to-day experiences with them. Trust is fragile, however, and can be quickly shattered. This fact leads to the next point.

- *Friends forgive.* We humans are wonderful but also weak. We all make mistakes, and we all hurt one another, most of the time without intending to. When we hurt someone, it is difficult to find the words to express sorrow and regret and to ask for forgiveness. When we have been hurt, accepting once again the risks that trust involves can be even more difficult. Friends must work at learning the skills of asking for and granting forgiveness.

- *Friends experience freedom, not fences.* Freedom relates closely to trust. When friendship exists, we do not feel trapped by the other person. A sure sign of the absence of true friendship is the presence of jealousy. If all contacts with others cause a friend to be suspicious or fearful, then friendship did not exist in the first place. This idea relates to the last point.

- *Friendship builds more friendships.* We want to share our friendships with others. Constantly wanting to be alone with a person is often a sign that the relationship is not one of friendship but of dependency. When we learn to be friends with another person, that experience gives us the skills and desire to build more friendships. ♥

Finding Answers to Life's Longings

In the Catholic Christian vision, it is no accident that we are full of aches and longings, that we feel so incomplete. We were created by God with a built-in **longing for happiness**, and we will be restless until we find happiness. The ache is there for a reason, God's "reason," so that we might be moved to search for *true* happiness and ultimately find it.

Our longings, then, are not cause for despair. Rather, our emptiness can be seen as the spaciousness we need to help us discover that what truly fulfills us also fulfills God's desire for us. Unfortunately North American society does not often see our longings in this light; instead, it offers many short-cuts to happiness.

Society's "Answers"

When we speak of our society's "answers" to the needs raised by our longings, it is good to recall that we are social creatures. We need society, and in fact we *are* society. All of us play a part in the development of society's answers. So when we examine society, we also examine our own part in society.

The Western society we live in provides us with some ready-made answers to what will make us happy. In many cases society points us in some good, worthwhile directions, such as "Stay in school" or "Learn to express yourself." But too many of the answers and values we get from society point us to illusions of happiness, not the real thing. Let's take a look at some of these values, the recommended habits and assumptions about life that society offers us as the way to fulfillment.

Popularity

Is **popularity** the answer, the key to filling up the ache in us? That is often the message we get from our society. Consider the following ways people are encouraged to behave when around others their age whose opinions are important to them:

- A group of boys stands in the hallway and makes fun of an overweight girl who walks by. One boy wants to be accepted by the crowd, so he joins in the ridicule even though he knows he will later feel guilty about doing so.
- A group of girls spreads rumors that could destroy someone's reputation. One girl disapproves but says nothing in protest because she doesn't want the group to lash out at her.
- Everybody who is anybody is going to get together on Friday night to "get high." One girl doesn't really want to get into drugs, but she doesn't want to be rejected by those who do.
- Although she is afraid of the hazards of getting involved in sex, a ninth grader feels terribly pressured by her peers to become sexually active.
- A young Catholic person who enjoys religion and even likes going to Mass does not dare let others know. After all, doesn't everyone say that religion is boring and only for people who have no real life?

If we can just fit in and win everyone else's approval, the big ache in us will be healed. That is what the value of popularity says.

Consumerism

Our economy is driven by the notion that people are primarily consumers who seek and acquire new products. Many of these products are totally unnecessary. The message we get from society, particularly from advertising, is that these products will bring us the happiness we are longing for. The attitude that acquiring unlimited material possessions is the key to fulfillment is known as **consumerism.**

16
For each example given here of the pressure to be popular, assign a rating from 1 to 5 of how typical this kind of popularity-seeking behavior is (a) in yourself and (b) among your friends. Let 1 represent "not at all typical" and 5, "extremely typical." Then write a paragraph about how strong the pressure to be popular is in you and your friends.

17

Rate each of the following statements from 1 (strongly disagree) to 5 (strongly agree):

- Buying things I want makes me feel happy.
- Advertising entices me to want the latest consumer items.
- I wish I had more money than I have.

In writing, summarize your thoughts on how you rated yourself.

So while much of the world goes hungry, we spend billions of dollars each year on junk food. While many in the world do not have enough clothing, we buy and then quickly discard the latest fashions. Young people are a major target of advertisers, who try to pressure them to buy everything from junk food to brand-name shoes to the latest in sound systems. Each of us must carefully weigh the degree to which we are influenced by this cultural drive to acquire more and more things that fail to bring lasting joy.

Individualism

"Look out for yourself" is another answer to life's longings that we often hear from society. This is the value of **individualism.** Individualism can be positive. A commitment to the dignity and rights of the individual is at the center of a democratic way of life and, indeed, central to our religious beliefs as well. And it is also true that a person can contribute to the world only if he or she has taken the time and the energy to develop and grow as an individual. In other words, we cannot contribute what we do not have.

When individualism is carried too far, though, a sense of responsibility to others and to the community as a whole is lost. The value of service to others is replaced by the belief that I must take care of myself first and last. The notion of sacrificing any of one's desires for the sake of the common good is considered old-fashioned. When the single moral guideline of our society becomes "I have to do my own thing," we forget our need to be part of a caring community. Many people in our society have apparently achieved individual success, only to find that they are now dying of loneliness.

Immediate Gratification

Our society is often described as a "feel good" society. Much human behavior seems to be based on the conviction, "If it feels good, do it." Suffering is viewed as evil, even if the suffering is done out of care and concern for loved ones. As a result, when people experience inevitable loneliness or pain in life, they immediately want to block it out with alcohol, drugs, or perhaps more consumerism ("I'll feel a lot better if I just buy something new").

Immediate gratification means that we want and expect our needs to be met right now—not tomorrow and certainly not in a few years. This inability to be patient has harmful effects on human relationships. Many people view as friends only those who always make them feel good. As soon as a relationship requires sacrifice or commitment of them, they become fearful and want to cast it aside. They feel as free to discard friendships as they would a pair of blue jeans that is no longer fashionable. Without patience—the ability to wait—relationships cannot grow and flourish.

Sexual Permissiveness

The belief that loneliness and longing will go away if we just find sexual satisfaction is a notion thrown at us constantly by advertising and the media. Sex is used to sell products as varied as soft drinks and cars. Underneath the ads, the message is, "You will be happy if you have this car (or this drink) because look who will be attracted to you! They'll be climbing all over you!"

Let's consider the attitude of **sexual permissiveness** in terms of the values already discussed.

- The impulse to engage in sexual activity at a young age is often driven by the desire to be popular, to be accepted and viewed as "with it" by others.
- For many people in our society, sexual relationships are just one more consumer item to be tried out and discarded as easily as a new video game.
- Because of society's emphasis on individualism, many people are terrified of the thought of true commitment to another person, the kind of commitment required if sexual expression is to be wholesome and life giving.
- Because of the desire for immediate gratification, many people are impatient with the struggle and growth that will always be part of caring relationships.

18
Pretend a debate is going on inside you between these two sides:
- I have to take care of myself first and last.
- I have to be concerned about the good of the whole society.

Write out some of each side's statements from the debate. Which side wins?

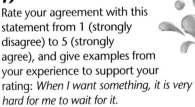

19
Rate your agreement with this statement from 1 (strongly disagree) to 5 (strongly agree), and give examples from your experience to support your rating: *When I want something, it is very hard for me to wait for it.*

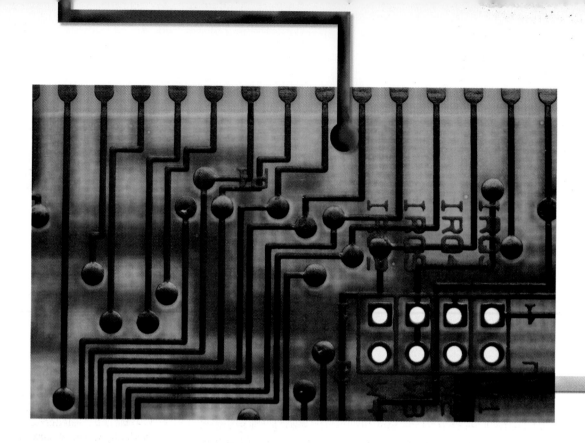

These negative characteristics of our contemporary approach to sexuality are reflected in the nearly epidemic problem of teenage pregnancy—more than one million teenage girls in the United States become pregnant each year. Many of these girls and the boys and men who were involved with them probably engaged in sex thinking that it was the thing to do, that it was so natural there was surely nothing wrong with it, or that it was a response to a desire for immediate gratification that could not and should not be denied. Certainly many others who become pregnant believe that they were expressing an honest love and commitment. Yet the sad fact remains that most of these girls discover pain and even tragedy rather than joy, and they are often left to face the consequences alone. Too many give in to the pressure to have an abortion to get rid of the consequences of their behavior—another quick, instant "solution." The boys' and men's lives, too, are poorer, not richer, for having brought about new life without a willingness or readiness to take on the responsibilities that accompany sexual activity.

Sexual permissiveness seems to offer an answer to life's longing, but it is a shallow answer with potentially tragic effects, including sexually transmitted diseases and AIDS.

Technological Fixes

Our society is based on a belief in progress, with an almost religious faith that technology will take care of our every need; we will always have **technological fixes** for our

20

Which of the following sentences best represents your view? Explain your answer in a paragraph.

- The prevailing values and attitudes around sexuality in our society are healthy and balanced.
- The prevailing values and attitudes around sexuality in our society are too permissive.
- The prevailing values and attitudes around sexuality in our society are too restrictive.

problems. So, for instance, if our planet is filling up with garbage, we can let the next generation deal with it because by then technology will have solved all the pollution problems. Or if I am in pain, a medicine or treatment will take this pain away. Technology to the rescue! If I have done serious damage to my heart through smoking, I can have surgery to make it all better, even a heart transplant! If I have gotten pregnant, I can have an abortion. If I am bored or lonely or hurting, I can watch a video or tap into a computer network to take away this feeling. Or I can drink alcohol or take a drug that will numb me.

Deep down we find it impossible to believe that technology is limited. This "techno-addiction" may temporarily fill the space in us that is yearning to be filled with true happiness—but not for long.

The Need to Be Critical

During adolescence, people become intellectually capable of evaluating and criticizing everything they took for granted in childhood. Being critical is not simply a matter of finding fault with something we dislike. In **effective criticism** we take something we have learned—whether from parents, teachers, pastors, or others—and turn it over in our mind and question it. In the process we may find that our previous understanding needs to be updated. For example, consider a child who has developed a negative attitude toward people of other races. This attitude may have come about from comments made by a respected relative or family friend. In adolescence this young person develops the intellectual capacity to be critical of her or his past understanding and, upon reflection, may find that the attitude is in fact wrong and based on false assumptions.

The need to be critical goes beyond what we have learned in the past. We also need to be constructively critical of all the messages about happiness that bombard us. Television, videos, the Internet, ads, music, magazines, and computer games are powerful message carriers, often linked with consumer products. They surround and even saturate us; it is impossible to live in society without being influenced by the media. They are especially geared to captivate the minds and hearts of the young, and many teenagers soak up hours each day of media messages about what is valuable in life. We can approach the media in one of two ways: as a child, ready to be spoon-fed whatever they offer; or as a maturing adolescent who exercises critical intelligence.

21
Rate your reaction to the following statement from 1 (strongly disagree) to 5 (strongly agree): *I believe technology can solve just about any problem.* Explain your rating in writing.

The media surround and even saturate us with images of violence. *Student art:* **"Telegenetics," mixed media by Jaime Maiorano, Sacred Heart High School, Kingston, Massachusetts**

To be critical of the media does not mean shutting down television, music, and so on. After all, they have many good things to offer. The media, at their best, convey youth culture by expressing the great longings, dreams, hurts, and fears of young people's hearts. But let's face it. The media are not always at their best. Much of what they have to offer is junk food for the mind—a diet of violence and brutality, exploitation, greed, sexual permissiveness, and crudeness. But rather than simply turn away from the media, young people can benefit from taking a good, long look at the menu and deciding what is worth eating. They can become more selective. A familiar saying goes, "You are what you eat."

Take, for example, the area of music. We can enjoy music passively, allowing it to fill us up with its points of view. Or we can listen consciously and critically to the music that fills our life. We can reflect on song lyrics and try to discover what values they promote. In many cases they will be good and wholesome and true—no sugarcoating on life, just an honest expression of how it feels. But listening critically helps us get beneath the surface to discover, What is being said here? What is being proposed as the way to fill the emptiness in life, to satisfy the human heart's longing for happiness? By asking critical questions, we can decide if we want to accept a particular message as a guideline of our own beliefs and values. We become our own best music critic.

New Questions

Adolescence is the period when you can *be* reflective about life because now you are capable of **reflection**, careful thought or meditation. It is also the time when you are reaching out for relationships that are different from those of your childhood. You are coming into your own as a growing young person, with all the stresses and agonies that involves.

Now more than ever you may reflect on the aches and longings that never seem to go away, that eternal quest for happiness. Now more than ever you may be able to go beyond the shallow answers to life's longings that are offered by society. You may find yourself asking new questions you never asked before:

- Is there something deeper than the answers society offers?
- Why am I here? What's the purpose of my life? What will help me make sense of my life?
- What will really fill this longing in me?
- Is there something beyond what I see?
- Is there a God? And if so, does God care for me?
- If God exists, why is the world so full of hate, suffering, and misery?

22
If "you are what you eat" is true, what effects do you think your diet of media culture (like the music you listen to and TV shows or videos you watch) is having on you as a person?

These are religious questions, and they emerge from a growing maturity. Notice they are not religious questions in the same category as, Why do I have to go to church? That is a good question, too, but the above questions are more fundamental and radical than that. And you are ready for them. We will take up the "God question" in the next chapter, on faith, which is the basis for the remainder of this course on Catholic Christianity.

For Review

- Briefly describe society's answers to life's longings.
- What does it mean to be critical of something we have learned, seen, or heard in the media?
- What are some religious questions many people begin to ask during adolescence?

Our Heart Is Restless

More than fifteen hundred years ago, a young man from northern Africa was studying in Italy. He was leading a turbulent life, getting into all kinds of trouble and making his mother sick with worry about how he would "turn out." But he had something quite wonderful going for him: he was a searcher. He knew he was longing for happiness, and he knew that no matter how much he tried to find it (in all the wrong places), he came up short of real happiness. It was beyond his grasp. But he kept searching.

At last, partly through a wise teacher who introduced him to a new spiritual vision of life, this young man turned his life around and became a Christian. Years later, in his autobiography, he reflected prayerfully on what he had learned through all his searching. Addressing God, Augustine wrote: "You have made us for yourself, and our heart is restless until it rests in you."

Ultimately we are made for union with God in this life and forever. All our longings for happiness point finally to the One who created us out of love and set us forth on this restless, joyous, wonder-filled journey of life. The young man who recognized this was **Augustine**, who was later named a bishop and, after his death, a saint. Today he is considered one of the greatest thinkers and leaders in the history of Christianity. And it all began for him with a young man's searching heart.

23
Have you found yourself asking any of the questions on page 30 in the last year or so? If so, which ones? Write down any thoughts you may have had about these questions.

"Saint Augustine's Vision," by fifteenth-century painter Carpaccio

2

Faith:
Responding to God's Invitation

A Question of Worldviews

Let's begin this chapter with a Jewish folktale.

Two men set out on a journey together. The friends took a donkey to carry their packs, a torch to light their way at night, and a rooster. The rooster sat on the donkey's head during the entire journey.

One of the men was deeply religious; the other was a skeptic, one who doubts all forms of faith. On the journey they frequently spoke about the Lord. "In all things, God is good," said the first companion.

"We will see if your opinion bears out on the trip," said the second.

Shortly before dusk the two men arrived in a small village, where they sought a place to sleep. Despite their frequent requests, no one offered them a night's lodging. Reluctantly they traveled a mile outside of town, where they decided to sleep.

"I thought you claimed that God is good, " the skeptic said sarcastically.

"God has decided this is the best place for us to sleep tonight," replied his friend.

They fixed their beds beneath a large tree, just off the main road that led to the village, and tethered their donkey about thirty yards away. Just as they were about to light the torch, they heard a horrible noise. A lion had killed the donkey and carried it off to eat. Quickly the companions climbed the tree to avoid danger.

"You still say God is good?" the skeptic asked with anger.

"If the lion hadn't eaten the donkey, he would have attacked us. God is good," his companion declared.

Moments later a cry from the rooster sent them further up the tree. From this new vantage point, they saw a wildcat carrying the rooster away in its teeth.

Before the skeptic could say a word, the man of faith declared: "The cry of the rooster has once again saved us. God is good."

A few minutes later a strong wind arose and blew out the torch, the only comfort the men had in the black night. Again the skeptic taunted his companion: "It appears that the goodness of God is working overtime this evening," he said. This time the believer was silent.

The next morning the two men walked back into the village for food. They soon discovered that a band of outlaws had swept into town the previous night and robbed the entire village of all its possessions.

With this news the man of faith turned to his friend. "Finally it has become clear," he cried. "Had we been given a room in the village last night, we would have been robbed along with all the villagers. If the wind had not blown out our torch, the bandits who traveled the road near the place where we slept would have discovered us and taken all our goods. It is clear that in all things, God is good."

These two traveling companions had two entirely different ways of looking at life. As the story suggests, the way we see the world around us and all reality—our **worldview**—influences how we experience life. Some people, for example, experience life as an unending series of difficulties or disappointments. Others might see the same events either as exciting opportunities or as challenges.

How Do We Get a Worldview?

Our worldview may partly result from how we were raised in a certain family and culture. Our relationships with other people and our particular life experiences have a great deal to do with how we view life. The personality or temperament we inherited may also play a part. Yet when all is said and done, our worldview is not simply imposed on us. It is something we freely choose and say yes to, not all at once but in thousands of ways over a lifetime.

Chapter 1 said that certain kinds of questions tend to emerge in a person's adolescence—about the meaning and purpose of life, how to fill the longing in life, the existence of God, and why the world is full of suffering if there is a good God. Questioning in this way is a sign of growing maturity. The answers we eventually find can play a major role in determining the worldview we take. Our worldview, in turn, may affect whether we view our life as meaningful and rich with promise or as absurd and tragic.

Matters of the Heart and the Head

Worldviews are matters of the heart as well as the head. They are expressions not only of our *thoughts and beliefs* about life and the world ("head issues"), but also of our *feelings and attitudes* about life and the world ("heart issues"). When we answer the questions that help develop our worldview, we rely on both our head and our heart. Our mind's ability to answer a question is just as important as what we feel in our heart about that question. One or the other may dominate as we answer a particular question, but both have a role. Think back to our two traveling companions. The religious man's strong belief in a good God overcame his feelings about their situation, while the other man's lack of belief made his negative feelings about their situation even stronger. The men came to different conclusions, but each demonstrated worldviews that contain elements of both heart and head.

Faith in God is one kind of worldview. In this chapter we will look at issues of faith in God, beginning with what faith is. But first we need to acknowledge some limitations we have in speaking of God and the things of God.

Struggling to Speak of Great Mysteries

A language problem immediately crops up in any discussion of faith in God or matters of God. As human beings we are limited in what we can say about God because the mystery of God is immensely beyond us. Anything we say is going to seem quite trivial next to the great mystery of God. It is like trying to take all the water in the earth's oceans and pour it into a tiny paper cup. Our mind is just a paper cup compared with the ocean of God.

So we must speak of God with a great deal of humility. We need to recognize that no matter who we are or how smart we are, our descriptions of God and how God works and relates to us are never going to capture all that God is. We can only try, in our struggling and limited human way, to understand.

Our worldview comes partly from how we were raised in a certain family and culture.

When we speak of God, we must realize that we are using metaphors about God. **Metaphors** are means of expression that try to describe, by comparison with something else, a trait or characteristic of a person or thing. For instance, a husband might say to his wife, "You are the light in my life." Of course this does not mean that the woman is actually a lamp, but rather that she cheers her husband and offers vision and hope and joy, like a lamp in a dark room that casts its light into all the corners, dispelling the darkness and gloom. The metaphor of light tells us something important about the character of this particular woman. Even so, it cannot tell us everything about her; her husband would be the first to admit that it falls far short of describing her completely!

The same is true of our descriptions of God. We speak in metaphors about God—for instance, God as father or mother, as supreme being, as ruler or majesty, as living bread, as ocean—to compare God with what we *do* know from our human experience. But all the images in the world cannot come close to describing the great mystery of God.

1

Think up a metaphor for God that is somewhat original—not typically used to describe God. Write a paragraph about what this metaphor is trying to convey about God and how well you like it as a descriptor of God.

For Review

- What is a worldview? How do we get a worldview?
- What is a metaphor? Why are we limited to speaking about God in metaphors?

The Meaning of Faith

To help us understand what faith means, let's begin with a story about two friends.

Eddie and Vince went to the same Catholic grade school and spent much of their childhood years together—playing sandlot baseball, hanging out in each other's homes, putting up a lemonade stand to make a few nickels every summer, biking all over, doing homework together, checking out every trash can in the area for aluminum cans to recycle for money. When it turned out they would be going to the same Catholic high school, they were really happy. The old friendship would stay alive.

Once they hit high school, Vince went out for junior varsity sports, easily making the football team and the baseball team. Eddie tried out, too, but didn't make either team. So he joined the band, playing saxophone. That was fun; it was an award-winning marching band. Their new schedules put them on different tracks, in different worlds. But Eddie and Vince still laughed and enjoyed each other's company. They had some classes together, and they occasionally joined up for a movie or pizza. Whenever Eddie felt left out of Vince's world, he would console himself by thinking about the great time they would have next summer, when all the sports and band schedules were not in the way. They were still friends; there was no question about that. They would *always* be friends.

One day as Eddie was hurrying down the hallway to get to class, he heard a familiar voice just around the corner by the lockers. It was Vince. Eddie slowed down a little, figuring he'd stop for half a minute and chat. Then he heard loud laughter from some other guys; Vince was so good at entertaining people. But before Eddie turned the corner, he was stopped cold by the next words out of Vince: "Yeah, I have to admit, he's kind of a loser—thinks he's such a big deal when he puts on that band uniform. Eddie tries to be so cool with the sax, but it just doesn't work. It's pathetic!"

2
Write down what you imagine Eddie must have thought and felt when he heard Vince's remarks about him. Express it as you think Eddie would express it to himself.

Faith: Trust and Belief

The story of Eddie and Vince serves to illustrate the meaning of faith at the human-to-human level. We are not talking about faith in God here. The story is about faith in a human person, or rather, destruction of that faith. But the process of putting faith in another human being is somewhat like putting faith in God. It involves both trust and belief, matters of the heart and matters of the head.

It's About Trust

We can grasp the significance of trust in our life by reflecting on what happens when our faith in another person is destroyed. For example, put yourself in Eddie's place in the story of the two friends. Play out in your imagination what will happen between Eddie and Vince in the future because of Vince's betraying remarks. Of course we can hope that Vince will apologize and decide to be a more trustworthy friend, and that Eddie will find it in his heart and gut to forgive Vince. But at this moment Eddie has lost all trust in Vince. Understandably, Vince's remarks would be devastating to Eddie, especially if he has no other friends. The incident might even destroy Eddie's trust in people generally.

Faith in God, like faith in a human being, is about trust. When we say we have faith in certain friends, relatives, teachers, coaches, pastors, or other important persons in our life, we usually mean that we *trust* them. We all yearn for

Trust is a matter of the heart—a whole attitude about life.
Student art: **Untitled, pencil drawing by Kelly Snook, Mercy Academy, Louisville, Kentucky**

people who care for us in such authentic ways that we know we can rely on them—friends with whom we can share our deepest feelings and thoughts, and people whose love can give energy and purpose to our life. When we find a trustworthy friend or older guide, we realize we have been given a special gift.

In religious faith a person invests **trust** in God. This process, like trust in human beings, is a **matter of the heart**—a whole attitude and movement toward God. A person who trusts God is aware of God's love and loves God in return, shares his or her deepest thoughts and feelings with God, depends on God when in trouble, and has a sense that God will always be there, even when times are tough and it isn't clear how things will turn out.

The issue of trust in God is closely related to another issue—whether life itself is trustworthy. That is, is life basically good, and can we approach it with hope? Or must we live with an attitude that trouble is around the corner, "just waiting to get me"? Those two attitudes toward life are actually two worldviews, similar to the worldviews of our two traveling companions in the folktale that opened this chapter.

It's About Belief

Faith in God is not only a matter of the heart, of a trusting attitude toward God. It is also a **matter of the head**, of **beliefs** and convictions about God. Let's return to Eddie and Vince to see how this "head" dimension works out when faith in another person is broken.

If you had asked Eddie to list his beliefs and convictions about Vince before the hallway incident, he might have said: "Vince is a true friend. He's smart and talented, and he has a great sense of humor. He's really honest and considerate. He'll go far in life because he has high goals and standards for himself. He would never stab anyone in the back. He brings out the best in people, especially his friends."

Now imagine the list of beliefs about Vince that Eddie would come up with the day after the hallway incident: "Vince is a phony. He tells you one thing and thinks another. He may be talented and smart, but he'll never go anywhere in life because he's a hypocrite. All he wants out of life is to be popular at other people's expense. We used to be good friends, but now I wonder what he really thought of me all those years."

Eddie's beliefs about Vince are closely connected with his trust, or lack of trust, in Vince. His beliefs, in fact, are influencing his trust level, and the other way around as well: his trust level is influencing his beliefs about Vince. Belief and trust are two sides of putting faith in someone.

3
Of the two approaches to life described here, which one is closer to your own? In a paragraph, describe how your approach to life compares with these two.

4
Think about the person you trust more than anyone else in the world. List five beliefs you have about that person. Then do the same exercise again, but focus it on the person you *mistrust* more than anyone else.

You Can't Have One Without the Other!

THIS is a funny little story of an atheist, someone who does not believe in God. He is struggling with both belief and trust:

An atheist fell off a cliff. As he tumbled downward, he caught hold of the branch of a small tree. There he hung between heaven above and the rocks a thousand feet below, knowing he wasn't going to be able to hold on much longer.

Then an idea came to him. "God!" he shouted with all his might.

Silence! No one responded.

"God!" he shouted again. "If you exist, save me and I promise I shall believe in you and teach others to believe."

Silence again! Then he almost let go of the branch in shock as he heard a mighty Voice booming across the canyon. "That's what they all say when they are in trouble."

"No, God, no!" he shouted out, more hopeful now. "I am not like the others. Why, I have already begun to believe, don't you see, having heard your Voice for myself. Now all you have to do is save me and I shall proclaim your name to the ends of the earth."

"Very well," said the Voice. "I shall save you. Let go of that branch."

"Let go of the branch?" yelled the distraught man. "Do you think I'm crazy?" (De Mello, *Taking Flight,* pages 62–63)

The poor atheist is grasping at belief, but he lacks trust!

When it comes to faith in God, a similar relationship between trust and belief exists. Yes, religious faith involves trust in God, a matter of the heart. It also involves beliefs about God, a matter of the head. You can't have one—trust or belief—without the other and still have genuine faith.

People of genuine faith trust in God because of what they *believe* about God—that God is all-good; that God created them and holds them in love; that God wants their happiness; and (in the case of Christians) that God sent Jesus, God's own Son, to save them and the whole world out of love for them. Their trust in God enables them to hold these beliefs with even greater conviction.

A Gift, Not an Achievement

Faith is trusting in God and holding beliefs or convictions about God. This is the human part of a dynamic relationship with God. But before we go any further, we need to clarify the Catholic Christian understanding about how a person comes to have faith at all.

God Makes the First Move

It would be a mistake to see faith as something that a person works at and strives toward, as if it all depends on the person. The Catholic Christian understanding of faith is that human beings are created by God with a built-in desire for God; it is written in their hearts. They may not always recognize it as a desire for God; they may simply experience it as a restlessness or a searching. But it is there, in each and every single person.

Having created us with a built-in longing for God, God does not then abandon us to wander aimlessly on our own. God is constantly trying to reach us, to .get through to us, to reveal something of God's own self to us. In Catholic terminology God's self-disclosure to human beings is called **Revelation.** God is always moving among us and inviting us into life with God. (Later in this chapter we will explore the various ways Revelation takes place.)

So God—not we humans—makes the first move. The human yes to God's invitation, the response of faith, is only the second move. And God is not neutral about how each human being responds to the invitation. God longs for a yes response from each of us, and pours out the help, the grace of God's movement in our life, to enable us to respond.

A Free Gift and a Free Response

It is God's nature to love, to give God's own self freely to us. But it is our nature as human beings to respond to God's love freely. We can choose to put our faith in God—or not. Nothing or no one can *make* us believe, even God's grace poured out in us, and certainly not our parents or teachers or anyone else who seems to be encouraging us to have faith. The response of genuine faith is a free act of giving our trust and belief to God; it cannot be coerced, forced, or bought.

A Lifetime Offer

You may have met people (or perhaps you think this way) who ask if you have been saved, if you have made your decision for Jesus. "Do you *believe?*" is the first question, and the next is, "*When* were you saved? When did you make your decision for Jesus?" That way of thinking presumes there is one moment in time when we make a definite, once-and-for-all decision to have faith, and after that there is no question about it.

Although that might be the experience of some people, the Catholic understanding of faith differs from that one. It presumes that the response of faith is given through a lifetime of decisions, not just one. Every day, God is offering life, and every day, in many small and large decisions, people can choose to trust in God and try to deepen their beliefs about God. Because it is a matter of daily decision, sometimes people are less wholehearted in their response than at other times. One's faith may wax and wane, being a strong, brilliant torchlight in one season of a person's life and a small, flickering matchlight in another season. At times, too, the light of faith in a person's life may go out completely. God, however, is always offering the invitation to come back to faith. It is "a lifetime offer" as well as "the offer of a lifetime"!

The invitation to faith, then, is a gift freely offered to every human person by God, and the response of faith must be freely chosen by the person if it is to be faith at all. People of faith do not *achieve* faith; rather, they choose to *accept* what God is offering them all the time. Their response is a

5
If you have ever been coerced or pressured into saying yes to something, describe briefly in writing how you felt about it. Then write a paragraph agreeing or disagreeing with this statement: *If you love someone, you will never try to coerce or pressure the person into doing something.*

6
Would you rather be offered the invitation to faith as a one-shot offer or a lifetime offer? Explain your answer in a one-page essay.

whole vision of life, which enables them to address the deep human questions: Where do I put my trust? What is there to believe in?

For Review

- What are the two aspects of faith in God?
- Is having trust in God a matter of the heart or a matter of the head?
- How do trust and belief influence each other?
- How does the process of coming to faith get started?
- Explain the Catholic understanding of the ways we respond to God's invitation to faith.

When We Do Not Have All the Answers

This discussion about faith being a gift from God and our response being freely chosen should not leave you with an idea that faith is necessarily easy, or that it provides ready answers to everything. God's invitation and our response are not a matter of "Just sign up here, and you'll never be confused again," or "A trouble-free life, guaranteed." On the contrary, the deepest kind of faith is the kind that has been struggled over and that has held up, even though all the answers have not been provided in a neat package.

The Story of Brenda

Here is a true account of a time when members of a high school community found they didn't have all the answers:

> Brenda was one of those special persons who comes along so rarely in life that people wonder if the world deserves them. Although she was naturally bright and a great student, Brenda never bragged about her accomplishments or acted superior. In fact, she often offered to help friends study for exams, and she volunteered to tutor kids in lower grades. Brenda had a low-key wit and said funny things in such a quiet way that she immediately put people at ease. She was especially popular at parties because people felt comfortable whenever she was around.
>
> Brenda was also a gifted gymnast who seemed to be totally at home on the parallel bars. Yet what impressed

Faith never guarantees a trouble-free life.
Student art: Untitled, mixed media by Rita O'Donnell, Saint Peter's High School, New Brunswick, New Jersey

people was not just her routines on the bars. Rather, they were captivated by the joyous look on her face and the sparkle in her eyes. She was a young woman in love with life and everything and everyone in it. Her spirit warmed anyone who met her.

As a cheerleader for the girl's basketball team, Brenda enjoyed leading cheers for others. The cheerleaders had a favorite cheer that involved multiple leaping somersaults. They always saved it for that time in a game when the team needed a great boost in a tough situation or wanted to celebrate a game that was going their way.

One night the team was flying high—playing their best game in memory against a school that had won the conference championship the year before. The fans were as excited as they had ever been, stomping and yelling nonstop. During a crucial time-out, the cheerleaders went into their somersault cheer. Brenda could do this cheer with her eyes closed. But of course she kept them wide open, her incredible smile lighting up the gym. However, something unexpected happened. Brenda lost her balance at one point, and the somersault move turned into an awkward jumble of limbs, with Brenda struggling to get her balance. But she could not, and she fell to the floor, landing on her head.

After her head and shoulders crashed onto the gym floor, Brenda quickly tried to stand up, but she felt dizzy and sat back down. Her fellow cheerleaders crowded around. A doctor hurried to her aid. Her parents were there moments later. Brenda was carefully helped off the floor and to the training room near the gym. The doctor said that she had to go to the hospital's emergency room for X-rays. "Just as a precaution," he added. Brenda said she was okay and wanted to return for the end of the game. Her parents insisted that she listen to the doctor, and Brenda finally agreed.

Brenda died later that night.

The next morning the news swept through the school. People thought it was all a mistake or somebody's idea of a sick joke. Then over the school's P.A., the

7

Imagine yourself as the student editor of the school newspaper, trying to write your editorial column the week after Brenda's tragic accident. What would you write to try to respond to the question in everyone's mind: "Why? My God, why?"

When tragedy occurs, it is hard for us to comprehend it.
Student art: "Ring of Friends," oil painting by Amy Westerman, Holy Cross High School, Louisville, Kentucky

principal made the announcement that Brenda had died during the night due to bleeding in the brain. "There was nothing that could be done."

People tried to figure out how the usually easy move for Brenda had turned into a fatal accident. Even more, they tried to understand *why* it had happened. A year later the memories of Brenda's funeral and all the grief had not dimmed. Yet her friends had begun to heal from the shock. Some of them were now able to recall fond memories and even to tell an occasional funny story about Brenda. Others would laugh, for a brief moment forgetting that she was gone. Then the pain would come back, and the agonizing question would linger in the air like a plea: "Why? My God, why?"

Responding to Tragedy

Few of the details of this real story have been changed in this account. You may know a similar story involving the death of a very special person. Every year high school students all over the country grieve the loss of friends who die in car accidents or drown during swim parties. They watch in silent horror as classmates with cancer suffer through their last months of life. The same question haunts many of us: Why would God let this happen?

Answers That Fail to Satisfy

In Brenda's death we are faced with questions that do not have obvious or easy answers. Even her schoolmates who had a strong faith in God could not make sense of Brenda's death. It seemed totally absurd to them. The answers that some religious people give at such times—"It must have been God's will," "God wanted to take her home to heaven," or even, "God wanted to teach us all a lesson about how fragile life is"—were completely inadequate. A neatly packaged answer that would make sense of Brenda's death was not possible.

The lack of satisfactory answers to life's tragedies convinces some people that there must not be a God, or at least not a God who loves and cares for us. How could a loving God let such things happen?

A Christian Response: Deepened Trust

We certainly cannot assume that God arranges tragedy and suffering for some grand purpose. A truly honest Christian response to the question of why suffering occurs, is that we do not know why. Although we believe that Brenda is with God in her death, we do not have all the answers about why she died. Life has a mysterious dimension, and some things are simply beyond us. What Christians do know is that even the worst suffering imaginable can bring forth life in abundance. This was demonstrated by the aftermath of Jesus' torturous Crucifixion and death on the cross. For Jesus, the Resurrection followed his terrible suffering and death. For us today, new life and growth can spring forth from suffering of any kind.

Christians believe something further about Jesus: In Jesus, God became human and walked, lived, and suffered among us. And God continues to be with us and for us in our pain, loss, and suffering. The Christian response to suffering is to deepen trust in God. It is to hang in there and keep believing that goodness can eventually come forth from suffering, and that God's grace is given to us when we suffer and when we grieve.

Why would a loving God let bad things happen to innocent people? *Student art:* "Suffer the Little Children," linocut print by Mary Gattas, Saint Agnes Academy, Memphis, Tennessee

8
Recall and briefly write about an incident from your own life that prompted you to ask, "Why would God let this happen?" Explain how you answered that question.

For Review

- Give three examples from the text of inadequate answers to the question, Why would God let tragedy happen?
- What is an honest Christian response to tragedy?

How Can We Know About God?

How do we know that God is with us when we suffer? How do we know that God even exists? These are difficult questions that are too often assigned easy answers. Yet most of us have experienced the need for in-depth answers, with honest attempts to respond to our questions at both the heart and the head levels.

The first consideration when we are trying to come to a knowledge of God is, Does God exist at all, and how do we know? We have to deal with this question if any of the other material in this course is going to make sense. Discussing the truth of Christianity or Catholicism, for example, makes no sense without first spending some time on the more basic issue of whether God exists.

Lots of easy answers to what is sometimes referred to as **"the God question"** are available. Such answers can either affirm or deny God's existence. Here are some typical answers:

- Of course God exists. That's just the way it is.
- You have to take it on faith.
- I have always believed.
- I don't believe in what I can't see, and I don't see God.
- The universe is a random accident, not a creation by God.

Some people may feel that such pat answers are enough for them. Frequently, however, these answers fail to satisfy people. More sophisticated answers are expected—and deserved.

Signs of God's Existence

We cannot set up a scientific experiment to prove absolutely that God exists, like proving beyond question that the earth is round. Yet we do have signs of God's existence, if we keep our eyes and mind open.

In the Convictions of Persons Who Care for Us

We can believe in God because others who care about us have taught us to do so—perhaps parents, teachers, or pastors. Believing in God *only* because others have taught us to is not the best reason for having faith, but when we are young and not fully able to take on the mystery of God for ourselves, it is the usual way we begin to believe.

Yet we cannot rely completely on others' faith convictions for a reason to believe in God. The faith of others can lead us to faith in God, but we must not mistake one for the other. People can let us down. For example, what if those who have cared for us and whom we love choose not to believe and trust in God? Does that mean that we follow their lead away from faith? What about young people who are tragically abused by those who are supposed to be caring for them and who claim to be persons of faith? Certainly such victims would seem to have more reason not to believe in God than to believe. So we must look for other sources of evidence upon which to make a sound decision about God.

9
Have you ever been awestricken by something in nature? If so, explain the experience in a paragraph.

In Human Reason

Fortunately human beings are created with intelligence. Through their own experience and thought processes, looking at themselves and the world around them, they can come to an understanding that God exists.

From experience with the natural world. Many scientists who study the intricacies of the natural world are coming more and more to the conclusion that a world like ours could not exist by chance, that its wonderful beauty and order point to a mysterious origin.

We do not have to be a scientist, though, nor an "outdoor type," to be awestricken by the wonders of creation. All of us can find something to marvel at if we just take the time.

If you can, take some time to go outside on a clear, peaceful night and stretch out on the grass. Find a place where the darkness is deep. Watch the night sky and simply let it speak to you. Avoid trying to analyze anything. Just relax and observe. Or spend some time watching the ants that make anthills in the cracks of the sidewalk, or the spider weaving a web in the corner of a room or window frame. Such moments of contemplating both the immense and the small wonders of creation can expand our heart and mind.

The glories of nature may give us a very personal sense of mystery. When we consider creation—from the immensity of the universe down to the tiny world of the ants, and the infinitely smaller reality of the atom—and realize that all of nature holds together somehow, we want to ask how? . . . or by whom?

From experience of ourselves as human persons. Chapter 1 spoke of the built-in longing for happiness that is part of every human being. We experience ourselves, too, as

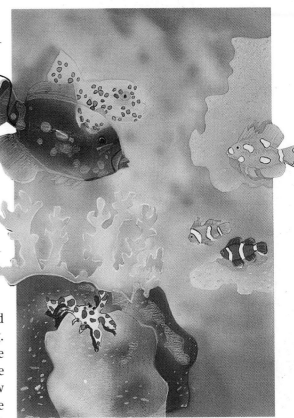

The marvels of creation make us wonder how such order and beauty could have come about.
Student art: "Look at the Fish," mixed media by Stephanie Przedwiecki, Saint Wendelin High School, Fostoria, Ohio

more than our physical body. We are conscious; we fall in love; we make deep friendships; we debate; we create; we dream and plan for the future. We desire truth, moral goodness, and beauty. All these point to a spiritual dimension in us. Our humanness must have a spiritual origin.

In Universal Belief Throughout History

The vast majority of the world's people claim a belief in **Sacred Mystery.** Perhaps they were all taught this belief and merely accept what they have been told. More likely, many of these people find their religious beliefs confirmed in their life experiences. Something beyond their family background and upbringing convinces them of the reality of a God—or sometimes of multiple gods.

This belief in some kind of divinity has been with humankind throughout history and even before recorded history. Scientists are now able to trace human culture back some forty thousand years to the time of the cave dwellers. Amazingly, evidence of religious belief and ritual exists even among those early humans. Since prehistoric times, all cultures have developed religions, with ritual and worship as a part of them. Thus belief in God—at least as the belief in some power beyond us—seems to be a basic trait of human culture.

In the Experience of Being Loved

Love relationships can put us in touch with the sense of Mystery in life. This is true both when we reach out in love to another person and when we experience another person's love for us.

Almost more remarkable than the experience of loving someone is that of being loved by another. Most of us at times doubt our own value, worth, and goodness. When we realize that someone loves us for ourselves, however, the experience can be wonderfully freeing. By the same token, we should not be surprised to discover that people who are lonely, hurt, or abused often find that believing in God is difficult—at least when God is pictured as loving and caring, because they have not experienced any human examples of God's love.

The gift of another's affection and concern can fill us with the sense of the basic goodness of life and with the belief that such goodness can come only from a gracious and loving Creator.

As human beings we can come to know of God's existence through the natural means and experiences described in this section. Not everyone believes in God, however. **Atheists** (who deny the existence of God) and **agnostics** (who say we cannot know whether there is a God) offer dif-

As humans, we are conscious; we desire truth, goodness, and beauty. Our humanness must have a spiritual origin.
Student art: "A Modern Day Thinker," oil painting by Amy Westerman, Holy Cross High School, Louisville, Kentucky

ficult questions and arguments against having faith in God. Many cite, for instance, the **problem of evil:** Why do evil and suffering exist in the world if there is a loving God? This question was raised earlier in connection with the story of Brenda's tragic death. The senseless pain of innocent people, natural disasters that wipe out the lives of thousands, the incredible cruelty that people inflict on one another, the Nazi death camps, and so on, are experiences that haunt believers and challenge religious faith. Faith in God is not always easy; it can be very hard to believe. But for many throughout history, faith has brought deep and genuine healing and joy.

Revelation: God's Self-Disclosure

Human beings have a built-in desire for God and a capacity to believe in God, although not all people are believers. But if we do believe in God, what kind of God do we believe in, and how do we decide that? Where do we get our understandings of God? How do we arrive at certain beliefs about the qualities possessed by God and about the nature of the relationship between God and people or, more personally, between God and me as an individual?

If God is to be known to us, we must rely on God's self-disclosure. God reveals to us what we could never discover on our own. Our own reasoning abilities take us only so far, and God has to do the rest.

God Longs for Intimacy with Us

Revelation is the self-communication or self-disclosure of God, in which Sacred Mystery is made known by God to human beings. We may wonder, Why does God wish to reveal or disclose Sacred Mystery to us?

Revelation is based on the belief that God created people in order to enter into a personal, intimate relationship with them, a relationship in which both God and humans fully reveal themselves to each other. God, of course, does not have the fears about being shy or embarrassed that you and I normally have when we think of revealing our innermost thoughts or our deepest feelings! God's gift of self can be totally free because God is God.

10
Think of a time when you disclosed to another person something personal about yourself that was at least a little bit hard to share. Describe in writing what the experience was like, positive or negative.

Clearly God would enter into such a relationship only if God cared deeply for people. So the concept of Revelation implies a God who loves and cares for us enough to take the initiative, to become one with us in our history, constantly revealing Sacred Mystery to us. God longs to have a deep, intimate relationship with us.

This is another way of saying what was said earlier—that faith is a gift from God. The only way we ever come to faith, to a believing and trusting relationship with God, is because God invites such a relationship. Faith in God is initiated only by God and sustained by both God and the person.

How Is God Revealed?

Besides all the ways God is revealed to us through our natural capacities as human beings (recall the signs of God's existence), God's Revelation has also been experienced and understood by people throughout history in four other ways.

Within individual experience. One way that the Revelation of God takes place is within personal life experiences—God communicates directly to and with individuals. This results in a deeply personal sense of union with God. The individual then responds with a whole new outlook and attitude toward life. Several Christian churches emphasize the need for this kind of personal religious experience if we hope to gain salvation.

The Bible includes many stories of such individual encounters with God, such as the experiences of Moses and Saint Paul. But God is also revealed in the less intense, everyday experiences of people like ourselves. For example, a high school student addresses God in these excerpts from an original prayer:

> As I walk into the hallway in school,
> I am kindly greeted by my friends;
> In their acceptance I hear your voice.
>
> . . . .
>
> At night, during dinner,
> My parents inquire about how my day went;
> In their love and concern I hear your voice.
>
> (Alaine Gherardi, Academy of the Holy Angels,
> Demarest, New Jersey)

God's Revelation in personal experience is not reserved for mystics and saints—it is open to all.

Through the events of history. Sacred Mystery is also revealed by God through the events of history that a community or a people live through and experience together. In the tradition of Jews and Christians, this is called **salvation history**, the history of the People of God. These marvelous events throughout history include the Exodus and, for Christians, the death and Resurrection of Jesus, events we will take up in later chapters. Jesus himself is seen by Christians as the fullest Revelation, the one in whom God was totally revealed, God's only Son.

Within sacred writings or scriptures. Many of the major world religions possess special writings that they see as revealing the wisdom of God in unique and holy ways. These are called scriptures, which literally means "writings." The Hindu scriptures are known as the Vedas, and Islam's holy book is called the Koran, or Qur'an. Of course Jews and Christians revere the Bible, although for Jews the Bible consists of the first part of the Christian Bible, known as the Hebrew Scriptures or Old Testament. Just how God is revealed in the Jewish and Christian Scriptures is a subject of much debate and discussion, and we will return to that question later in this course.

Through religious teachings and statements of faith. Scriptures are written down at a certain point in time, and historical events and personal experiences of God happen at particular times to particular persons. These writings and experiences reveal God to us. But to better understand these "messages" from God, people must reflect on them for a long time and live them out. This is why religious teachings and statements of faith are so important. They take the community's or people's experiences of God's Revelation in the past and try to distill and summarize the community's understanding of them into clearly stated teachings. Such teachings of faith are known as doctrines or dogmas. For Catholicism the Tradition of church teachings has always been very significant as a means of transmitting God's Revelation. We will look at Catholic Tradition in more depth throughout this course, but particularly in chapter 8.

For Review

- Briefly describe four different sources of evidence of God's existence.
- What is Revelation? On what belief about God is this concept based?
- Briefly describe the ways that God's Revelation takes place.

Faith and Religious Practices: The Same or Different?

We have been using the word *faith* throughout this chapter, but you may be wondering: Where does religion come in? Are faith and religious practices the same thing? The answer is no; they are related but not the same thing. Here is a way to understand the difference.

Religious Practices: A Way to Express Faith

When we feel something deeply, we have to express that feeling. For instance, if we want to encourage somebody during an athletic event, we may applaud and cheer. If we care a lot about some people, we may hug them, kiss them, or give them gifts. If we feel angry, we may scream and pound the wall. All these actions are natural attempts to express inward feelings in outward ways.

Our wonderfully human need for expression is part of our experience of religious faith, too. Throughout history people have struggled to find ways to express outwardly what they have experienced and come to believe about God. This is precisely what **religious practices** are all about. They are the attempt by peoples and communities throughout history to express their shared faith through outward signs—including symbols, celebrations, statements of belief, and codes of behavior. Exactly how this is done in any one community depends both on its particular understanding of God and on the available expressions—symbols, celebrations, statements, and codes of behavior—that are recognized and understood by that community. This is the major reason that we have so many different religious traditions in the world.

Buddhist monks worship in a temple in Bangkok, Thailand.

Faith, then, is like the love we have for a friend. A religious act is like the hug we give our friend—the way we express our love. But someone else might express love in a different way—through a smile, a pat on the back, affectionate teasing. Those different gestures of love are somewhat like the different religious traditions in the world, which are the ways that various peoples and communities have found to express their faith in God.

They Need Each Other

So faith and religious expressions are not the same, but they need each other very much. Love that goes unexpressed by gestures or words dries up after a while. Likewise, faith that goes unexpressed eventually drifts off into the air because it does not seem real and concrete anymore.

And think of it the other way around. Have you ever known people who act "mushy" with everyone, hugging and acting affectionate all the time, but somehow it doesn't feel genuine? That is like religious practices that do not express a genuine faith. If faith is not present, religious expressions have no basis and will eventually become meaningless, empty, and boring. To an outsider such practices seem hypocritical, and at times they are.

Is There a Crisis of Faith?

Are teenagers today undergoing a crisis of faith? Sometimes we hear this, but we need to sort out what is really happening among young people.

Recent surveys demonstrate that 95 percent of teenagers in the United States believe in God, and about 74 percent pray at least occasionally. These statistics suggest that no crisis of faith exists. On the other hand, many teenagers—and their parents as well—are not completely satisfied with the ways their religious faith is expressed. In fact, they may be turned off by religious practices. So for them it is more a crisis of religious practices than faith.

Expressing Faith Is Not Easy

Discomfort with religious practices is hardly surprising and need not be the cause of exaggerated concern. Even as individuals we do not find it easy to express our deepest feelings to one another. Clearly and comfortably expressing outwardly what we feel inside is extremely hard work and can seem nearly impossible.

Telling It Like It Is!

BACK in the era of the Hebrew Scriptures, God's people got off track sometimes. They put tremendous emphasis on doing all their religious observances and practices correctly—like sacrificing their animals and their harvest—but they lost a sense of what it was all about, which was faith in their God. This was evident because they became unjust, and they exploited poor people.

At such times prophets would speak up on behalf of God, telling the people in loud and blunt ways that their religious practices were worthless without the justice that showed their faith in God. Here the prophet Amos conveys God's message to the people in scathing terms:

I hate, I despise your festivals,
and I take no delight in your solemn assemblies.
Even though you offer me your burnt offerings and grain offerings,
I will not accept them;
and the offerings of well-being of your fatted animals
I will not look upon.
Take away from me the noise of your songs;
I will not listen to the melody of your harps.
But let justice roll down like waters,
and righteousness like an ever-flowing stream.

(Amos 5:21–24)

11
Have you ever been insincere, that is, have you ever expressed or said something outwardly that you didn't really mean inside? Describe in writing what that was like and how you felt about it.

A Question, an Answer

I don't know Who—
or what—
put the question,
I don't know
when it was put.
I don't even
remember answering.
But at some moment
I did answer
Yes to Someone—
or Something—
and from that hour
I was certain
that existence
is meaningful
and that, therefore,
my life,
in self-surrender,
had a goal.
(Dag Hammarskjöld, *Markings*)

12
Have you had the opportunity
to be around people—adults
or teenagers—that you would
describe as deeply faith filled?
What effect have they had on you?
Write about your experiences.

What is true for us as individuals is just as true for a religion in its attempts to express the faith shared by its members. That is precisely why religious practices do not always appeal to us, why we cannot expect to feel excited every time we go to Mass, and why the words that we use to describe God or pray to God seem to fall short. But we should never stop trying to let our religious practices truly express our faith.

Questioning Faith Because of Religious Practices

A dissatisfaction with religious practices can lead to a crisis of faith. For instance, many people feel frustrated with their religious upbringing, with the lack of meaning in public worship, or with disagreements over specific religious or moral teachings. Because they are questioning their particular religious traditions, they assume their faith in God is gone. But that is not necessarily the case.

For example, you have probably known people who say they do not believe in God, and maybe you put yourself in that category. When asked why they do not believe, most of these people say they are unhappy with *religion* as they have experienced it. The danger here is that they are "throwing the baby out with the bath water." In other words, they reject a good thing (faith) because it is related to something they are dissatisfied with (religious practices).

Celebrating Faith

Perhaps the religious expressions some people have been involved in have lacked a dimension of personal faith in God. If a community practicing its religion has little or no sense of faith, the religion can seem boring and meaningless. But when a shared faith relationship with God is present, the members of that community hunger to express their faith together, and that brings about spirited and nourishing religious celebrations and practices that are very much alive. Teenagers need to be with and celebrate with other people of deep and genuine faith—both adults and other teens—if they are to embrace their religion enthusiastically.

Faith and religious practices are different, but they do go hand in hand and need each other.

The Challenge of Responding

The challenge that eventually confronts each of us is to make a personal response regarding all the matters discussed in this chapter.

- We are all confronted with the decision of whether to believe and trust in God. In Christian terms that means responding to God's invitation to faith with a yes or a no. Our yes or no may not always register at 100 percent; we are likely to waver and shift as we go through different experiences and periods of development. And, as was said earlier, our yes or no may be given not all at once but in many opportunities over a lifetime.

- If our response to God's invitation is yes, we confront another decision: How do we live out that relationship with God in our life? Will we live it out within a certain religious tradition? If so, which one?

Muslims, members of the religion of Islam, bow to the one God, whom they call Allah.

This last point does not imply that all religions are the same, or that what one believes makes no difference, or that one religion is as good as another. Not at all. Certainly most religions are sincere in their conviction of their own truth, have valuable insights into God and the nature of God's relationship with people, and are worthy of our respect and study. The Catholic church recognizes the human right to **religious freedom,** and "rejects nothing of what is true and holy in [non-Christian] religions," according to its document on non-Christians (*Nostra Aetate,* number 2). Nevertheless, Christians believe that God has revealed the fullest depth of divine mystery in Jesus Christ. But even as Catholic Christians live their faith, the church calls on them to

13
From what you know of non-Christian religions, name something that is "true and holy" in one of them.

"acknowledge, preserve and encourage the spiritual and moral truths found among non-Christians" (number 2).

Each of us must search for the truth with sincerity and open-mindedness. But it is not meant to be a lonely search, undertaken on our own. That is why children are usually raised in a specific religious tradition, so that they will be surrounded by caring people of faith when they become old enough to search for answers to their deepest questions about life.

Perhaps this course in Catholic Christianity will be a significant help in your search. Whether you were raised Catholic or not, this course can offer you insights into the faith heritage that has inspired many of your teachers and those who founded your school, possibly your parents, and millions of great and even heroic people who have gone before you.

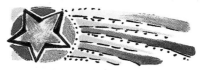

For Review

- What is the difference between faith and religious practices? Why do they need each other?
- How can a crisis of religious practices lead to a faith crisis?
- Why do young people need to be around people of faith and not just people who follow religious practices?
- What is the Catholic church's attitude toward non-Christian religions?

A Testimony of Faith

A little more than fifty years ago, a young woman about your age struggled with questions of faith in God amid the terrible reality of the Holocaust, or *Shoah*, of World War II. The Nazi regime under Adolf Hitler, intent on creating a "pure" white race, herded millions of Jews and others they considered undesirable into concentration camps. In the camps, death by execution, disease, or starvation was almost certain. In an attempt to escape such a fate, Anne Frank, a Jewish thirteen-year-old, and her family went into hiding in Nazi-occupied Holland in 1942. For the next two years Anne kept a diary. In the following excerpt Anne writes of maintaining, and even deepening, faith in dangerous, life-threatening circumstances:

We've been strongly reminded of the fact that we're Jews in chains, chained to one spot, without any rights, but with a thousand obligations. We must put our feelings aside; we must be brave and strong, bear discomfort without complaint, do whatever is in our power and trust in God. One day this terrible war will be over. The time will come when we'll be people again and not just Jews!

Who has inflicted this on us? Who has set us apart from all the rest? Who has put us through such suffering? It's God who has made us the way we are, but it's also God who will lift us up again. In the eyes of the world, we're doomed, but if, after all this suffering, there are still Jews left, the Jewish people will be held up as an example. Who knows, maybe our religion will teach the world and all the people in it about goodness, and that's the reason, the only reason, we have to suffer. . . .

Be brave! Let's remember our duty and perform it without complaint. There will be a way out. God has never deserted our people. Through the ages Jews have had to suffer, but through the ages they've gone on living, and the centuries of suffering have only made them stronger. The weak shall fall and the strong shall survive and not be defeated! (*The Diary of a Young Girl,* pages 261–262)

After two years in hiding, Anne and her family were discovered and sent off to concentration camps. Anne died less than a year later, one of six million Jews who died in the *Shoah.* Her diary was left behind, though, and her father published it after the war. It has inspired tens of millions of readers with its testimony of faith in God and the goodness of humanity. Anne's Frank's spirit certainly did survive the *Shoah.*

Catholic Christianity is grounded in, and founded on, the history and religious tradition of the Jews. In other words, Christianity was born out of the faith experience and religious expression of the Jewish people. Therefore, if we understand Judaism we will develop a stronger understanding of the Catholic heritage. Jesus was born into a devout Jewish family. As a child he was educated in the Jewish faith, and as an adult he became a Jewish teacher and prophet. He proclaimed his vision of God and the meaning of life to the Jews. The earliest followers of Jesus were Jews, and they were the founding members of the religious community that today we recognize as the church.

So we will turn next to Judaism and the history of God's people in the time before Jesus.

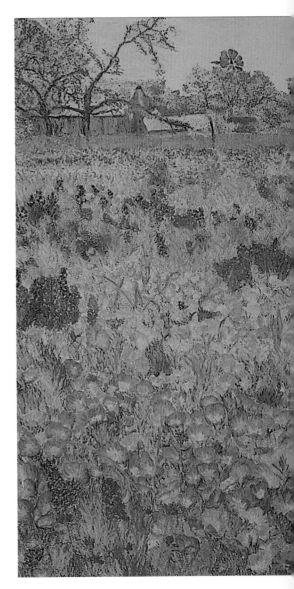

Anne Frank's testimony of faith speaks of her hope in the goodness of God and life itself.
Student art: Untitled, oil pastel drawing by Melanie Weickel, Mercy Academy, Louisville, Kentucky

3

Judaism:

Discovering Our Religious Roots

A People of the Promise

God holds out an invitation to every single human being—the offer to live intimately with God, responding with trust and belief to the love that God pours out in us. As we saw in the previous chapter, human beings are free to respond with faith to God's invitation, or not to respond at all. And faith is not typically an "all or nothing" response. Like the love between a couple that ideally grows and deepens in a marriage over many years together, the human response of faith in God usually grows and becomes more mature over a lifetime.

Like a Marriage Bond

Think of a couple on their wedding day. They pledge a special bond with each other, and they intend that it will last forever. When they make their marriage vows, or solemn promises, they know that their life together will be quite a journey, full of rugged and smooth places, although they do not know in just what ways it will be rugged or smooth. Plenty of uncertainty lies ahead of them. If they are insightful about how most marriages go, the couple may realize that in the course of their life together, they will probably take each other for granted at times and let each other down. They will also inevitably hurt and disappoint each other. But on the day they make those vows, they pledge that they will be true to each other "in good times and in bad, in sickness and in health . . . all the days of my life." They say, in other words, "I have faith in you, and I will *keep faith* with you always."

1

Is there someone in your life who has been faithful and supportive to you even when you have let that person down? If so, describe that person in a paragraph, including a sentence that begins, *This person is a little bit like God because . . .*

The promises of marriage are a special bond that can unite the couple through all the ups and downs of life. Sometimes one or both persons may be unable or unwilling to live up to the promises. But the ideal is that the couple stay committed to each other as marriage partners through their whole lives.

In a way, the bond between God and a person of faith is like that. But the bond uniting God and the believer has one crucial difference: God *never* lets the person down; God is always faithful, even when the person lets God down.

God's Covenant: A Special Bond with a Whole People

A life of love with God is offered to each person individually, and we can respond with faith as individuals. In the tradition of Catholic Christianity, though, a person's relationship with God is much more than a matter of "me and God." God reaches out to all creation and desires to enter into a loving relationship with all human beings as a community, not just as individuals. To reach all humanity, God chose to have a special bond with one group of people *as a people,* acting in the midst of their history. Through them, God intended that all human beings might eventually come to know and love God.

The solemn promise between God and the people whom God has chosen is called the **Covenant.** Like marriage promises (which are even called a "marriage covenant"), God's Covenant with the people is a pledge of faithfulness forever—a pledge that God will never give up on them and will love them "in good times and in bad." For their part the people pledge their faithful love, too—to love God, one another, and all God has created. But as we will see, they are not as good at keeping their promise as God is!

Our People, *Our* Family, *Our* Roots

Who are the people God has chosen through this Covenant? Ultimately God chooses all people and desires union with all of them. But this chapter tells the story of that People of God, the **Jews**, who were chosen by God at a particular time in history, and with whom God continues to have a special relationship. In ancient times, long before Christianity came on the world scene, the Jews—as a people, not just as individuals—were the ones who carried God's promise of faithful love. Christians and Jews share a special heritage.

We know that Jesus was a Jew. He felt their hopes and dreams and longings, spoke in their language, thought as they thought, prayed their prayers, remembered their history, celebrated their holy feast days, read their Scriptures, heard and told their wisdom. He was a Jewish man in every respect. The story of the Jews and their relationship with God is also Jesus' story, his "family background." We cannot understand Christianity without getting inside the mind and heart of Jesus. And we cannot get inside Jesus' mind and heart without understanding his Jewish roots. Thus, for Christians, the story of the Jews before Jesus is *our* story as well. The people with whom God chose to have a loving bond are also *our* people. Their past is *our* past.

The Need for a Sense of the Past

Just imagine what happens to persons who cannot remember their own past, where they came from and what their history has been. You have probably heard of such people, who for some reason have completely lost their memory. These people suffer from something called amnesia. Maybe

Jewish boys in present-day Jerusalem are schooled in the traditional practices of prayer and devotion by a rabbi at the Western Wall.

2
Write about one incident from your family's past, even going back to your parents' or grandparents' lives before you came along, that helps explain why your family is the way it is today.

they suffered a bad blow to the head and cannot remember who they are or recognize their own relatives. All recollection of home and workplace is lost. In a way, their identity is lost with their memory. Rebuilding an amnesiac's life and identity is a slow and painstaking process. But as memories are triggered for the person by small events, even hearing a song on the radio or smelling a certain aroma, the sense of who he or she is begins to take shape again.

Without a sense of the past, our present life, like an amnesiac's, would be filled with confusion and loneliness. We need to know where we came from or else we do not recognize who we are. And so it is with groups of people, too. A family needs some sense of its past to understand who it is in the present. A nation does as well. So does your school and your town. So, too, does a religion.

Catholic Christianity has emerged out of a history that stretches back nearly four thousand years, to the beginning of what would come to be known as **Judaism**, the religion of the Jews. We cannot expect to understand Catholicism without a sense of that past. In this chapter, then, we are going to briefly explore the history and heritage of the Jewish people up to the time of Jesus.

More Than Just History

The story of the Jews goes beyond history in our usual sense of that term, for we are dealing with more than a series of historical events involving certain people on clearly defined dates. Rather, we are exploring salvation history, the story of God's action and Revelation among a people throughout their history. That story revolves around the Covenant that God made with the Jews, the promise to be faithful to them and to bring salvation to the whole world through them as a people.

Let's start at the beginning of the story. Some of it may be familiar to you, but some of it may not. It will help you to refer to the timeline of events in biblical history on page 63.

For Review

- Compare and contrast the bond between marriage partners with the bond between God and a person of faith.
- What is the Covenant between God and the people God has chosen? How is it like a marriage covenant?
- Why is it necessary to understand Judaism in order to understand Catholic Christianity?

The Beginnings of a People

Abraham, Father of Biblical Faith

Abraham lived in a region of the Near East about eighteen hundred years before Jesus. He belonged to a group of tribal people known as the **Hebrews.**

The Covenant Begins

According to the Hebrew Scriptures of the Bible (also known as the Old Testament), God called Abraham out of his obscure life as a wandering shepherd, or nomad, told him to go to a new land where God would be with him, and gave him a remarkable promise. God promised that from Abraham and his family would come a great nation, and

that all families of the earth would be blessed through him. Abraham's descendants would be more numerous than the countless stars in the heavens. Because Abraham's wife, **Sarah,** had never had any children and was now old and past her childbearing years, this seemed like a strange promise. But Abraham trusted in God and set off with his family to **Canaan,** the Promised Land.

This relationship between God and Abraham was the beginning of the Covenant, which God would renew again and again with the Jews throughout their long history. As a physical sign of the people's commitment to that Covenant, their male children from Abraham's time on were circumcised.

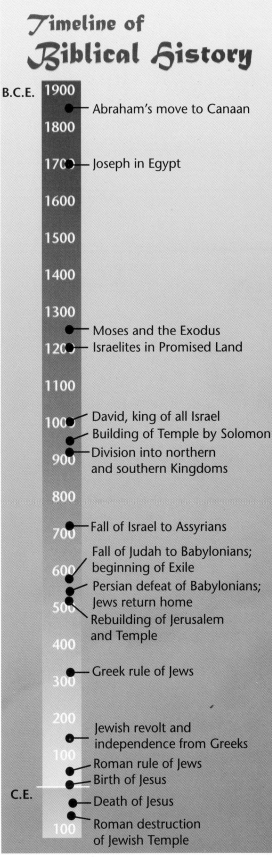

Timeline of **Biblical History**

B.C.E.

- 1900 — Abraham's move to Canaan
- 1800
- 1700 — Joseph in Egypt
- 1600
- 1500
- 1400
- 1300
- — Moses and the Exodus
- 1200 — Israelites in Promised Land
- 1100
- 1000 — David, king of all Israel
- — Building of Temple by Solomon
- 900 — Division into northern and southern Kingdoms
- 800
- 700 — Fall of Israel to Assyrians
- 600 — Fall of Judah to Babylonians; beginning of Exile
- — Persian defeat of Babylonians; Jews return home
- 500 — Rebuilding of Jerusalem and Temple
- 400
- 300 — Greek rule of Jews
- 200
- — Jewish revolt and independence from Greeks
- 100 — Roman rule of Jews
- — Birth of Jesus

C.E.

- — Death of Jesus
- 100 — Roman destruction of Jewish Temple

3

Do some research on the religion of Islam. Find out at least one belief or practice that is similar to something in Christianity or Judaism. Write a report describing that belief or practice.

4

Think of a situation today in which you, someone you know, or a whole group of people could be as forgiving of another who has hurt them as Joseph was of his brothers who had sold him into slavery. Write about how difficult it might be to forgive, and about the good that might come from it.

Jewish and Muslim sacred sites exist side-by-side in Jerusalem today, reminders of the common "father" of these two religions—Abraham.

The One God

The belief in many gods is called **polytheism**. The world in which Abraham lived was polytheistic—people worshiped all kinds of gods. Abraham struggled with the mystery of the many gods. However, once he had been called by the God of the promise, he began to realize that there was one God above all other gods. He decided to be faithful to that God and no other.

This faith of Abraham developed into **monotheism**, or the belief that only one God exists. That belief would later become central to the three world religions that today trace their origins back to Abraham: Judaism, Christianity, and Islam (the religion of the Muslims). These three religions are connected by their common worship of the One God, the God of Abraham.

Abraham's Descendants, the Israelites

Amazingly, Abraham's wife, Sarah, did give birth to a son, named **Isaac**. (Another son of Abraham by a different woman was Ishmael, from whom Muslims believe they are descended.) Isaac married, and his wife, **Rebekah**, had a son, **Jacob**, to whom God later gave the name *Israel*, meaning "one who has contended with divine and human beings." (This name came from the story of Jacob's wrestling with a mysterious, angel-like being one night.) The people who descended from Jacob thus became known as the **Israelites**. Centuries later they would be known as the Jews.

Patriarchs and Matriarchs

So the origins of Judaism are traced to Abraham, the father of biblical faith; his son, Isaac; and grandson, Jacob. These three men are called the **patriarchs** of the Jewish faith, and their wives—Sarah, Rebekah, and **Rachel**—are called the **matriarchs**. Jacob and Rachel's son **Joseph** is also considered one of the patriarchs.

Joseph in Egypt

Jacob had twelve sons altogether, with his favorite being his beloved Joseph. Jacob demonstrated this by giving Joseph a special long robe, often referred to as the "coat of many colors." You may remember the story of how Joseph's favored status caused his brothers to become extremely envious of him. In their hostility the brothers tried to kill him, but then decided instead to sell him as a slave to some merchants who were on their way to Egypt.

Joseph, however, was so talented that he gained great authority and status in **Egypt.** Moreover, he was as virtuous as he was talented. Years after he had been sold into slavery, Joseph forgave his brothers for what they had done to him, and he invited them and his father to leave the famine-stricken Canaan and join him to live comfortably in Egypt.

Under a series of kindly Egyptian **pharaohs** (or kings), the Israelites (Jacob's descendants) continued to live prosperously in Egypt. If the story had ended there, we might be able to say that "they lived happily ever after." But the story is only beginning.

For Review

- What promise did God give to Abraham?
- What three monotheistic religions trace their roots back to Abraham?
- Name the patriarchs and matriarchs of the Jewish faith. Why were the people who were eventually called Jews known as the Israelites?
- How did the Israelites end up living in Egypt?

From Slavery to Freedom

The time of peace and prosperity in Egypt under sympathetic rulers ended for the Israelites when they were enslaved by cruel pharaohs who burdened them with the backbreaking jobs of making bricks and constructing public buildings. This oppressive slavery devastated the Israelites, and they yearned for freedom. Hundreds of years later the answer to their dreams came in the person of the man most revered to this day by faithful Jews. That man was **Moses.**

Moses, the People's Greatest Leader

Moses was the son of Hebrew slaves, but he was raised in the pharaoh's palace. You probably recall the story of how the baby Moses, condemned to death by the ruthless pharaoh along with all Israelite baby boys, was found in a basket on the Nile River bank by the pharaoh's daughter.

The Revelation of a God Named Yahweh

When Moses grew up, personal encounters with God led him to realize he had a mission—to save his people. God told him that he, Moses, was to lead the Israelites from slavery to freedom. As God's sign of intimacy with the people, the holy name of God—"I AM WHO I AM," or **Yahweh** in Hebrew—was revealed to Moses.

The name Yahweh is difficult to translate into English. Some other translations are "I am the One who is present," "I bring into existence all that is," or simply, "I am." The name hints at the very nature of God, one who is both present and yet beyond us. The Jews later held the sacred name in such reverence that they refused to pronounce it out loud, even passing over the word *Yahweh* when reading it in their Scriptures and substituting for it a Hebrew word meaning "Lord."

The Exodus: Escape from Slavery

After a mighty moral struggle with the Egyptian pharaoh, Moses eventually did lead the Israelites in an escape out of Egypt, but the pharaoh's soldiers and chariots pursued the Israelites to catch them and bring them back. No one would ever forget the awesome story of how God saved the Israelites by parting the waters of the sea and leading them across on dry land, then making the waters close back over the Egyptian charioteers when they tried to cross in hot pursuit. The Egyptians drowned in the sea, and the Israelites were free!

This miraculous event of God's freeing the Israelites from slavery, called the **Exodus**, became the central story of God's saving love for Israel. (Historians date the event at about 1250 B.C.E.) Ever after that the people recalled with joy and gratitude how God had freed them from slavery so they could return to Canaan, the **Promised Land.** Whenever they doubted God's love for them, the Israelites only had to remember that God had acted directly in their lives and their history. Moses, their leader, had led them in trusting the God who would never leave them, who could always be counted on. They believed that God's promises to Abraham would be fulfilled—that they would be a great nation someday in their own land, a light to all the other nations. They were a people with a destiny.

The Passover Feast

The Exodus and the events leading up to it are remembered every year to this day in the Jewish feast of **Passover**, with its special memorial meal, the **Seder.** In this meal Jews recall how the Israelites ate a meal of lamb, sacrificed to God, and unleavened bread before they fled Egypt in great haste, to be freed and saved by their God. In recalling the events of the past, Jews bring the liberating power of the Exodus right into their midst in the present. Later in this course we will learn about the role of this ritual meal in the life of Jesus and in the sacrament that Christians call the Eucharist.

The Israelites would never forget the Exodus, the story of God's freeing the people from slavery.
Student art: "Free at Last," three-color linocut print by Julie Oattis, Saint Agnes Academy, Memphis, Tennessee

5
Have you ever felt trapped or oppressed? Describe in writing what it was or is like. If you have been freed from that oppression, tell how it happened and what you experienced. If you are still feeling unfree, describe your longing for freedom.

In the Desert

Having escaped from Egypt, the Israelites knew that God was with them. However, once out of Egypt, while they wandered in the desert, they grumbled at Moses about their severe surroundings and lack of food; they even moaned that they would rather be enslaved in Egypt than die in the desert. Despite their doubts, God took care of them by sending them manna (a bread-like substance that they found on the ground) and quail (small birds) to eat.

The Sinai Covenant

After many days, the Israelites encamped in the desert at the base of **Mount Sinai**, waiting direction from Moses about where to go and what to do next. In an encounter on the mountaintop between Moses and Yahweh, which is told with great drama in the Book of Exodus, God sealed the loving relationship with the people that had begun with the promise to Abraham hundreds of years before. This pledge between God and the Israelites became known as the **Sinai Covenant.**

The scriptural story depicts Yahweh calling Moses to the top of the mountain and giving him this directive:

> "Thus you shall say to the house of Jacob, and tell the Israelites: You have seen what I did to the Egyptians, and how I bore you on eagles' wings and brought you to myself. Now therefore, if you obey my voice and keep my covenant, you shall be my treasured possession out of all the peoples. Indeed, the whole earth is mine, but you shall be for me a priestly kingdom and a holy nation. These are the words that you shall speak to the Israelites." (Exodus 19:3–6)

Moses returned to the people and told them what Yahweh had said, and they agreed to do whatever God asked of them. In one of the most powerful scenes in the Bible, Yahweh again encountered Moses on the mountaintop and presented him with the Law. The **Law** described the Israelites' end of the bargain—in other words, their responsibilities in the sacred Covenant between God and them. The cornerstone of the Law given to Moses, or the **Mosaic Law**, is what we now call the **Ten Commandments.**

A Law That Frees

With their acceptance of the Law as a code of both individual and communal behavior, the Israelites forever changed and elevated the human understanding of morality, our sense of what is right and wrong. It was a great moral leap forward, a code that truly did make the Jews "a light

The Sinai Desert, with Mount Sinai in the background
Facing page: Stone tablets, like those on which the Ten Commandments were said to have been written, from an Egyptian temple in the Sinai Desert

to the nations" (Isaiah 42:6), that is, a light to all peoples who were Gentiles, or non-Jews.

The Mosaic Law (or **Law of Moses**) did not carry the restrictive or negative meaning for the Israelites that today we may associate with laws, which we see as limiting our freedom and locking us in. For the ancient Israelites and for faithful Jews today, the Law promotes freedom because it is an expression of God's loving intention for the people. The Law is all about how to love God and one's neighbor. For Christians as well, the Ten Commandments of the Law are the foundation of morality.

The Covenant with its Law was somewhat like a loving marriage, which entails mutual responsibilities of the spouses to each other. The Jews did not see the responsibilities of the Mosaic Law as a burden but as a way of expressing their love and concern for one another and their devotion to the God who had freed them.

Although for Christians the Ten Commandments are the most familiar part of the Law, the Law is far more extensive than that, speaking to almost every aspect of the lives of the Jews. In Jesus' time some Jews were more negative in their understanding of the Law, trying to live exactly by the letter of the Law rather than by its loving spirit. For instance, some Jews, citing God's commandment to rest on the Sabbath, would not even help someone in trouble if it was the Sabbath day. Jesus condemned those who lived only by the letter of the Law, not because he rejected the Law but because he loved it and did not want to see it misused.

Wandering for Forty Years

Once again it would be wonderful to say, "And they lived happily ever after." But of course that is not what happened.

The Israelites, who had been chosen and freed by a tender and loving God, soon lost sight of how gracious God had been to them. While Moses spent forty days on the mountaintop receiving the Law from Yahweh, the people down below grew impatient. As a diversion they built an idol of metal—a golden calf made of melted-down jewelry—and had a festival to honor it, and offered sacrifices to it. Already they were worshiping a false god.

The Ten Commandments

THIS is the account from the Book of Exodus of God's giving the Ten Commandments to Moses:

Then God spoke all these words:

"I am the LORD your God, who brought you out of the land of Egypt, out of the house of slavery; you shall have no other gods before me. . . .

"You shall not make wrongful use of the name of the LORD your God, for the LORD will not acquit anyone who misuses his name.

"Remember the sabbath day, and keep it holy. Six days you shall labor and do all your work. But the seventh day is a sabbath to the LORD your God. . . . For in six days the LORD made heaven and earth, the sea, and all that is in them, but rested the seventh day; therefore the LORD blessed the sabbath day and consecrated it.

"Honor your father and your mother, so that your days may be long in the land that the LORD your God is giving you.

"You shall not murder.

"You shall not commit adultery.

"You shall not steal.

"You shall not bear false witness against your neighbor.

"You shall not covet your neighbor's house; you shall not covet your neighbor's wife, or male or female slave, or ox, or donkey, or anything that belongs to your neighbor."

When all the people witnessed the thunder and lightning, the sound of the trumpet, and the mountain smoking, they were afraid and trembled and stood at a distance. (20:1–18)

Although Moses was furious with the people when he found out what they had done, he and God did not abandon them. However, the people did not soon reach the Promised Land. For forty years they were lost and wandered in the desert, learning through many mistakes, hardships, and triumphs to trust more deeply in the God who had saved them. In their best moments the people knew that Yahweh was with them every step of their long journey, even when God seemed absent.

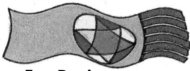

For Review

- Who was Moses, and what mission did God give him?
- What was God's name as revealed to Moses?
- What was the Exodus? How do Jews to this day celebrate and remember the Exodus?
- What was the Sinai Covenant, and how is the Law given to Moses related to that Covenant? What is the cornerstone of the Law?

The Promised Land

Moses himself never reached the Promised Land. He died just before his people entered the fertile territory of Canaan, promised to Abraham's descendants by God as a land "'flowing with milk and honey'" (Exodus 3:7). Today this land is variously identified as **Palestine**, **Israel**, or the **Holy Land.**

Taking Over the Land

Joshua, Moses' assistant, led the Israelites into Canaan. But it was not a peaceful entry. The people who already lived there were not happy to see the Israelites laying claim to the land. The period that followed was filled with constant warfare between the Israelites and other tribes, as well as between the Israelites and the city dwellers of the region. As they had in the desert, the Israelites at times abandoned Yahweh, choosing to worship false gods instead. It was in those times of infidelity to Yahweh that they fell into the worst trouble. When they relied on their own power instead of God's, they met with disaster and were defeated by their enemies.

During these struggles, men and women called **judges** were periodically appointed to bring the people back to reliance on Yahweh. Israel's judges did not have the legal func-

6
Recall a time when you felt "lost in the desert," wandering around not knowing what to do about some problem, making mistakes and going through hardships. Write a one-page reflection on what you learned from the experience.

7
Agree or disagree with this statement and explain your answer in writing: *Today God takes the side of one country or group over the other in war.*

Facing page: A sculpture of David as a young soldier battling the giant Goliath with his slingshot.

tions of today's judges. A judge was more of a ruler or a chief. But unlike a kingship, which is passed on from father to son, judges were recognized by the ways they made the spirit of Yahweh evident. For example, **Samson**, perhaps the most familiar of the judges, was capable of superhuman feats because "the spirit of the LORD rushed on him" (Judges 14:6).

The people saw their struggle for the Promised Land as God fighting for them in the person of the judges, who were their leaders. As the Israelites gradually conquered the land, it was divided up among the twelve tribes of Israel, each tribe claiming its descent from one of the twelve sons of Jacob.

A Kingdom for the Israelites

Over a period of about two hundred years, the Israelite tribes, led by the judges, spread over the land just east of the Mediterranean Sea. All the Israelite tribes worshiped Yahweh; that was what they had in common.

The United Kingdom Under David

The Israelites could have gone on as twelve tribes with a loose unity, but something else was needed if they were to become a great people, a light to the nations. That something else came in the form of a united kingdom of all the twelve tribes, led by the remarkable young shepherd and soldier, **David**. Chosen by God and anointed by the prophet Samuel, David became king of all Israel about one thousand years before the time of Jesus. He set up the capital of the nation at **Jerusalem**, and the era of his royal kingdom became synonymous with the "glory days" of Israel.

David was a human being with many failings; he made some significant mistakes and sometimes violated the trust of his people. But he was totally devoted to Yahweh and kept the people faithful to the Covenant. The story of David shows us that then as now, God can act through persons who have great weaknesses and flaws and who sin.

For centuries after David's death, the Jews longed for a return to that time when their dream of being a great nation seemed to become reality. They saw God's promise continuing through David's line. Therefore, whenever things got bad and it looked as though the people might be wiped out, they put their hopes in the descendants of David to deliver them.

After David's death, his son **Solomon** became king and built a beautiful **Temple** in Jerusalem; this became the focus of the people's worship. With such a magnificent Temple for Yahweh and a luxurious palace for the king, it seemed that the glory days would keep going on. But that was not to be the case for Israel.

Jeremiah, the Young Prophet

JEREMIAH, one of the major prophets in the Hebrew Scriptures, was called to be a prophet at a young age. He was a quiet young man with the personality of a mystic, but God called him to be an outspoken critic of society, its rulers, and the unfaithfulness of Israel to the Covenant. In return he was scorned and held in contempt. Jeremiah was whipped, accused of treason, imprisoned, and even thrown into a muddy cistern, or pit, and left to die of starvation in the mud, although the concern of an Ethiopian man saved him from death.

Through it all Jeremiah remained faithful to what God had requested of him. He delivered a message that was at once pessimistic because of Israel's failure to keep the Covenant, and optimistic because he believed in a God of hope and promise, whose love was unending.

In the opening passage of his book, Jeremiah recounts God's call to him and his own reluctance to answer:

Now the word of the LORD came to me saying,
"Before I formed you in the womb I
    knew you,
and before you were born I consecrated
    you;
I appointed you a prophet to the
    nations."
Then I said, "Ah, Lord GOD! Truly I do not know how to speak, for I am only a boy." But the LORD said to me,
"Do not say, 'I am only a boy';
for you shall go to all to whom I send
    you,
and you shall speak whatever I
    command you.
Do not be afraid of them,
for I am with you to deliver you,
    says the LORD."

(1:4–8)

Things Break Down

Solomon was rich, powerful, and famous for his wisdom, but he was far from a model king. He ruled the people oppressively and began to fall away from true worship of Yahweh. The unity of Israel under David and its faithfulness to the Covenant broke down. After Solomon's death, the kingdom split into two kingdoms—the **northern kingdom**, called **Israel**, and the **southern kingdom**, called **Judah**—with constant rivalry between them. Judah retained the capital city of Jerusalem with its great Temple.

A succession of kings of both kingdoms followed; many of them were corrupt and idolatrous. Injustice to poor people and worship of false gods were continuing temptations and sins of the kings and their wealthy courts. The people were not well served by these kings; they were a disgrace to the memory of King David, who, though a flawed person, had loved Yahweh with all his heart.

Prophets: Calling the People Back to God

In both Israel and Judah great **prophets** questioned the injustices of the wicked kings and tried to call the people back to their Covenant with Yahweh. Contrary to the image we may have of a prophet, their role was not simply to predict the future. Rather, they were critics of their society and of the injustices that were a sign of the people's failure to be faithful to the Covenant. They told what *could* happen if the people did not turn around their hard hearts. Some prophets were fiery critics of empty religious practices—empty because they were not accompanied by justice for the poor.

Isaiah told of Yahweh's distress at how the people had turned their backs on God and the Covenant:

> Hear, O heavens, and listen, O earth;
>> for the LORD has spoken:
> I reared children and brought them up,
>> but they have rebelled against me.
> The ox knows its owner,
>> and the donkey its master's crib;
> but Israel does not know,
>> my people do not understand.
>
> Ah, sinful nation,
>> people laden with iniquity,
> offspring who do evil,
>> children who deal corruptly,
> who have forsaken the LORD,
>> who have despised the Holy One of Israel,
>> who are utterly estranged!

(Isaiah 1:2–4)

Sometimes the prophets succeeded in bringing the nation to its senses. All too often, however, they were rejected, ridiculed, and scorned. But the goal of the prophets was not to be popular; it was to interpret events from God's point of view, no matter how angry it made the king or the people with power. You may be familiar with the names of some of the prophets besides **Amos** and Isaiah—for instance, **Elijah, Hosea, Micah, Jeremiah,** and **Ezekiel.** These prophets, some of the greatest figures in Jewish history, were outsiders and loners, speaking the truth and suffering the consequences.

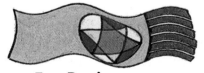

For Review

- What was the role of the judges in the Promised Land?
- Who was David, and why was he a focus of hope for the Jews for centuries after his death?
- How did the Israelites' faithfulness to the Covenant break down, and how did the prophets try to intervene?

8
Who are some modern-day prophets, people who are telling truthful messages to society or the world that most people do not want to hear? Describe in writing one such prophet and her or his message.

Crushing Defeat and Painful Exile

Although a few kings attempted to reform the nation, the Israelites and their kings by and large did not heed the warnings of the prophets. The prophets said that the people were paving the way for their own destruction by turning away from the Covenant, and they were right. Eventually the greater powers of the region crushed both kingdoms.

First the northern kingdom of Israel with its capital, **Samaria**, fell to the huge empire of the **Assyrians**, in about 722 B.C.E. The Israelite citizens of the north were dispersed and never returned again to their land. This was the beginning of what would become known as the **Jewish Dispersion** (sometimes called the Diaspora), the settling of the Jews outside the Promised Land.

The Babylonian Exile

Later, in 587 B.C.E., Jerusalem, the capital of the southern kingdom of Judah, fell under the enormous might of the **Babylonian Empire.** Many of the Judahites were forced to march about six hundred miles to their place of exile in Babylon. Babylon was a sophisticated city devoted to the accumulation of wealth, and its people were intolerant of the Jewish religion. The Jews were strangers in a strange land, having apparently lost everything.

The experience of the **Babylonian Exile** was about as crushing a blow as the Judahites could imagine. Their beloved city of Jerusalem and their magnificent Temple were destroyed. Everything familiar to them was gone, with no hope of its return. And the haunting questions kept coming before them: Where was Yahweh in all this? Had Yahweh abandoned them? Maybe Yahweh was not so powerful after all. Maybe the Babylonians had a mightier god than Yahweh.

Many people of the twentieth century have been forced into exile by war.
Student art: **Untitled, charcoal drawing by Saribel Daza, Notre Dame High School, San Jose, California**

Song of a Sorrowful People

ONE of the most touching psalms in the Hebrew Scriptures was sung by the Jews during their exile in Babylon, as they poured out their soul over the loss of Jerusalem, or Zion. It even includes the honest and perhaps shocking sentiment of wanting to get vengeance on those who had harmed them.

If you have ever moved away from a place you loved or had things you cherished torn away from you, you may identify with the feelings expressed by the exiled Jews in Psalm 137:

> By the rivers of Babylon—
> there we sat down and there we wept
> when we remembered Zion.
> On the willows there
> we hung up our harps.
> For there our captors
> asked us for songs,
> and our tormentors asked for mirth, saying,
> "Sing us one of the songs of Zion!"

> How could we sing the LORD's song
> in a foreign land?
> If I forget you, O Jerusalem,
> let my right hand wither!
> Let my tongue cling to the roof of my
> mouth,
> if I do not remember you,
> if I do not set Jerusalem
> above my highest joy.

> Remember, O LORD, against the Edomites
> the day of Jerusalem's fall,
> how they said, "Tear it down! Tear it down!
> Down to its foundations!"
> O daughter Babylon, you devastator!
> Happy shall they be who pay you back
> what you have done to us!
> Happy shall they be who take your little
> ones
> and dash them against the rock!

Renewal in the Midst of Exile

This devastating experience for the Jews in exile, however, did not ultimately defeat their spirit. True, some Jews lost their faith during this period and tried to blend into their pagan surroundings. But for many others the Exile led to deeper thought, more serious reflection on the meaning of what the prophets had been telling them all along, and sincere repentance. They began to see that Yahweh had not abandoned them in Jerusalem; rather, *they* had abandoned Yahweh, and that was why they were in exile.

Instead of losing heart because they had no glorious temple to offer sacrifices in, the Jews began to worship more informally. They prayed and studied in what became the forerunners of their later **synagogue** services (and of the Christian Liturgy of the Word, as well). They held simple services in which they prayed and retold the ancient stories of how Yahweh had saved them so many times in so many ways. They prayed intently, singing psalms from the heart about how they longed for Jerusalem (or Zion, as they also called their beloved city). They poured out their soul honestly to God. Yet they praised God even in their sorrow.

9
Recall a time you felt abandoned and exiled, cut off from all your familiar comforts, surroundings, and even friends. Reflect in writing on your feelings at the time and how you got through the experience.

10
Think of an example of someone who stops doing something wrong because he or she is scared of punishment or simply wants to look good. How does that person differ from someone who stops doing the same wrongful thing because his or her heart has been deeply changed? Explain the difference in writing.

The Sabbath, a day set aside each week for rest, prayer, and study, became extremely important to the Jews during the Exile.
Student art: Untitled, oil painting by Holly Esposito, Bishop Kearney High School, Brooklyn, New York

The Jews were purified by the experience of the Exile. They became closer to God, not through a powerful kingdom or a magnificent temple, but through the communal process of turning around their hearts. They began to realize that God was making a *new* Covenant with them: "'I will put my law within them, and I will write it on their hearts; and I will be their God, and they shall be my people'" (Jeremiah 31:33). Now God would work in each person's heart, as well as in the people as a whole. This was a marvelous gift of the Exile.

A Sabbath for the Jews

The practice of the **Sabbath**, the sacred day of rest and worship, became extremely significant to the Jews during the Exile. It marked them as different from the Babylonians, who carried on their business every day. It also reminded the Jews that although business and work were important, ultimately they were a people chosen by God, given a promise by God, and never abandoned by God. This relationship with God was honored by setting apart a special, sacred time away from all the earthly concerns that dominate day-to-day life. The Sabbath was an important practice at the time of Jesus, and it continues to be central to Jewish life and worship today.

People of the Book

Another development during the Exile was the collection of the people's ancient stories into the Hebrew Scriptures.

Writing and compiling the people's stories. Prior to this time, the stories were told orally. Some stories, rules,

prayers, and songs from a variety of oral sources had been written down, but they were not pieced together and edited into a whole. This was perhaps the most significant happening of the Exile, and without it we would not have the Bible as we know it.

The **Book of Genesis**—with its wonderful stories of Creation, Adam and Eve and the first sin, Noah and the flood, and of course Abraham and the patriarchs—was compiled during the Exile. Various versions of the stories had been passed along for centuries in oral and written form, but they had not been put together coherently. The stories that make up the Bible were not generally written at the time the events happened. Some were recorded centuries later. Many accounts, such as the Creation stories, were written down as the exiled Jews attempted to understand and preserve their worldview. The **Creation stories** are not considered historical, but they helped the Jews understand their origins.

The meaning of the Creation stories. The essential religious truths of the Creation stories were deep in the people's bones: God made the earth and all of Creation, and they were *good*. The earth belongs to God, and everything in it deserves to be treated with the greatest respect. All of Creation is a gift from God and is completely dependent on God. Human beings are made in God's image. These convictions were part of what it meant to be a Jew. A deep sense of the goodness of life was the heritage of every Jew, and Jesus himself would have learned this sense as a child at his mother's knee, hearing the ancient stories of Creation.

The Scriptures, with their wonderful accounts of God's love for the Jews, became the basis for the Jews' continuing faith. During the Exile they no longer relied on having a temple but became **"people of the Book."** The Covenant became "portable." The people's faith and worship could now go with them wherever they went.

11
Reflect on this statement in writing: *If modern-day people took the Creation stories seriously, the world would be a better place.*

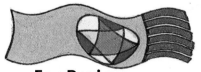

For Review

- What was the Babylonian Exile?
- What was the new Covenant proclaimed by the prophet Jeremiah?
- Why did the Sabbath become so important to the Jews during the Exile?
- What significant development during the Exile made it possible for the Jews to bring their faith and worship along with them wherever they went?

The Jews were ruled mostly by oppressive Greek and Roman dictators in the centuries after the Exile.
Student art: Untitled, linocut print by Anthoney Woodard, Gonzaga Preparatory High School, Spokane, Washington

After the Exile

Approximately fifty years into the Exile in Babylon, the **Persian Empire** conquered the Babylonian Empire. Suddenly the Jews were set free, allowed to return home to Jerusalem. Many of those who had remained faithful, called the **Remnant**, returned joyfully to their homeland of Judah. (The terms *Judaism* and *Jew* are derived from the word *Judah.* Those terms began to be used after the Exile to describe the religion and people of ancient Israel.)

The Faithful Practice of Judaism

The returning Jews rebuilt the city of Jerusalem and built a new Temple, although they never regained the political power that the Israelites had known in the days of David and the united kingdom. However, the purifying of the Exile had led to a deep conversion. God's law, as the prophet Jeremiah had said, had been "written on their hearts." The people no longer engaged in the kind of idolatry and extreme oppression of poor people that had brought them into ruin and exile. Jewish leaders were conscientious about maintaining a strict and pure form of their faith. Judaism was practiced with integrity.

A Series of Oppressors

The Greeks

The Persian Empire, which was relatively kind as ruler over Judah, did not last very long. Persia was defeated by Greece under the empire builder Alexander the Great, so the **Greeks** became the Jews' overlords for nearly three hundred years. And cruel they were. Some of the most powerful stories of the Jews' courage emerged from this period, as they faced their Greek dictators and tried to fight them off, meeting with some success. They gained their independence and kept it for seventy years.

One Jewish holiday, **Hanukkah**, or the Festival of Lights, comes from the remembrance of how the Jews rededicated the Temple after the Greeks had defiled it.

The Romans

Just sixty-three years before the time of Jesus, Palestine (the name given by the Greeks to the area east of the Mediterranean) came under the rule of the **Romans.** By then the Jews were scattered all over the **Roman Empire,** and Jerusalem in Palestine had become the religious capital for all these far-flung, dispersed Jews. It is estimated that 10 percent of the population of the Roman Empire was Jewish. The Jews were city dwellers who moved frequently from place to place. The Romans, with their incredible building program and efficient methods of governing outlying areas like Judah, made travel throughout the Empire easier than it had ever been. But despite their efficiency, Rome's identity as an oppressive dictatorship was never in doubt.

The Longing for a Messiah

During this time many Jews of deep and simple faith recognized that they could not survive as a people on their own. They put all their hopes in the coming of a savior to rescue them from oppression. Some of the prophets' writings in the Hebrew Scriptures, especially Isaiah's, pointed to the coming of someone sent by God to bring lasting joy and peace to the people. The Jews thought that perhaps now was the time.

Most Jews believed that this "anointed one" of God, or the **Messiah,** would come from the line of David, the beloved king who had united the people almost a thousand years earlier and brought Yahweh's favor to them. The people saw the coming of the Messiah as the fulfillment of the Covenant; the Messiah would fulfill all God's promises of a prosperous and peaceful homeland. Yes, the Jews were under Roman rule, and yes, times were bad and they were poor and oppressed. But God would not abandon them in their need.

12
Ask your Jewish friends or acquaintances, or look up the information in a book of Jewish customs, about the story behind the feast of Hanukkah. Write up a summary of the story.

The Star of David has become a familiar symbol of Judaism.
Student art: "Starlight," oil pastel drawing by Beth Zunkiewicz, Saint Wendelin High School, Fostoria, Ohio

So the Jews longed for a savior, but who the Messiah would be was unknown. They had a variety of ideas about what this savior would be like. Some expected a great military leader who would triumphantly re-establish them as a political power. The prophet Isaiah's writings, however, spoke of a **"suffering servant,"** one who would save the people by suffering for them. As you can imagine, this image did not have as much appeal as the image of a powerful military conqueror who could bring back the glory days of David.

Groups Among the Jews

By the time Jesus was born, the dream of the Messiah had reached a peak in the thoughts and hopes of many Jewish people. All kinds of ferment were going on among the Jews in Palestine with respect to what might be coming.

Many factions and power groups were active within Jewish society. The group known as the **Sadducees** rigidly followed the laws of Judaism according to the letter of the Law, as written in the Hebrew Scriptures. As a priestly class they were also committed to proper worship and the offering of daily sacrifices in the Temple in Jerusalem. However, they were fairly accommodating to the Romans, preferring to compromise with them in exchange for being allowed certain positions of power.

13
What different kinds of "saviors" are people looking for today? Write down examples of at least four varied expectations people have of those who will rescue them from their problems.

Another faction, the **Pharisees**, believed that the Law could be interpreted and expanded to better direct the lives of people in every detail. The Pharisees of Jesus' time added so much burdensome "fine tuning" to the Law that this would later cause Jesus to come into conflict with them during his ministry.

Another group was the **Zealots**, so named because of their revolutionary zeal to overthrow the Roman Empire by force.

Social Classes at the Time of Jesus

EVERY society develops social classes or groups: the haves and the have-nots, the rich people and the poor people, the politically powerful and the oppressed. The world of Jesus' day was no different.

A great imbalance existed between the rights of men and those of women. This inequality was found in every culture of the time and still exists in our world today. In Jewish society the husband and father was recognized as the head of the household, with his wife and his children subject to his will. A law mandated that women wait on men but not eat with them. Women were also restricted to worshiping only in certain areas of the Temple in Jerusalem. Such practices help us to understand why in the Gospels the willingness of Jesus to talk and relate with women was the cause of so much controversy.

As in our own society, social standing in Jesus' time was based to a great extent on wealth. A wide gap separated the relatively few rich people from the many people who were very poor. A small but significant middle class existed, consisting of shopkeepers and persons in trades such as carpentry and fishing. Jesus, in fact, came from the middle class. But the vast majority of people lived in poverty. During his ministry Jesus would have much to say about this situation of wealth and poverty.

Some groups of Jews were clearly identified as social outcasts. For example, the Samaritans traced their origins back to the northern tribes of Israel, to those Jews who stayed on and never were sent into exile after defeat by the Assyrians. Although they worshiped Yahweh, the Samaritans were not accepted as true Israelites because they had intermarried with pagans and did not practice a pure form of Judaism. In fact, they were detested even more than pagans because they did not worship Yahweh "properly."

Other social outcasts included people with leprosy or other diseases. To us this rejection may seem to be terribly cruel—and it is. But again we must remember the unique characteristics of the time. For example, disease and poverty were seen as signs of the presence of sin and as punishments by God. A physically sick or mentally ill person was believed to be possessed by a demon. So fear, rather than outright cruelty, led many Jews to reject or avoid the sick people who were frequently encountered on their roads.

With our modern knowledge of illness, we might look down upon the Jews' fearful superstition. Yet think about this: with less reason we still fear illness and sick people. More to the point, these hardhearted attitudes described in Jewish society are everywhere in evidence today.

What Happened Just After Jesus?

Into this situation of division among the Jews and oppression by their Roman overlords, Jesus was born.

Judaism certainly continued after Jesus, although not with its center at the Temple in Jerusalem. The Temple was totally destroyed by the Romans in 70 C.E. as a response to a Zealot revolt. It was never again rebuilt. But the Jews had been well prepared by the Exile for carrying on their faith without the Temple. They knew they did not have to offer sacrifices in the Temple to please God, that they could worship through devotion to God's Word, their Scriptures. The Pharisees further developed the tradition of the synagogue, centered on the Hebrew Scriptures, as the basis of Jewish worship. Because the Scriptures could be taken anywhere, Judaism spread all the more throughout the known world.

14
Look up the story of the destruction of the Temple by the Romans in 70 C.E., and the valiant but losing defense of the fortress, Masada, where the Jews held out against the Romans. Or watch the video *Masada,* which tells the story. Write a report on these events.

Ruins of a second-century Jewish synagogue at Capernaum, in Israel

Jesus: Fulfillment of the Longing for a Messiah

The story of the Jews is essential to understanding the Christian faith, because their story marks the beginning of the Christian story. Christians recognize **Jesus** as the Messiah longed for by the Jews and the fulfillment of God's Covenant with the people.

A scale model of the great Jerusalem Temple, which was destroyed by the Romans in 70 C.E.

At the beginning of his ministry among the Jewish people, Jesus was aware that he had a divine mission. As a young man, following his Baptism and forty days of fasting and prayer in the Judean desert, Jesus went into the Jewish synagogue of his hometown, Nazareth. Here is the dramatic scene as told in the Gospel of Luke:

When [Jesus] came to Nazareth, where he had been brought up, he went to the synagogue on the sabbath day, as was his custom. He stood up to read, and the scroll of the prophet Isaiah was given to him. He unrolled the scroll and found the place where it was written:

"The Spirit of the Lord is upon me,
  because he has anointed me
    to bring good news to the poor.
  He has sent me to proclaim release to the captives
  and recovery of sight to the blind,
    to let the oppressed go free,
  to proclaim the year of the Lord's favor."

And he rolled up the scroll, gave it back to the attendant, and sat down. The eyes of all in the synagogue were fixed on him. Then he began to say to them, "Today this scripture has been fulfilled in your hearing." (4:16–21)

The next chapter takes up the story and message of Jesus, whom Christians see as God's fulfillment of the Covenant made so long ago to Abraham.

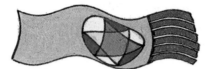

For Review

- After the Exile, how did the Jews who returned to Jerusalem practice their faith?
- Which empires oppressed the Jews after the Exile and up through the time of Jesus?
- In what belief did the Jews put their hopes for an end to their oppression and suffering?
- What happened to Judaism immediately after Jesus' death?
- Who is recognized by Christians as the Messiah longed for by the Jews?

The *Shoah,* in the twentieth century, was an attempt to wipe out the Jews as a people. This remarkable people and religion contiue to survive with deep faith.
Student art: Untitled, linoleum mixed media by Sean Finley, Gonzaga Preparatory High School, Spokane, Washington

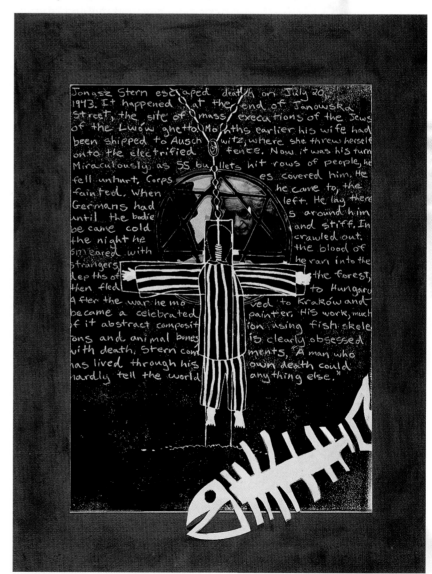

A Reflection on Judaism

Before we move on to Jesus and Christianity, let's pause to reflect on what Judaism means to the world today.

The history of Judaism has extraordinary features. It did not develop like any other religion the world has ever seen. God's grace, along with an incredible degree of faithful persistence and steadfastness, combined to make Judaism truly "a light to the nations."

In ancient times whenever a tribe of people turned from a nomadic life of wandering to an agricultural way of life, as the Hebrews did, their god became just one more god among many worshiped by the people in that locale. But this did not happen to the Jews and their God. Their history was different from that of all the other tribes and nations. Through great determination and by overcoming what seemed unbeatable odds, they remained true to Yahweh.

Again, after the Jews were scattered first by exile and then by the final destruction of their Temple, a historian might predict that their religion would come to an end. But instead the Jews discovered a renewed sense of their faith.

Judging by what has usually happened throughout history to small nations with no military power, the Jews should never have survived. In the twentieth century the *Shoah* destroyed six million Jews—fully one-third of their entire population. Still this remarkable people and their religion continue to survive.

Its extraordinary history alone makes Judaism a religion worthy of admiration. We can be sure that God is with the Jews today, keeping the Covenant with them and rejoicing in their great gifts of faith in the One God and their keen sense of morality. These are gifts that Judaism continues to give to the world.

15
Arrange with a rabbi to visit a synagogue or temple in your community or a city nearby, and find out about the contemporary life and concerns of the Jewish congregation there. Summarize what you learn in a report.

4

Jesus:

Revealing God in Humanity

Who *Is* This Man?

When Jesus stood up to read from the scrolls in the synagogue in Nazareth, as we saw at the end of chapter 3, he was known to people there as a local boy, now a grown man. Jesus had been raised in Nazareth in the home of Joseph, a carpenter, and his wife, Mary. He had accompanied his parents to the synagogue in his youth, learning the prayers and the Scriptures of his people. Most likely he went to school in a room attached to the synagogue, where he learned Hebrew and became devoted to the Law and God's Covenant with the Chosen People. Jesus faithfully followed the Jewish practices like the Sabbath rest and the dietary customs. He participated in the Jewish festivals and went on pilgrimage to the Temple in Jerusalem. Jesus was thoroughly Jewish in mind and heart. He identified with his people's longing that God's promise to them would be fulfilled—that they would be a great and free people, living in peace and justice with one another and being the source of light and hope to all other peoples.

So picture the scene, as the Gospel of Luke recounts, when Jesus stood up that day in the synagogue and read from the prophet Isaiah:

"'The Spirit of the Lord is upon me,
    because he has anointed me
        to bring good news to the poor.'"

(Luke 4:18)

1

Imagine yourself fifteen years from now returning to the hometown where you grew up and announcing that you have an important mission—to bring peace and justice to your hometown and the world. List some comments you imagine people might say about you.

Civil rights leader Martin Luther King Jr., who was assassinated in 1968, is considered by many to be a modern-day prophet. In Jesus' time people wondered if Jesus might be a holy prophet of Yahweh, or even *more* than a prophet.

2

How would *you* answer Jesus' question? Write out your answer as if you are talking directly to Jesus.

Then he finished the passage, sat down, and said, "'Today this scripture has been fulfilled in your hearing'" (Luke 4:21). Jesus' fellow Nazarenes must have been startled. They probably wondered: "Who does Jesus think he is? Does he think *he* is the fulfillment of God's promise to Israel? Isn't he just one of us, a hometown boy? Or is he more than that?"

Preacher? Prophet? or More?

Many of Jesus' followers, admirers, and even detractors in his day wondered about this same question: Who *is* this man? At the time Jesus began his ministry, it was not uncommon for wandering preachers to gain a following, often with a message that God was about to make everything different for the Jews. Was Jesus another preacher or rabbi, great and gifted but nothing more than that? Or was he a genuine prophet of Yahweh, in the revered Hebrew tradition of Jeremiah, Isaiah, and Ezekiel? Or was he something else?

Matthew's Gospel tells us that toward the end of his life and ministry, when Jesus asked his disciples, "'Who do you say that I am?' Simon Peter answered, 'You are the Messiah, the Son of the living God'" (16:15–16).

Truly God, Truly a Man

Peter's answer is the one that Christians have echoed for nearly two thousand years. Christians believe that this man from Nazareth, Jesus, is also the Christ—the Anointed One, the Messiah, and the Son of God. Within a few centuries of Christianity's beginning, this understanding of Jesus was expressed as the doctrine of the **Incarnation.**

What does the word *incarnation* mean? At its root it means "made in flesh." In Christian belief Jesus is God's own Son made present in human flesh—**truly God and truly a man.** Jesus has both a divine nature and a human nature.

Why would God become a human being? That is a great mystery of love. Perhaps a **parable**—a story about ordinary, everyday reality that points to a greater truth—will help us understand why. Read this story about a little boy named Juan.

A Parable

Juan was a boy about six years old who lived in Spanish Harlem, in New York City. His family was poor, so Juan had few toys. Many times he went out into the alley behind the apartment buildings to bounce a ball off the brick walls or to pick through the garbage to find something to play with.

One day when Juan was scavenging, he found a glass bowl covered with grime. Because he had so few things, Juan saw a beauty in that bowl that we would probably miss. He was very excited. He took his discovery gently in his hands and carefully climbed the steps up to the apartment his family lived in. Then Juan carried the bowl to the kitchen sink and began to clean it. When he was finished, Juan was delighted because he discovered that his bowl was perfect. No scratch or chip marred its beauty. Juan gingerly carried the bowl to the kitchen table, sat down, and admired the bowl. Juan was happy.

After a short time, however, the thrill of discovery began to wear off, and Juan started to get bored. Then he had an idea. He would decorate his bowl. So Juan went down to the street and picked up a handful of shiny pebbles and pieces of wire and sticks. He took what he had collected back to his apartment, sat down

again by his bowl, and set to work. Juan placed the pebbles on the bottom of the bowl and pretended they formed a roadway. Next he placed the wire and sticks among the pebbles and pretended they were bushes and trees. Then Juan had another idea. He got an old tin can, cut it in half lengthwise, placed it over the roadway, and pretended it was a tunnel. When Juan was finished, he looked upon his bowl with great pride—it was beautiful! Juan was happy again.

Once more, however, the wonder and charm of the bowl began to fade for Juan, and he began to lose that special thrill he had felt. Finally Juan realized what he was missing; he had no one with whom to share his bowl, no one to enjoy what he had created. So Juan went to his mother. "Mama," he said, "can I buy a goldfish to put in my bowl?" Juan's mother thought for a long time, knowing they had very little money. When she looked into Juan's eyes, however, she did what all mothers tend to do. She said, "All right, Juan," and went to the cupboard and found a dollar. She placed it in Juan's hand.

Juan's feet seemed to fly above the sidewalk as he ran to the store on the corner. He bought a beautiful goldfish, ran back to his apartment, filled his new bowl with water, and gently dropped the fish into it. Then Juan began to talk to his fish: "Swim along the roadway, fish. That's why I put it there—to make you happy." The fish merely swam around and around in the bowl, unaware of Juan's handiwork. "Hey, why don't you swim among the trees I made for you? That's why I put them there—to make you happy." The fish just kept swimming in circles, ignorant of Juan's pleas. Finally Juan became so frustrated that he began to pound on the side of the bowl, demanding that his fish swim through the tunnel. Again no response. The fish kept swimming around and around.

Juan ran to his mother in tears. "Mama, why doesn't my fish listen to me? I keep telling him what's going to make him happy, but he won't do what I say. Why?"

Juan's mother was very wise and had been watching what was going on. Gently she took Juan on her lap and said: "Juan, the trouble is that you and the fish speak different languages. He doesn't understand what you're trying to tell him. The only way he could understand would be if you could become a fish, jump into the bowl, and swim along the roadway, among the trees, and through the tunnel. Then maybe the fish would watch you, see how you live in the bowl, and follow you."

So Juan spent a lot of time wishing he could be a fish.

3
Before reading any further, come up with your own explanation of the parable. What does Juan symbolize? the fishbowl? the fish? Juan's desire to become a fish? Write out your interpretation.

End of story—just a kid's story, it might seem. Yet if you read the first chapter of the Book of Genesis in the Bible, you will find that the Creation story, on which our parable is partly based, is not much more complicated. And the message of Jesus may be just as simple, simple enough even for children to understand. Let's take another look at the story of Juan and see what truth it tells us about God and God's relationship with us.

God's Longing to Reach Us

We live in this great goldfish bowl that we call the world. God created it and decorated it beautifully. But God and Juan both realized something was missing. God, like Juan, wanted to share this creation, this goodness. Out of that great longing to share, God created people—you and me. God's wish was that we would live together with God, sharing the wonders of Creation in harmony and love. With this gift, God was sharing not just the world, but God's own self. We call this great gift **grace**—God's life and love poured out to us.

But we know from the Hebrew Scriptures that even though God reached out to share life and love with human beings, humans did not always accept that love. They sinned. **Sin** means they ignored God and turned away from God; they insisted on having things their own way. Sinful human beings seemed remarkably dense—unable or unwilling to understand the love that God was trying to offer them.

We know, too, from the Hebrew Scriptures that God tried to get through to the people by acting in wondrous ways in their history, freeing them from slavery in Egypt through the Exodus. And when the people sinned, God sent great prophets—people who remind us of Juan pounding on the side of the bowl in frustration as he tries to get the fish to follow his commands. In a similar way the prophets jarred the people's conscience and called them back to an awareness of God's grace, only to see them erect new monuments to other gods and to their own greed. Like the fish in the story, the people could not or would not understand what God was trying to say. So they kept wandering around, ignoring the great life that God was holding out to them.

Juan, through his mother's wise words, was given a great dream, the dream of becoming a fish so he could show his little fish how to enjoy the wonders of his bowl. God had a similar longing—to reach people intimately by becoming one with them. Juan could only dream his dream. But Christians believe that God's longing became reality, for God became human in Jesus.

God created human beings to share Creation and God's own life and love with them.
Student art: Untitled, watercolor painting by Nate Scatena, University of San Diego High School, San Diego, California

God took on humanity in Jesus in order to walk along the roadways, among the trees, and through the tunnels of life just as we do, so that we might look at Jesus, see how he lived, and then follow his living model of life in God.

In the Christian Testament the Second Letter of Peter explains that the awesome reality of the Incarnation gives human beings the opportunity to "become participants of the divine nature" (1:4). By becoming human for us in Jesus, God offered us a share in divinity.

Really God?

Let's pause here to consider the challenge that some people raise about the Incarnation: "Isn't it a bit much to believe that Jesus was God? I can buy his being a good man, even a great prophet, and maybe the greatest human being that ever lived. But this God stuff—that's going too far!"

Ultimately, accepting that Jesus is God as well as a man is a matter of faith, but that does not make it unreasonable. Here is one way to think of it.

Recall your own experience of friendships. When we like someone, we want to be with that person. We try to communicate with him or her in as many ways as possible. When we are separated, we feel lonely and think about getting together again. This drive for togetherness is true of all love relationships.

Now consider this: God loves us, and that love is total, infinite, and unconditional because God *is* infinite love. Wouldn't God then want to be with us, to communicate with us, just as we do with our friends? There would be no better way for God to be *with us* than for God to become *one of us*.

The Gospel of John expresses this mystery as Jesus' own words: "'For God so loved the world that he gave his only Son, so that everyone who believes in him may not perish but may have eternal life'" (3:16).

Really Human?

Although some people have difficulty accepting that Jesus is truly divine, others have an equally hard time accepting that Jesus is truly human. They want to push him off into the heavens or make him a "semi-human," not a full one! This is somewhat the way the thinking goes:

Jesus was human, maybe, but certainly not like me. Surely he didn't feel down in the dumps as I do so often, or

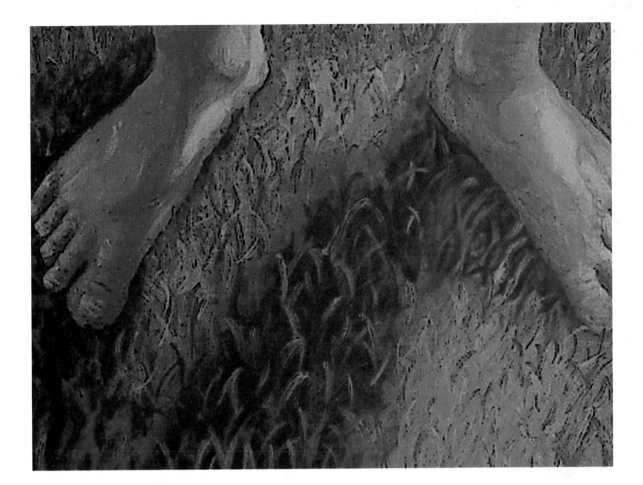

get as frustrated and angry as I do. He was always nice and kind and understanding. He wasn't even tempted to be anything but good. Certainly he never suffered the loneliness or the gnawing questions that I do. I mean, he was God, right? So how could he be like me?

Accepting Jesus as **fully human** is as important as accepting him as **fully divine.** If we do not accept Jesus as one who experienced life as we do—with all its limits, frustrations, loneliness, and fears—we will not be able to identify with him and try to live as he did.

Saint Paul says that Jesus became one with us in all things except sin. In other words, besides the joys of human life, Jesus experienced the same pain that we do in being human—the stress, loneliness, anger, and longing for acceptance. But he chose never to respond sinfully to these human experiences. Given the choice between popularity and telling people hard truths, he chose the path that ultimately turned others against him. Faced with a violent death, he did not command his disciples to kill in his name. He responded with **humility**—a total openness to the call of God that is the exact opposite of sinful self-centeredness.

Though fully divine, Jesus came among us as fully human, becoming one with us in all things but sin. *Student art:* **"On Sacred Ground," oil painting by T. J. Meeks, Holy Cross High School, Louisville, Kentucky**

Saint Paul urged Christians to have the same humble attitude as Christ Jesus,

> who, though he was in the form of God,
>   did not regard equality with God
>   as something to be exploited,
> but emptied himself,
>   taking the form of a slave,
>   being born in human likeness.
> And being found in human form,
>   he humbled himself
>   and became obedient to the point of death—
>   even death on a cross.

(Philippians 2:6–8)

4
Reflect in writing on which part of the mystery of the Incarnation is harder for you to understand or accept: (1) that Jesus is God or (2) that Jesus is human.

Remember the question Jesus put to Peter, "'Who do you say that I am?'" It was not obvious to Peter the first time he met Jesus that the answer to Jesus' question was, "'You are the Messiah.'" Peter discovered that over time. Peter got to know Jesus as a man, discovering him as a remarkable teacher, a loving guide, a generous friend, a gifted healer, and a courageous prophet. Gradually, though, Peter began to understand that Jesus was a man, yes, but more than that. He was "'the Messiah, the Son of the living God.'"

Christians have been proclaiming that truth with Peter since the earliest days of the church. Let's turn, then, to Jesus' life and message as a way of discovering for ourselves this God who reaches out to us and offers us a share in God's divine life.

For Review

- How did Peter answer Jesus' question, "'Who do you say that I am?'"
- What Christian belief is expressed in the doctrine of the Incarnation?
- Using the images from the parable of Juan, tell why God became human in Jesus.
- Give the quotes from the Gospel of John and from Paul's Letter to the Philippians that express the mystery of God's becoming human in Jesus.

The Great Councils on Jesus

ESPECIALLY in the early centuries of Christian history, various thinkers denied either the divinity or the humanity of Jesus. The church saw these challenges as heresies—false understandings of the essential truths of the Christian faith. **Arianism**, for instance, claimed that Jesus was more than human but less than divine. **Gnosticism** denied Jesus' humanity.

Some of the early gatherings of church leaders, called ecumenical (meaning "worldwide") councils, tried to clarify and define the truth that Jesus is fully God and fully human. Out of such gatherings as the **Council of Nicaea** in 325, and the **Council of Constantinople** in 381, eventually came the **Nicene Creed**, which all Catholics and many Protestants hold today as a basic statement of their beliefs. This is the creed recited at Mass in Catholic churches around the world.

Another significant event occurred at the **Council of Ephesus** in 431, when Mary, the mother of Jesus, was given the title **Mother of God**. This event not only recognized Mary's significance but also affirmed Jesus' humanity (because he was born of a human mother) and his divinity (because she was the Mother of God).

Then, in 451, the **Council of Chalcedon** was called to deal with a heresy that claimed that Jesus was divine but not human, that he only acted human, or played the role of a human being, while on earth. Once again the leaders of the church affirmed the basic Christian belief in the Incarnation, that Jesus is truly God and truly human.

Annunciation, by fifteenth-century artist Fra Angelico

Jesus' Life and Mission Begin

Jesus' Origin

The Gospels make it clear from the start that Jesus is worthy of special attention. Jesus' origin was amazing. According to the accounts written by Matthew and Luke, Jesus was not conceived in the usual way, but by the power of the **Holy Spirit**.

Jesus Is Conceived

Here, in summary, is how Luke describes the event known as the **Annunciation** (so called because of the angel's "announcement"):

A young Jewish girl, **Mary**, engaged to **Joseph**, a carpenter, was surprised one day by the appearance of an angel, Gabriel, in her hometown of **Nazareth** in Galilee. The angel announced to her that God had chosen her to bear a son who would be named Jesus and known as the Son of the Most High. (The name Jesus means "Yahweh saves.") When

Mary asked the angel, "'How can this be, since I am a virgin?'" (Luke 1:34), the angel told her that this child would be conceived in her womb not by a man but by the power of the Holy Spirit. Though perplexed, Mary gave her willing response: "'Here am I, the servant of the Lord; let it be with me according to your word'" (Luke 1:38).

Thus God became human through the power of God's Spirit and the consent of a young, unmarried Jewish girl who was open to surprises—especially to God's surprises.

As a pregnant, unmarried young woman, Mary could easily have been publicly disgraced. But her fiancé, Joseph, kept faith with her and with God's plan. Although hesitant

Mary, Full of Grace

MARY, the mother of Jesus, is held in great honor by Christians, particularly Catholic Christians, because of her unique role among all human beings as the Mother of God. Catholic tradition affirms that God prepared Mary for her role as the Mother of God by uniting her very closely with God from the first moment of her existence in her mother's womb. Unlike every other human being but Jesus, Mary was not born into the condition known as Original Sin, the alienation of the whole human race from God (see chapter 12 of this text for more information on Original Sin). She was "full of grace" from the moment she was conceived in her mother's womb. This special favor given to Mary is known as her **Immaculate Conception**. It did not exempt her from suffering; she endured great pain and sorrow in life. But she was and is always closest to God of any human being that ever lived, except Jesus.

Devotion to Mary is intense for many Catholics. For example, many poor and oppressed people experience her care for them in a very special way. Listen with your heart to Mary's own prayer of praise, the **Magnificat**, from Luke's Gospel account of Mary's visit to her cousin Elizabeth when both women were pregnant. In this great prayer, so Jewish in its spirit,

Mary proclaims her joy and hope that God's promises to the poor and the lowly will be fulfilled through the baby she is carrying in her womb:

"My soul magnifies the Lord,
    and my spirit rejoices in God my Savior,
for he has looked with favor on the
        lowliness of his servant.
    Surely, from now on all generations will
        call me blessed;
for the Mighty One has done great things
        for me,
    and holy is his name.
His mercy is for those who fear him
    from generation to generation.
He has shown strength with his arm;
    he has scattered the proud in the
        thoughts of their hearts.
He has brought down the powerful from
        their thrones,
    and lifted up the lowly;
he has filled the hungry with good things,
    and sent the rich away empty.
He has helped his servant Israel,
    in remembrance of his mercy,
according to the promise he made to our
        ancestors,
    to Abraham and to his descendants
        forever."

at first, he stood by Mary and married her even though Jewish Law would have justified his breaking off the engagement. Joseph was of the house (or lineage) of David, out of whose descendants the Messiah, you may recall, was expected to come. Joseph had to try to understand the blessing that was happening in Mary, which must have been very difficult for him. But his faith in God was stronger than his questioning.

Jesus Is Born

You are probably familiar with the Gospel stories of Jesus' birth, known as the **Nativity.** Jesus was born in the "City of David," **Bethlehem,** during a census being taken at the order of the Roman emperor. Luke's account tells of poor shepherds coming to the stable to worship the newborn baby. Matthew's account has wise men, or magi (non-Jewish foreigners from the East), traveling long miles, led by a brilliant star, to see and offer homage to the child. Luke's account lets us know that Jesus came as a source of hope for poor people and those on the fringes of society. Matthew's story adds the insight that Jesus came as a light to the nations, that is, to the Gentiles, or non-Jews.

The stories of Jesus' origin were meant to be wondrous accounts, indicating what an amazing thing had come about for humankind through the birth of this child.

His Early Years

Mary and Joseph had Jesus circumcised at eight days old, according to the custom of their ancestors. Several weeks later they presented Jesus, as firstborn male, to the Lord in the Temple, fulfilling another requirement of the Law.

Luke summarizes Jesus' years of growing up in Nazareth with the words, "The child grew and became strong, filled with wisdom; and the favor of God was upon him" (2:40). We can imagine that Jesus learned the carpentry trade of his father, and that they worked together in Joseph's shop. The boy must have been an extraordinary young person, learning great sensitivity and compassion from his parents, and becoming a keen student of Hebrew and religion in the synagogue.

We are not told much about Jesus' childhood, other than the story of how his parents, on a visit from Nazareth to Jerusalem when he was twelve years old, lost track of him there. The boy Jesus, mature for his age, busied himself by

5
Read the account in Matthew 1:18–25 of Joseph's dilemma over Mary's pregnancy. Imagine an inner monolog, or conversation with himself, that Joseph might have had in wrestling over what to do. Write up the monolog as if you are Joseph speaking to yourself.

The Church of the Annunciation in Nazareth, the town in Galilee where Jesus grew to maturity as a young man

6
Read the two Nativity accounts from the Gospels: Matthew 2:1–12 and Luke 2:1–20. Which one speaks most to your heart about the coming of Jesus into the world? Explain why in a paragraph.

7

Imagine you are one of Jesus' friends growing up with him in Nazareth. Describe in writing to another friend what Jesus is like at the age of fourteen or fifteen.

having an intense discussion with the learned teachers of the Temple. During years of growing into manhood, no doubt he was noticed by people in his hometown as being an unusually perceptive, faith-filled, and devout young person. Mostly, however, he led an ordinary life of obedience to his parents.

Baptized in the Jordan River

The next we hear of Jesus in the Gospels, he is about thirty years old, and he is presenting himself to John the Baptist—his cousin and a wandering prophetic preacher—to be baptized in the Jordan River. Jesus admired John's zeal in preaching a message of repentance. John had an urgent

The Jordan River in Galilee, where Jesus was baptized

sense that things were about to change drastically, and he wanted people to get ready for what was to come by being baptized. When Jesus appeared at the Jordan, John recognized that Jesus was greater than he, but Jesus insisted on being baptized by John. In Matthew's account of the **Baptism of Jesus**, we are told that

> when Jesus had been baptized, just as he came up from the water, suddenly the heavens were opened to him and he saw the Spirit of God descending like a dove and alighting on him. And a voice from heaven said, "This is my Son, the Beloved, with whom I am well pleased." (3:16–17)

Jesus knew that the great mission of his life lay before him, and that it was now beginning. The mission would involve pain and suffering, Jesus realized. But knowing that,

8

Think of a message that has sustained you in a time of need, given by someone who cares about you, communicated in words or in attitudes. Write out that message and what it means to you. If you cannot recall a sustaining message you have been given, write about one you would like to hear from a particular person.

he always carried within him the intimate message from God: "'This is my Son, the Beloved, with whom I am well pleased.'" That message would sustain him.

Tempted in the Desert

Before Jesus began his ministry, he first went off, led by the Spirit, for an extended time of prayer, fasting, and solitude in the desert wilderness. For forty days he ate nothing. By relying totally on God, Jesus prepared for his life's mission.

The Gospels tell us that the forty days in the desert were a time of great trial for Jesus—not unlike the forty years of trial that the Israelites experienced wandering in the desert after they escaped from Egypt. In what is known as the **Temptations in the Desert**, Jesus was tempted by the devil three times to give up his complete dependence on God and accept the easy and attractive forms of power offered by the devil. Jesus (unlike the Israelites) prevailed in the struggle with temptation. He kept his focus on the only true source of power that would sustain him during his ministry. That source was the One whose message Jesus carried deep in his heart: "'This is my Son, the Beloved.'"

After this great desert struggle with temptation, Jesus was filled with the Spirit and an unshakable sense of purpose. He returned to Nazareth, in his home region of **Galilee**, to preach. It was there and then that he entered his hometown synagogue, took up the scroll, and proclaimed the powerful words from Isaiah: "'The Spirit of the Lord is upon me. . . .'" Jesus took the prophetic words as his own, and he knew that God was with him completely, filling him with divine power and love. Jesus was now ready for whatever was to come.

For Review

- According to the account in the Gospel of Luke, how was Jesus conceived?
- What two different insights about Jesus are given to us in the Nativity stories in Luke's and Matthew's Gospels?
- What was the intimate message from God that Jesus received at his Baptism?
- What happened to Jesus during his forty days in the desert wilderness? How did this prepare him for his coming ministry?

The Public Ministry of Jesus

A Community of Disciples

One of the first things Jesus did as he began his ministry was to gather a community of disciples around him, people who would learn from him and carry on his mission even after he was gone. The closest of these disciples to Jesus were the **Twelve**, the men we call the **Apostles.** You are probably familiar with some of their names—like **Peter** (also called Simon), **Andrew, James, John**, and **Judas Iscariot**, the one who eventually betrayed Jesus.

The Gospel of Mark portrays Jesus calling some of the Apostles to follow him. Some were rough fishermen who seemed to be unlikely candidates to lead a spiritual and religious revolution, but Jesus saw in them something they did not see in themselves. He had a way of drawing people out, recognizing and affirming those who thought they were not particularly talented or gifted. Picture the scene and the magnetism of Jesus as he attracts his followers:

> As Jesus passed along the Sea of Galilee, he saw Simon and his brother Andrew casting a net into the sea—for

Fishermen left behind their boats and nets to follow Jesus.
Student art: "Reflections in Water," linocut print by Sara Nicol, Saint Agnes Academy, Memphis, Tennessee

they were fishermen. And Jesus said to them, "Follow me and I will make you fish for people." And immediately they left their nets and followed him. As he went a little farther, he saw James son of Zebedee and his brother John, who were in their boat mending the nets. Immediately he called them; and they left their father Zebedee in the boat with the hired men, and followed him. (Mark 1:16–20)

Jesus apparently had quite an effect on people. Several times the Gospels report that individuals left everything behind to follow him. And Jesus *needed* to affect them deeply if they were to join him in the work to which he was dedicated.

The Mission: Proclaiming the Kingdom of God

What was the mission given by God that Jesus was so passionately set on? It was to proclaim the **Kingdom of God**—to preach it as a reality that was coming, but even more than that, to live the Kingdom in the present. Jesus knew that people would never catch on to the goodness and glory of God's Kingdom unless they experienced it for themselves. So Jesus dedicated himself to *living* the Kingdom in the midst of the people, not just talking about it.

What was Jesus trying to get across about the coming Kingdom by his own life and example? Many ideas were circulating at the time of Jesus about how God would restore Israel to its glory. Many people thought that God's Reign, or Kingdom, meant that the Jews, led by a military or political messiah, would triumph militarily and re-establish the ancient kingdom of Israel, as in the glorious era of King David.

Jesus had to be certain that people did not expect him to be that kind of messiah. He had no interest in setting up a geographical nation with borders and worldly power. Most important, that was not the kind of Kingdom that God wanted either. The Kingdom that Jesus proclaimed and lived was entirely different from what so many people expected. It was a Kingdom of love, not of political rule or power.

9
Think of someone you know who recognizes and affirms other people, who draws out others and helps them see their own talents and gifts. Write a character sketch of that person, telling how she or he affects others.

10
Imagine a situation of a young person today who is pressured to fit into others' expectations but sincerely wants to break out of those expectations and follow the genuine voice of conscience. Write up a brief scenario of what might happen in the situation.

God Is Our Father

How did Jesus know with such confidence what God wanted? Jesus *knew.* He knew it with all his being because he was intimately related to God, aware of God's life within him, loving him and moving him to take each new step in his mission.

Jesus knew that the God of his ancestors—of Abraham and Sarah, Isaac and Jacob, Moses and David—was also the One who tenderly called him Beloved and Son at his Baptism. He called that God **Father.** At times Jesus addressed God as *Abba,* which means "my own dear father." His sense of Sonship was as intense as it was familiar and personal.

Yet, although the Son's relationship to his Father was unique, Jesus did not think of his relationship with God as exclusive. He told the crowds who followed him as he preached in the towns and countryside of Galilee that God was not only "*my* Father" but "*our* Father." He taught people to pray simply and trustingly to God as Father, without try-

ing to impress God with fancy language. When he taught his disciples how to pray, Jesus presented them with a simple and profound prayer that had roots in the Jewish tradition. This passage from the Gospel of Matthew shows Jesus teaching that prayer, known by Christians as the **Lord's Prayer:**

> "When you are praying, do not heap up empty phrases as the Gentiles do; for they think that they will be heard because of their many words. Do not be like them, for your Father knows what you need before you ask him.
>
> "Pray then in this way:
> Our Father in heaven,
>> hallowed be your name.
>> Your kingdom come.
>> Your will be done,
>>> on earth as it is in heaven.
>> Give us this day our daily bread.
>> And forgive us our debts,
>>> as we also have forgiven our debtors.
>> And do not bring us to the time of trial,
>>> but rescue us from the evil one.
>
> For if you forgive others their trespasses, your heavenly Father will also forgive you; but if you do not forgive others, neither will your Father forgive your trespasses."
> (6:7–15)

We Are All Loved by God

Living in the Kingdom of God meant living in the Father's love, surrounded by that love, breathing it, being saturated by it, and letting it be the guiding element behind social and community life. Jesus knew the love of God the Father in the closest way. That experience of love became a fire in him that he longed to share with everyone. He wanted everyone to know God's love for them and to realize not only in their head but in the depths of their being what it meant to be a child of God.

How did Jesus live the reality of God's love for everyone? As God's own Son, Jesus was the embodiment of God's love. He put flesh on God's love. It was as if Jesus was throwing open his arms to say: "Look! God's love is wider and deeper than anything you can imagine. We are *all* God's children. Come and join us in this great, wide love!"

So Jesus' powerful message to people about God was that God is our Father, and we are all loved by God.

11
Change the prayer from Our Father to Our Mother and then reflect on the meaning of each phrase. Write a brief summary of your reactions. What insights about God does this shift in language give you?

12
Reflect on the following question in a paragraph: *If we are all loved by God, why do so many people not feel or experience that love?*

The Kingdom of God Is Among You!

Jesus' Actions: Signs of the Kingdom

Every page of the Gospels shows God's love and God's Kingdom being manifested in Jesus' actions.

Healing and life-restoring miracles. Jesus cured sick people and relieved suffering of all kinds. Many people in his time were considered unclean and were outcasts because of a disease such as leprosy or a long-term hemorrhage in a woman. Conditions like blindness and epilepsy were believed to be the result of sin. But Jesus saw true faith in these suffering people; he embraced them and offered the healing power of God, for their spirit as well as their body, whenever they presented themselves to him in genuine faith. Three Gospel stories even tell of Jesus bringing people back to life after they had died.

Nature miracles. The Gospels record that on several occasions Jesus performed miracles in nature. In the miracle of the loaves and fishes, he fed thousands of people by relying on God's providence to provide food when there was not enough for all. Another time he calmed a fierce storm that terrified the disciples who were with him in a boat at sea.

The Gospel accounts of miracles may challenge our modern way of understanding nature and science. But most significant is what the miracles reveal about Jesus and his teaching. Jesus was so filled with the love of God that when faced with suffering, he compassionately healed; when faced with chaos, he restored calm. These actions reveal vital characteristics of the Kingdom of God that Jesus proclaimed.

Inclusion of outsiders. Jesus welcomed children when others saw them as a bother or not worthy of his attention. He ate dinner with sinners and those who were considered "lowlife." He treated as his friends those who were rejected or thought inferior in his society: foreigners, women, the unclean, the insane, the poor, the sick. He stood up for people who had no power and no esteem from others.

Love of enemies. Jesus taught that people should love not only their friends but their enemies as well:

"I say to you that listen, Love your enemies, do good to those who hate you, bless those who curse you, pray for those who abuse you. . . .

"If you love those who love you, what credit is that to you? For even sinners love those who love them. If you do good to those who do good to you, what credit is that to you? For even sinners do the same. . . . But love

13
Have you ever seen healing take place in a person—healing of body or spirit that seemed like a special gift, perhaps even a miracle of grace? If so, write about what you saw or experienced.

14
Give three examples of kinds of people considered to be "lepers" in our society or in your school—that is, people rejected by others as inferior and not deserving of respect.

your enemies, do good, and lend, expecting nothing in return. Your reward will be great, and you will be children of the Most High; for he is kind to the ungrateful and the wicked. Be merciful, just as your Father is merciful." (Luke 6:27–36)

Jesus not only taught love for enemies, he lived it. He forgave those who persecuted him and betrayed him. Even as he hung on the cross dying, he forgave those who put him to death.

The confronting of hypocrisy and religious legalism. Sometimes when Jesus conveyed the mystery of God's love, the message was harsh. He could not stand hypocrisy and injustice, and he let people know that. In particular the Pharisees and the Sadducees debated with him about the fine points of the Jewish Law. In one incident in a synagogue, the Pharisees questioned Jesus about healing on the Sabbath, which they understood to be a day of total rest. But Jesus responded by asking the Pharisees:

> "Suppose one of you has only one sheep and it falls into a pit on the sabbath; will you not lay hold of it and lift it out? How much more valuable is a human being than a sheep! So it is lawful to do good on the sabbath." (Matthew 12:11–12)

Then he healed the withered hand of a man in the synagogue. Angered by this, the Pharisees plotted against Jesus.

Jesus loved the Law, but he could not bear to see it abused as a way to control people and put them down. He demonstrated God's love for all by challenging hypocrisy and showing that religious legalism had no place in God's Kingdom.

The Least Are the Greatest

In the Kingdom of God as Jesus lived it and taught it, the usual values and priorities of the world are turned upside down. Those who have less really have more. The poor are truly rich. Those who want to be in the highest places of prestige are really in the lowest places. People considered unworthy are the most worthy. The most powerful ones are really the weakest, and those who are weakest are really strongest. The foolish are really wise, and those who think themselves wise are foolish. A person who wants to lead must first become a servant. Those who want to gain their life must first lose it.

In God's Kingdom, the poor are truly rich, the weakest are really the strongest, and those thought unworthy are actually most worthy. *Student art:* Untitled, pencil drawing by Sarah Johnstone, Mercy Academy, Louisville, Kentucky

The Beatitudes:
Turning the World's Values Upside Down

ESUS, in the Sermon on the Mount, given in Matthew's Gospel, proclaims to the crowd the **Beatitudes**, the values and the lifestyle that characterize those who live in God's Kingdom now and who will someday live God's promises to the full:

"Blessed are the poor in spirit, for theirs is the kingdom of heaven.

Blessed are those who mourn, for they will be comforted.

Blessed are the meek, for they will inherit the earth.

Blessed are those who hunger and thirst for righteousness, for they will be filled.

Blessed are the merciful, for they will receive mercy.

Blessed are the pure in heart, for they will see God.

Blessed are the peacemakers, for they will be called children of God.

Blessed are those who are persecuted for righteousness' sake, for theirs is the kingdom of heaven." (5:3–10)

Jesus lived these values by paying attention first of all to the poor and those on the margins of society, by insisting on serving his disciples rather than lording over them, and, most of all, by giving his life on the cross.

Parables of the Kingdom

Jesus had another way besides the example of his actions to get across what the Kingdom of God is like. He taught truths about God and the Kingdom by using parables, intriguing little stories and images that piqued people's curiosity and then delivered a point they were not expecting to hear. The images were familiar—a sheep, a coin, a seed—so

15
If Jesus were here in our society today, what kind of hypocrisy would he confront? What kind of strict legalism might he question? Give two examples of hypocritical attitudes or behaviors that Jesus would criticize.

his audience understood that Jesus knew them and their concerns. Jesus kept his listeners on their toes. With his talent for telling just the right story, Jesus was probably one of the most fascinating teachers of all time.

You are probably familiar with the **parable of the lost sheep.** A shepherd seeks out the one lost sheep in a hundred, leaving the other ninety-nine to take care of themselves. Jesus was trying to give the message: "God is like that. God cares about the people who are lost, the sinners, the ones everyone else has given up on. If you want to be like God, then you too must seek out the lost ones who have gone astray. And if you are lost, know that God is trying to find you and bring you back home."

The **parable of the good Samaritan** is also a familiar one. In the story a man is robbed, beaten up, and left for dead on the side of the road. Several prominent and respectable religious men pass by and do not help him. Only a Samaritan man stops to help, one who, in the eyes of Jesus' Jewish audience, is a despised foreigner. Jesus' message about the Kingdom was something like: "Don't be surprised if people you see as outsiders are the ones who enter the Kingdom before you 'respectable' ones! God's Kingdom is for all who are open to God, regardless of what they own, how much power they have, or how high a position they hold in society."

Although Jesus' message was of God's love for all, and his whole ministry was about inviting people to share that love with one another, he became a controversial figure and the subject of much concern by the ruling authorities.

16
Do you know of someone who is "lost"? Write a brief meditation on how God's love could be expressed to that person so that he or she would not feel so lost.

The Response to Jesus

When a remarkable and loving figure passes through history—the kind of person who demands a response from those who encounter her or him—two things can happen.

First of all, many people take notice of and cling to the person. Some people reacted to Jesus this way. He came among a people, remember, who at the time were under the thumb of the Romans. The Jews' long and difficult history had led them to a passionate yearning for the one who would save them, the one who would relieve them of their suffering—the Messiah.

Jesus was hardly what the Jews expected. Many were looking for a take-charge military leader; Jesus told them to turn the other cheek. They wanted to become masters of their destiny; Jesus told them to humble themselves and to serve. They wanted wealth; Jesus told them to give everything to the poor.

Jesus told people to give everything to the poor.
Student art: "Homeless," color pencil drawing by T. J. Meeks, Holy Cross High School, Louisville, Kentucky

17
What kind of responses would Jesus get if he came into our world today? Write up an imaginary newspaper story describing how various groups react to him and what steps they take to deal with him and his challenge.

Despite all this, many of the Jewish people found Jesus irresistible, for they knew he offered them the kind of freedom that could not be gained from wealth and war. Surely many people listened, found Jesus' message impossible to accept, and walked away. Many others, however, followed and staked their lives on this man and his message. The world is so hungry for love that when a loving person is finally met, we find that person especially attractive. So Jesus came upon the scene, and in a dramatic fashion, people began following him in great numbers.

A second thing often happens when this kind of leader emerges in history. The powers that be—that is, the political, social, and religious leaders of the time—are threatened by the new leader and new ideas they cannot control. Many Jewish leaders refused to accept Jesus as the Messiah whom they had awaited. They were also irate that Jesus dared to criticize those who twisted the Jewish heritage, which he loved so deeply. Those he criticized included the legalists, who taught a spiritless form of the Law, and the pompous leaders who deemed themselves superior to the poor and the powerless. These elites deeply resented Jesus. And even the Romans feared him. He threatened their base of power by stirring up the people's desire for freedom and equality. No doubt about it—this fellow was not only controversial, he was dangerous.

Eventually a plot was arranged to get rid of Jesus by having him executed as a criminal. As you know, he was crucified, died, and was laid in a tomb for burial. But of course that was not the end of the story; it was only just beginning.

Chapter 5 looks at the events surrounding Jesus' death and the remarkable happening that followed three days after. It also searches out the meaning of those events for us today.

For Review

- How was Jesus' idea of the Kingdom of God different from what people expected the Kingdom to be?
- How did Jesus address God? What name for God did Jesus use that indicated his intimate, personal sense of Sonship?
- What powerful message about God did Jesus preach and live by his example?
- List five ways that Jesus' actions manifested God's love and God's Kingdom.
- Give five examples from the text of the upside-down values of the Kingdom of God.
- Offer two examples from the text of the parables of Jesus, and describe the point made in each one.
- Briefly summarize the various responses to Jesus that people had in his time.

Love One Another

Jesus left his followers with the example of his love for them, a love that went so far as to give up his life for them. John's Gospel recounts that at the meal shared with his disciples the night before he was put to death, Jesus said to them:

> "This is my commandment, that you love one another as I have loved you. No one has greater love than this, to lay down one's life for one's friends. You are my friends if you do what I command you. I do not call you servants any longer, because the servant does not know what the master is doing; but I have called you friends, because I have made known to you everything that I have heard from my Father." (15:12–15)

The meal that Jesus shared with his friends was the Last Supper. It was a celebration of love, a way of experiencing God's Kingdom in the time they had together before Jesus was arrested and put on trial. Christians today celebrate that supper in the Eucharist. Through it they share again and again the powerful love of Jesus, thus bringing God's Kingdom into their midst as Jesus did in his life and death.

18
If people in your school, neighborhood, or wider community were to take Jesus' message to heart, "'Love one another as I have loved you,'" how might things be different in those circles? Write a description of what your school, neighborhood, or community might be like.

5

Jesus and the Paschal Mystery:

Finding Life Through Death

The Last Supper: A Meal of Self-Giving Love

The night before he died, Jesus gathered his closest friends, the Twelve, to share a special meal, which we now call the **Last Supper**. This occasion is remembered every year among Christians on **Holy Thursday**. The circumstances in which that meal took place will help us understand its meaning for us today.

The Passover Seder

The place was the city of Jerusalem, center of Judaism and home of the revered Temple. The season was the feast of Passover in the spring, the holy days when faithful Jews remembered how Yahweh, their God, had freed the Israelites from slavery in Egypt so many centuries before. Every year they recalled with passionate gratitude how God had not abandoned them to their oppressor, the pharaoh. They told the story of the Exodus again and again, of how God had rescued them by parting the sea and leading them through on dry land to freedom on the other side.

Every Passover, the Jews kept that memory alive with a special meal, the Seder, in which they retold the story of the Exodus and poured out their thanks to God for all that God had done for them. This meal also kept alive in the Jews the hope that God would not abandon them now in the midst of their trials, and that God would one day free them from every form of oppression they suffered.

Toward the Final Confrontation

It was this deeply joyful memorial meal that Jesus longed to share with his disciples during the Passover in Jerusalem. But the occasion was not a lighthearted, happy moment for Jesus and his friends. Something ominous was in the air; they recognized that some of the Jewish authorities were closing in on Jesus, plotting to destroy him.

Jesus had entered Jerusalem with a triumphal welcome the week before the Passover. Jewish crowds who were there for the feast days waved palm branches and cheered his arrival on a humble donkey. Christians now remember this event every year on **Palm Sunday**, also known as **Passion Sunday**.

A Catholic parish celebrates Palm Sunday, which recalls Jesus' triumphant entrance into Jerusalem.

It was clear to the authorities that Jesus had a tremendous following. Furthermore, he was claiming to be sent from God—that was blasphemy! As if that were not enough, this "wandering preacher" had the nerve to challenge the operations of the Temple itself, claiming that the Temple might even be swept away someday! Jesus' challenge to the authorities reached a highly dramatic point during a visit to the Temple:

[Jesus] entered the temple and began to drive out those who were selling and those who were buying in the temple, and he overturned the tables of the money changers and the seats of those who sold doves; and he would not allow anyone to carry anything through the temple. He was teaching and saying, "Is it not written,

'My house shall be called a house of prayer for all the nations'?

But you have made it a den of robbers."

And when the chief priests and the scribes heard it, they kept looking for a way to kill him; for they were afraid of him, because the whole crowd was spellbound by his teaching. (Mark 11:15–18)

Jesus was confronting the very guardians of the Law, the **chief priests** of the Temple and the Pharisees. No way could they tolerate such a bold attack on all they stood for. In addition, the Roman rulers were beginning to see that Jesus' presence in Jerusalem at Passover time could stir up trouble, inciting the passion of the crowds and possibly causing a riot against the Romans. He had to be done away with.

As Jesus and his disciples gathered for the Passover Seder, Jesus sensed that his final confrontation with the authorities was near.

Bread and Wine: "My Body . . . My Blood"

With the awareness that his time of great suffering was close, Jesus led his friends in the celebration of the Seder. They told the ancient story of the Exodus, poured out thanks to God, sang the psalms of liberation. Then it came time to bless and share gratefully the unleavened bread and the cup of wine, as their ancestors had done for centuries. But at that meal, when Jesus blessed the bread and the cup, he did something different than the usual ritual. With tender love he identified the bread, blessed and broken, with his own body, which was soon to be given up and broken in death for all humankind. And he identified the cup of wine with his own blood, which was about to be poured out in sacrificial love for all. Here is the way Matthew's Gospel tells it:

While they were eating, Jesus took a loaf of bread, and after blessing it he broke it, gave it to the disciples, and said, "Take, eat; this is my body." Then he took a cup, and after giving thanks he gave it to them, saying, "Drink from it, all of you; for this is my blood of the covenant, which is poured out for many for the forgiveness of sins. I tell you, I will never again drink of this fruit of the vine until that day when I drink it new with you in my Father's kingdom." (26:26–29)

Broken and Shared

MARIAN Dolores Schumacher, a Maryknoll sister, describes a kind of "little eucharist" in the everyday life of some children in the poor country of Bolivia:

It was nearly 9 p.m. when I heard a faint knock on the door of our Sisters' house in Riberalta, Bolivia. It was Franci, a regular visitor—only 7 years old. He wore an oversized, air-conditioned T-shirt and his usual whimsical smile. His mother had sent him to ask for bread. I gave him a cookie to eat while I collected some things in a bag. When he left the house, his little brother came out of the darkness to join him. Immediately Franci gave him the remainder of the cookie, which he had saved.

In John's account of the Last Supper, we get another glimpse of Jesus' great love. During the meal Jesus got up from the table, took a towel and a basin of water, and washed the feet of his friends, as a servant would do. This was his way of teaching them by his example to serve one another in love.

The Last Supper is the origin of the Eucharist, which will be discussed further in chapter 9. When Catholics celebrate the Eucharist, also called the Mass, they break bread as Jesus did at the Last Supper, in memory of him. They recognize that Jesus himself is present with them in the bread and the wine—that the bread *is* the body of Jesus broken for them, and the wine *is* the blood of Jesus poured out for them. In sharing the bread and the wine, they proclaim that Jesus' sacrifice of love is now and forever with them. They believe that in the presence of Jesus they are united in love with God and one another. For Catholics this is the great meaning of the Eucharist, which literally means "thanksgiving."

2
Reflect on someone whose example has taught you something important about serving others, about pouring out one's life for others. Write about that person in a one-page essay.

For Review

- What was the purpose of the Passover Seder, at which Jesus celebrated the Last Supper? On what day of the year do Christians now remember the Last Supper?
- What did Jesus do when he blessed the bread and the wine at the Last Supper?
- What do Catholics believe about the meaning of the Eucharist?

Accepting Death on a Cross

The Gospel accounts tell us that before the supper ended, Judas Iscariot, one of the Apostles, left the room. Jesus had an idea of what was in Judas's heart, that Judas was about to betray him by handing him over to the authorities. Jesus also realized that in spite of all their claims of loyalty, most of the other disciples would soon desert him to face his persecutors alone. They would be too frightened to stay by his side. Jesus would go to his death abandoned by most everyone around him. The terrible ordeal of suffering that he was about to face is called his **Passion**.

The Agony in the Garden

Before his Passion, though, Jesus walked with his friends across a valley to the Mount of Olives, where many people who came to Jerusalem for the Passover would camp at night. There, in the **Garden of Gethsemane**, among the olive trees, Jesus prayed in dreadful anguish to his Father that he might be spared from "drinking the cup" of suffering and death that awaited him:

> "Abba, Father, for you all things are possible; remove this cup from me; yet, not what I want, but what you want." (Mark 14:36)

As Jesus agonized over what was about to happen, he came to accept it because he trusted in his Father's love for him. He was ready for what lay ahead. Meanwhile his disciples slept on, unaware of what Jesus was going through.

The Arrest and Trial

When the chief priests and the elders arrived to take Jesus, Judas indicated who Jesus was by greeting him with a kiss. The authorities then moved in on Jesus. A disciple, rushing to Jesus' defense, drew his sword and cut off the ear of the high priest's servant. Jesus insisted there would be no such violent resistance: "'Put your sword back into its place; for all who take the sword will perish by the sword'" (Matthew 26:52).

Now deserted by his terrified disciples, Jesus was led off to face his accusers. Before the **high priest** of the Temple, he was accused of **blasphemy**—claiming a divine status—and of threatening the Temple. Those holding Jesus mocked him, blindfolded him, spat in his face, beat him, and hit him in the face. Then Jesus was handed over to the Roman governor, **Pontius Pilate**, who had the legal authority to sentence someone to death. Despite misgivings about condemning a

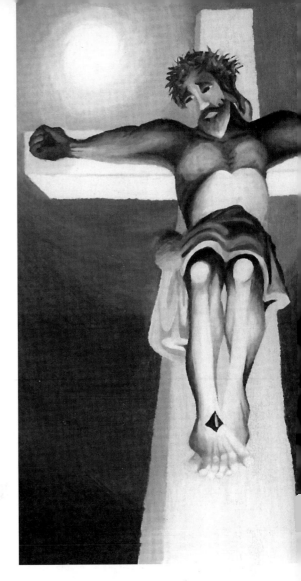

Student art: "Crucified," charcoal drawing by Saribel Daza, Notre Dame High School, San Jose, California

3
Has anyone ever let you down when you were going through an awful time in your life, that is, the person failed to be there for you when you needed him or her? If so, describe in a paragraph what that felt like.

man who seemed innocent, Pilate yielded to the pressure of the chief priests and the mob they had stirred up. He condemned Jesus to be crucified.

The Crucifixion and Death

Death by crucifixion was one of the cruelest, most torturous methods of capital punishment known in the ancient world, a method so horrifying that the Romans would not inflict it on Roman citizens, only on foreigners. Crucifixions were not uncommon at that time in Palestine.

The Scourging

First Jesus was scourged with a whip, probably made of metal- and bone-tipped strips of rawhide; his flesh was literally torn from his body. He was mockingly dressed in a purple robe, the color of royalty, and a crown made from a thorny bush was pounded onto his head. He was then

Who Killed Jesus?

GOSPEL accounts make it clear that some Jewish religious leaders were the instigators behind Jesus' execution, and that they received the help of the Roman government. The execution was ordered and carried out by the Romans. Some versions of the Passion and death, especially John's Gospel, seem to identify "the Jews" in a more general sense, not just some of their leaders, as being responsible for Jesus' death. Who really was responsible?

Biblical scholars tell us that references to "the Jews" in John's Passion account probably reflect the period when that Gospel was written, 90 to 100 C.E., when tensions were especially high between the Christians and the Jews. At the time of Jesus' death, most Jews were not against him, nor would Jesus' followers have said that "the Jews" killed Jesus. After all, the disciples considered themselves and Jesus to be good Jews; Jesus' followers had yet to identify themselves as members of a religion called Christianity. They would have said that certain leaders in their own religion conspired with the Romans to have Jesus executed.

Unfortunately the history of relationships between Christians and Jews has been marked by tragic misunderstanding. Seeing the Jews in general, instead of a few leaders, as responsible for Jesus' death, church and civil leaders in many eras of Christian history persecuted innocent Jewish people, even putting them to death for **deicide** (meaning the killing of God). Too many Christians, even today, use their blame of Jews for the death of Jesus as an excuse to discriminate against them. Prejudice against Jews, or **Anti-Semitism,** is still a serious problem in our society and in many other parts of the world.

In the last several decades the Catholic church has clarified in numerous official documents that Jews as a people are not to be blamed for the death of Jesus. There have been encouraging signs of love and cooperation among Christians and Jews, as they work together on projects of mutual concern and discover anew how close their traditions are and how much they have in common.

The Hurt of Ridicule

BEING humiliated by ridicule can be as painful as a physical blow, or even more so. Tara Coohill, an eleventh-grade student at St. John Villa Academy in Staten Island, New York, recalls what a new arrival to her school went through and how Tara responded:

Last week, my friends and I were sitting at our same isolated spot in the noisy lunchroom discussing our weekend activities. As usual, we had spent the weekend together—a tight-knit group that knows each other as well as we know ourselves. When Ciyo walked in, a sudden hush fell over the room. Ciyo is a girl from India who recently enrolled in my school. Everyone stopped what she was doing and stared uneasily at her. I noticed Ciyo's shoulders slumped a bit as she realized that no one was about to invite her to join them. I saw her quietly sit at an empty table in a corner of the room and bury her head in a book. The snickers and laughter that filled the silence were clearly directed at this lonely girl.

I was suddenly ashamed of my friends' actions and of myself. Why didn't we do anything to make this girl feel comfortable? Why didn't we give her the same respect we show other new girls who have been introduced to us? I think this is because Ciyo looks different from us. She dresses differently and talks with a slight accent. I started thinking our lack of civility showed something lacking in us and not her.

Ciyo has not been viewed by us as a person, but rather as a "foreigner." My friends assumed that she was unapproachable and wouldn't have anything worth contributing to the group. They judged her before getting to know her. Their feelings of superiority may be based on a fear of the unknown. Her customs, her lifestyle, her appearance are so different from theirs. They find it easier to ridicule what they don't understand than to adjust their views and accept something out of the ordinary.

I think that Ciyo feels like an outcast and believes that she hasn't been given a chance to show her true talents, abilities and good qualities. On her first day at school, Ciyo looked forward to making friends. After being wounded so deeply by the other students, she is no longer sure that she wants to fit in with them. She has tried not to be so vulnerable, but anyone can see that this experience has hurt her deeply.

On that day last week, I had an important decision to make. I stood up quickly and walked over to Ciyo's table. I could feel everyone's eyes on me as I introduced myself to her. I invited her to join my friends, and she hesitatingly came to my table.

It took a while—and a lot of hard work—to get a conversation going, but eventually Ciyo started to talk about herself. Her family didn't seem so different from ours. . . . I could see some of my friends thinking that Ciyo was a teenager too—different from us in some ways but similar in others. . . .

I know that people's attitudes do not change suddenly and that it will take time for our friendship to develop. If we can put aside our arrogance and become more sensitive to others' feelings, we may find our lives enriched by new friendships.

Recall an incident from your experience when a person—yourself or someone else—was being ridiculed or mocked. Reflect on what the person was thinking or might have been thinking during the mockery. Write it up as an inner monolog (that is, a talk with oneself).

A contemporary pageant re-enacts the Passion and death of Christ.

ridiculed by the Roman soldiers as "King of the Jews." In all this suffering, Jesus was alone; his friends and followers were nowhere in sight.

Nailed to the Cross

The Gospels do not say much about the Crucifixion itself. From descriptions of other crucifixions of that era, we have an idea of what happened. It is likely that Jesus, already weak from loss of blood and beatings, was forced to carry a very heavy wooden beam on his shoulders for the quarter-mile walk to **Golgotha** (meaning the "place of the skull," the hill where crucifixions in Jerusalem took place). Some of the Gospel accounts say Jesus was helped by a man, Simon of Cyrene, who was pulled from the crowd to prevent Jesus from dying before he got to the execution site. Once there, Jesus' garments were stripped off him, reopening all his wounds, and he was laid with his arms stretched out along the wooden beam. The soldiers pounded spikes through his wrists into the beam. Next, the beam, with Jesus nailed to it, was lifted up and lashed to an upright beam, which his feet were then nailed to.

Jesus hung in this tortured state for several hours. In a crucifixion, death usually came by suffocation, as the victim struggled to push up his body and gasp for air. As Jesus hung there writhing in pain and gasping for air, he must have felt alone and abandoned by God. At one point, as the Gospels tell it, he cried out, "'My God, my God, why have you forsaken me?'" (Mark 15:34)—the first words of the Twenty-second Psalm, which would have been familiar to Jesus from its role in Jewish life and prayer.

As Jesus suffered and died on the cross, the Gospels tell us that some of the women who had followed Jesus watched in shock and grief from a distance. John's Gospel reports that several women, including Jesus' mother, and one male disciple ("the disciple whom [Jesus] loved," assumed to be John himself) stood near the cross. Others abandoned Jesus out of fear for their own life.

Love and Trust from the Cross

In spite of his struggle with feeling abandoned, Jesus did not despair. Calling on the great source of his love, his *Abba,* Jesus prayed for those who put him to death: "'Father, forgive them; for they do not know what they are doing'" (Luke 23:34). Finally Jesus, with his terrible agony at an end and being at the point of death, yielded himself over in trust to God with a loud cry, "'Father, into your hands I commend my spirit'" (Luke 23:46). With that, he died.

Freely accepting his death, Jesus remained faithful to his Father to the end. The giving of himself—his body and blood—at the Last Supper came to its full meaning in the sacrifice of his life on the cross the next day. Jesus' death was an act of perfect love for all humankind and of total trust in God's love for him.

Christians each year commemorate the day Jesus died as **Good Friday.**

Joseph of Arimathea, a wealthy disciple of Jesus, went to Pilate and asked permission to take Jesus' body away to be buried. Joseph then wrapped Jesus' body in a linen cloth and laid it in a new tomb, carved out of a rocky hillside. A large stone was rolled in place to cover the entrance. Because it was Friday evening, the beginning of the Sabbath, the women who were to prepare Jesus' body for burial with ointments and spices had to delay their work. Following Jewish Law, they would rest on Saturday and come back to the tomb on Sunday.

Student art: **Untitled, mixed media by Nate Scatena, University of San Diego High School, San Diego, California**

5
Focus on one of the things Jesus said while he was dying on the cross. Write a prayer to Jesus in response to what he was thinking and feeling.

For Review

- What did Jesus agonize about while praying in the Garden of Gethsemane? How did he resolve his struggle?
- Who was responsible for the death of Jesus?
- Describe the kind of suffering that Jesus probably endured in the Crucifixion.
- What were three of the last things Jesus said, according to the Gospel accounts quoted in this chapter?
- On what day of the year do Christians remember Jesus' death?

Love in the Midst of Death

PEOPLE in El Salvador remember fondly their great hero and pastor, Archbishop Oscar Romero. During a terribly violent time in the Central American country, this humble and courageous man stood up for the many poor and oppressed Salvadoran peasants who were victims of government persecution, torture, and mass killings. Eventually Romero was assassinated for the stand he took with the people.

Romero, like Jesus, knew he was taking a dangerous path that could lead to his own death. Soon after he became archbishop of the capital region of San Salvador in 1977, he was burying a close friend and priest who had spoken out on behalf of the peasants and been gunned down by a government-condoned death squad. At the priest's funeral, Romero said in his homily that was broadcast live: "'Who knows if the murderers are listening to this on a radio in their hideout. We tell you, murderous brethren, that we love you and that we ask of God repentance for your hearts.'"

Two months later Romero was burying another outspoken priest who had been assassinated. In the funeral homily Romero told a parable as a way to illustrate what this priest's life and death had meant. He told the story of a Bedouin, an Arab who was guiding a group of thirsty travelers as they made their way through the desert. The trav-elers were so thirsty that they kept seeing mirages, or illusions, of water in the distance and kept heading off toward the mirages. They were duped by their own thirst. The Bedouin guide kept saying to them, "Not that way, this way." When this happened several times, the travelers became angry with the guide, pulled out their guns, and shot him. But even as he lay there dying, the guide kept holding out his hand, pointing and pleading with them, "Not that way, this way."

Romero made the point with his parable that the priest he was burying had continued to show people the way of justice at great danger to himself, even though he would be murdered for it.

Less than three years after that funeral, on 24 March 1980, Archbishop Romero himself was gunned down while celebrating Mass. The day before at a cathedral Mass aired on the radio, he had pleaded with the soldiers and national guardsmen not to kill their own Salvadoran people, begging them to end the repression that held the country in its grip.

Like the six assassinated priests whom Romero buried while he was archbishop, like the Bedouin guide of the parable who was killed by the thirsty travelers, and most of all like Jesus, Romero loved his people passionately to the end and gave his life for them.

The Resurrection of Jesus

To Jesus' followers it must have seemed that all was lost. They remembered his passionate preaching that God's Kingdom was right in their midst, that a loving God who cared for poor people and outsiders would never abandon them. They carried with them the memory of the healings and miracles Jesus had performed, those times when God's power had broken through into their world through Jesus and made everything good and right again. It had seemed that God's ancient promises to the Jewish people were coming together in the Good News of Jesus. But now he was dead. Had all that been just a false hope?

Jesus' followers were a fearful, defeated group who scattered at the time of the Crucifixion, their hopes crushed by their leader's execution. Although some faithful followers remained, viewing the terrible events at a distance, most of the disciples just fled, afraid that Jesus' whole purpose and mission had been destroyed in his death. They thought it was all over and that they would be lucky to escape with their lives.

Jesus' death on the cross, however, was not the end of the story.

"He Has Been Raised!"

Here is one Gospel's account of what happened when the women came back to the tomb on Sunday to prepare Jesus' body for burial:

> After the sabbath, as the first day of the week was dawning, Mary Magdalene and the other Mary went to see the tomb. And suddenly there was a great earthquake; for an angel of the Lord, descending from heaven, came and rolled back the stone and sat on it. His appearance was like lightning, and his clothing white as snow. For fear of him the guards shook and became like dead men. But the angel said to the women, "Do not be afraid; I know that you are looking for Jesus who was crucified. He is not here; for he has been raised, as he said. Come, see the place where he lay. Then go quickly and tell his disciples, 'He has been raised from the dead, and indeed he is going ahead of you to Galilee; there you

6
Recall a time when you were disillusioned and discouraged, and it seemed that everything good was over. But it wasn't over. You came back; things got better. Write an account of what happened to you.

The proclamation of the early church. The early church made no attempt to *explain* the Resurrection; instead, the Gospels simply and powerfully *proclaimed* it. Belief in the Resurrection was unanimous in the early Christian communities. Saint Paul, whose letters to those communities are the earliest writings in the Christian Testament, wrote:

> For I handed on to you as of first importance what I in turn had received: that Christ died for our sins in accordance with the scriptures, and that he was buried, and that he was raised on the third day in accordance with the scriptures, and that he appeared to Cephas [Peter], then to the twelve. . . . So we proclaim and so you have come to believe. (1 Corinthians 15:3–5,11)

Paul proclaimed the Resurrection with great confidence, as did the Gospel writers. Belief in the Resurrection, and the depth of that belief, seem most reasonably explained by an actual, not an imagined, Resurrection.

If You Believe

The implications of believing in the Resurrection of Jesus are far reaching. If we believe in the Resurrection, then everything that Jesus stood for deserves our commitment—even if that commitment should lead us to pain and suffering, even to death. Believing that Jesus really was raised from the dead also fosters hope and trust in God in our own life. God did not abandon Jesus; God was with him in all things, even death on a cross, and God raised him from death to the glory of risen life. That same God will never abandon us, will be with us even in our death, and will raise us, too. This is the great source of hope for believers.

Before leaving this important part of this discussion, recall that believers spend a lifetime deepening their decision and convictions about the truth of Christian faith, making their commitment over and over again. So you need not feel pressured into having all your questions settled at this point. Youth is a good time for raising questions. If you ask good questions now, the answers you eventually arrive at will have more substance, depth, and maturity.

Belief in the Resurrection of Jesus is central for Christians, and so we have spent some time here on the rational

The Resurrection of Jesus

To Jesus' followers it must have seemed that all was lost. They remembered his passionate preaching that God's Kingdom was right in their midst, that a loving God who cared for poor people and outsiders would never abandon them. They carried with them the memory of the healings and miracles Jesus had performed, those times when God's power had broken through into their world through Jesus and made everything good and right again. It had seemed that God's ancient promises to the Jewish people were coming together in the Good News of Jesus. But now he was dead. Had all that been just a false hope?

Jesus' followers were a fearful, defeated group who scattered at the time of the Crucifixion, their hopes crushed by their leader's execution. Although some faithful followers remained, viewing the terrible events at a distance, most of the disciples just fled, afraid that Jesus' whole purpose and mission had been destroyed in his death. They thought it was all over and that they would be lucky to escape with their lives.

Jesus' death on the cross, however, was not the end of the story.

"He Has Been Raised!"

Here is one Gospel's account of what happened when the women came back to the tomb on Sunday to prepare Jesus' body for burial:

> After the sabbath, as the first day of the week was dawning, Mary Magdalene and the other Mary went to see the tomb. And suddenly there was a great earthquake; for an angel of the Lord, descending from heaven, came and rolled back the stone and sat on it. His appearance was like lightning, and his clothing white as snow. For fear of him the guards shook and became like dead men. But the angel said to the women, "Do not be afraid; I know that you are looking for Jesus who was crucified. He is not here; for he has been raised, as he said. Come, see the place where he lay. Then go quickly and tell his disciples, 'He has been raised from the dead, and indeed he is going ahead of you to Galilee; there you

6
Recall a time when you were disillusioned and discouraged, and it seemed that everything good was over. But it wasn't over. You came back; things got better. Write an account of what happened to you.

7
Have you ever experienced a mixture of "fear and great joy," like the women at the tomb? Write about why you felt both excited and afraid at the same time, and relate that to how the women must have felt when they learned that Jesus had been raised.

will see him.' This is my message for you." So they left the tomb quickly with fear and great joy, and ran to tell his disciples. Suddenly Jesus met them and said, "Greetings!" And they came to him, took hold of his feet, and worshiped him. Then Jesus said to them, "Do not be afraid; go and tell my brothers to go to Galilee; there they will see me." (Matthew 28:1–10)

The reality that Jesus was raised from the dead by God is called the **Resurrection.** It is the core belief of Christianity. Christians celebrate that central mystery of their faith every year on **Easter Sunday.** In fact, every Sunday is "the day of the Lord's Resurrection," a kind of "mini-Easter," a day to recall with joy that Jesus has risen and is with us in glory. For this reason, the Sabbath for Christians is on **Sunday.**

The Appearances of Jesus

The Gospels tell us that Jesus appeared to various people following the Resurrection. These appearances give us fascinating insights into the nature of resurrected life, or life after death. The appearances also offer a strong sense of the meaning and power of Jesus' presence to his disciples, and can help us understand the nature of Jesus' presence in the world today.

In one of his appearances after the Resurrection, Jesus shared a simple breakfast of fish with Peter and others on a lakeshore.
Photo: **The shore of the Sea of Galilee**

No Trumpet Blasts

The Gospels do not record that blazing trumpets, magical signs, or roaring crowds accompanied Jesus' appearances. On the contrary, he appeared simply and without fanfare. In John's Gospel account Mary Magdalene at first thought that Jesus was an ordinary gardener. Yet when he called her name, she suddenly recognized him. In another appearance, on the road to Emmaus, Jesus took a long walk with two terrified disciples who felt hopelessly lost after the Crucifixion. They did not recognize him until he broke bread with them. Jesus also appeared to some totally shocked and frightened disciples who felt at first that they were seeing a ghost. He told them they had nothing to fear, then asked if they had anything to eat. Jesus also shared a simple breakfast of fish by a lakeshore with Peter and others.

In all these accounts the people were shattered by what had happened in the Crucifixion. They were unprepared for the Resurrection and amazed by the One who was now present among them. In all cases Jesus brought overwhelming peace and joy.

Really?

Did the Resurrection and the appearances actually happen? Or was it all a hallucination, a figment of the imagination of the followers of Jesus? Or perhaps it was a hoax, a deception pulled off by a few close friends of Jesus who stole his body and hid it, then claimed he had risen? Could the Christian faith that has spread around the world for almost two thousand years be based on a falsehood?

Let's consider this challenge to the Christian faith.

Differing Accounts

The four accounts of the Resurrection in the Gospels of Matthew, Mark, Luke, and John tell a similar story: The women return to the tomb on Sunday to find that Jesus' body is not there. They are afraid, but then they are told by someone that there is nothing to fear, that Jesus has been raised from the dead. They go off to tell the news to others.

Yet inconsistencies exist among the four accounts. For instance, they differ in details such as these:

- who arrived at the tomb first
- which of the Apostles came next to the tomb
- who informed the women that Jesus was raised (an angel? a man? two men or angels?)

8
Write about a big event you experienced, like a rock concert or a major tournament. Record all the details you can recall. Then compare your account with someone else's in your class who was at the same event. List any differences in your accounts. Does this give you any insights about the Resurrection accounts?

- whether the women saw an angel roll away the stone or they discovered it already rolled away
- where the message was given that Jesus was raised (inside the tomb? outside the tomb?)
- whether Jesus himself appeared in the garden where the tomb was located

To a reader who is looking for a literal history of events, such inconsistencies can be disturbing. The reader may wonder why the Gospel writers couldn't "get the story straight." Is it because the whole thing was just made up?

It helps if we understand that the Gospels were written down some forty to seventy years after the events they describe. In the decades after Jesus' death, the stories of his life, death, and Resurrection were passed on by word of mouth in different communities of Christians. Naturally some of the details were lost or changed in the telling and retelling of the stories before they were actually written down. In addition, each Gospel was written within a particular Christian community of the first century. Each community was involved in a journey of faith, and the Gospel writers often arranged their accounts of Jesus' life, death, and Resurrection to best serve the faith needs of their own community. It is not surprising, then, that we find many differences among the four Gospels in the way the same incident or event is described. This does not mean that a given event never happened, but only that various memories of the event were handed down in various communities.

As we will see in chapter 7, on the Scriptures, the Bible is not intended to be a literal, factual history in the same way as a newspaper or TV news report. The Bible is a collection of stories of religious truth carried and handed on by God's people. Details of a given story might be some-

The tomb of Lazarus, Jesus' friend who was raised from the dead, in Bethany, Israel. The tomb in which Jesus was buried in Jerusalem was probably similar.

what unclear or inconsistent; even so, such a story can still reveal truth.

Thus the differences in the four Gospel accounts of the Resurrection need not stand in the way of belief in the essential truth of the stories—that Jesus was raised from the dead and appeared to his followers.

Evidence for the Resurrection

We cannot actually *prove* that the Resurrection took place in the same way that a police detective can prove what happened, say, in a burglary. Belief in the Resurrection ultimately comes down to faith, not proof. However, that does not mean that we have no good evidence that Jesus was raised from the dead. Let's look at some of that evidence.

The stories themselves. In some ways, the inconsistencies in the Gospel accounts make the Resurrection event more, not less, believable. If Jesus' disciples had indeed stolen the body and then made up the story that he was raised from the dead, they certainly would have been more concerned about getting the details of their story straight!

Another interesting feature of the Resurrection stories adds credibility to them. In all the accounts women are the first to hear and spread the news that Jesus has been raised. We know that Jesus valued women, but that was unusual in his era and culture. In the society of that time women were not valued as reliable witnesses for anything. Their word was not taken seriously. If the followers of Jesus had been trying to pull a hoax, they would not have developed an account of the Resurrection that so prominently features the witness and testimony of women. They certainly would have developed a more "credible" story line, with high-status witnesses.

The experience of the disciples. We know that Jesus' followers scattered in fear after his death, terrified for their own lives. Yet shortly afterward they were boldly and joyfully professing their faith in Jesus to everyone who would listen. They seemed to have lost all fear. And this was true not for just a handful of followers but for hundreds of people who had witnessed Jesus' appearances after the Resurrection. So deep was their conviction in Jesus' Resurrection that many of them would later die as martyrs rather than deny their belief in the Risen Jesus. This sense of conviction in hundreds of people, with the power of their faith passed on to the generations after them, would not likely have been the result of a mass hallucination.

9
Imagine how the story of Jesus' Resurrection would have been announced to a TV news crew by the Apostles if they had been trying to pull off a hoax and guarantee that people would believe their story. Write up the Apostles' script for the announcement.

The proclamation of the early church. The early church made no attempt to *explain* the Resurrection; instead, the Gospels simply and powerfully *proclaimed* it. Belief in the Resurrection was unanimous in the early Christian communities. Saint Paul, whose letters to those communities are the earliest writings in the Christian Testament, wrote:

> For I handed on to you as of first importance what I in turn had received: that Christ died for our sins in accordance with the scriptures, and that he was buried, and that he was raised on the third day in accordance with the scriptures, and that he appeared to Cephas [Peter], then to the twelve. . . . So we proclaim and so you have come to believe. (1 Corinthians 15:3–5,11)

Paul proclaimed the Resurrection with great confidence, as did the Gospel writers. Belief in the Resurrection, and the depth of that belief, seem most reasonably explained by an actual, not an imagined, Resurrection.

If You Believe

The implications of believing in the Resurrection of Jesus are far reaching. If we believe in the Resurrection, then everything that Jesus stood for deserves our commitment—even if that commitment should lead us to pain and suffering, even to death. Believing that Jesus really was raised from the dead also fosters hope and trust in God in our own life. God did not abandon Jesus; God was with him in all things, even death on a cross, and God raised him from death to the glory of risen life. That same God will never abandon us, will be with us even in our death, and will raise us, too. This is the great source of hope for believers.

Before leaving this important part of this discussion, recall that believers spend a lifetime deepening their decision and convictions about the truth of Christian faith, making their commitment over and over again. So you need not feel pressured into having all your questions settled at this point. Youth is a good time for raising questions. If you ask good questions now, the answers you eventually arrive at will have more substance, depth, and maturity.

Belief in the Resurrection of Jesus is central for Christians, and so we have spent some time here on the rational

10
What is your belief about the Resurrection? Does your belief about it affect your life in any way? Write up your reflections.

basis for that belief. But assuming that there truly was a Resurrection, what is resurrected life like? Where is Jesus today? What does the Resurrection mean for us, two thousand years later? We turn now to these intriguing issues.

For Review

1. Briefly describe the reactions of Jesus' followers at the time of his death.
2. What core belief do Christians celebrate on Easter Sunday and every Sunday?
3. What can be learned from the accounts of Jesus' appearances?
4. Summarize the evidence that supports Jesus' Resurrection.

What Does the Resurrection Mean for Us?

Perhaps the most significant thing for us about the Resurrection is what it means in our own life. The Resurrection is not simply about some distant, long ago reality that affected the earliest Christians. It points to a great mystery that is going on in us today, a mystery that unites many of

the realities we have already talked about in this course: the Exodus, the Passover, the Eucharist, Jesus' death, and his Resurrection, which gives meaning to everything else.

The Paschal Mystery

We call this great unified reality the Paschal Mystery. *Paschal* comes from the Greek word meaning "lamb." Each year at the Passover Seder, or paschal meal, traditionally a lamb that had been ritually slain was eaten. The Last Supper took place in the context of the Passover Seder, which is why we use the term *Paschal Mystery.*

The Paschal Mystery is a mystery, but not in the sense of being a tricky puzzle or something we will never understand. Rather, it is a mystery in the way that love is a mystery—a deep reality to be lived more so than a problem to be explained.

The **Paschal Mystery** is the reality that *Jesus has gone through death to life.* This is the apparently simple but profound truth at the heart of Christian life. And if we follow Jesus, we, too, will experience the small and large deaths of pain, sorrow, suffering, and physical death. But life, not death, will have the last word. The Resurrection means that ultimately death will be overcome by life, despair by hope, sorrow by joy, fear by trust, hate by love. Because of the Resurrection, all suffering can be transformed into new, abundant life. We can be united to Jesus in his suffering and death and thus in his risen life. Saint Paul tells his friend Timothy (and all of us):

> The saying is sure:
> If we have died with him, we will also live with him;
> if we endure, we will also reign with him.
>
> (2 Timothy 2:11–12)

The Paschal Mystery is not just about life *after* death. It is about life *now,* as we live it today. As we enter into the Paschal Mystery, embracing the difficulties and crosses of our daily life, we can experience glimpses of the glorious risen life that will be ours after our physical death, for eternity.

The Resurrection means that ultimately death will be overcome by life and despair by hope.
Student art: "Abandoned Children," linocut by Brandon Canepa, Saint Agnes Academy, Memphis, Tennessee

11
What is a difficulty or cross you face in your life? Imagine yourself embracing that difficulty with trust—taking it on and working it through—so that it leads to new life, risen life for you. Write about what might be involved in embracing your cross.

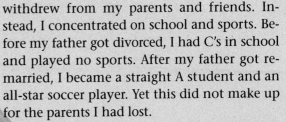

Through Death to Life: One Teenager's Story

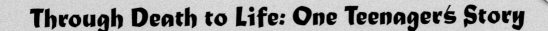

WHAT can the Paschal Mystery, the journey through death to life, mean for us today? The following account by a young man from La Salle High School in Pasadena, California, gives a sense of that:

About seven years ago, a major change occurred in my life. Yet to this day, I still do not know if it was for the best. When I was nine years old, my parents got divorced. I loved both of them, but I also hated them because they were doing this to me. My mother moved out. I then lived with my dad whom I had hardly ever talked to before the divorce.

At the end of the school year, my father and I moved to another city. Life was very hard for me. I had only one parent, and I had lost the other one that I cared for so deeply. And to make things even worse, we moved to a new city where I literally had no friends. My life seemed horrible. I can remember asking God why this was happening to me.

My father remarried. This made me extremely unhappy. First, I did not like the woman he was marrying and, second, I felt that she was trying to take my mother's place. I cried and yelled at my father for doing this, and again I asked God why? Until recently, I never found the answer to that question.

I felt that there was no one I could really trust to be always on my side. Because of this, I withdrew from my parents and friends. Instead, I concentrated on school and sports. Before my father got divorced, I had C's in school and played no sports. After my father got remarried, I became a straight A student and an all-star soccer player. Yet this did not make up for the parents I had lost.

At twelve years old, I never talked to my parents, except when I went into the kitchen to get something to eat. I thought everything was fine, but later I realized it wasn't. Because of all the things that had happened to me, I had isolated myself.

A day after I realized this, I called my dad at work, something I had never done before, and asked him if he could come home and talk. So he left work early and took me out to dinner. I told him how I felt and what made me feel that way. He just sat and listened. To me, that was one of the best nights of my life.

After my father and I had this talk, we started doing a lot of things together. We became father and son and developed an extremely close relationship. Three years later, we were best friends. I learned to tell my dad anything, and he always helped me with my problems. He even helped me make peace with my new stepmother. I don't think any of this would have happened, however, if I had not asked him to talk that one night long ago.

Our Redemption: Exodus to Freedom

What do the death and Resurrection of Jesus have to do with the Exodus, the Passover, and the Eucharist?

Recall the wondrous image of God freeing the Israelites from slavery in Egypt, leading them into the sea and parting the waters, bringing them to freedom on the other side. They were completely in God's hands, trusting God to bring them safely through the terror of the sea. And God did so—just as Jesus' beloved *Abba* brought Jesus through the terror of death on a cross to the risen life that awaited him. Jesus' death on a cross was our "exodus," our way to Redemption—freedom from sin in order to enjoy the new life of grace, a life lived in union with God. This is what is known as our **salvation.** We are saved from sin to live with God.

The Lamb of God

The Passover, as mentioned earlier in this chapter, was the Jewish commemoration of the Exodus. And the Last Supper, the first Eucharist, took place in the context of the Passover Seder. At the Seder a ritually slain lamb was eaten. In Christian symbolism, Jesus is the **Lamb of God**, through whose death (like the Passover lamb's) we come to freedom and salvation. Jesus, giving himself—his body and blood—in the Eucharist and on the cross, pours himself out for us like the lamb of the Passover. The image of Jesus as the Lamb of God is at the heart of the Eucharist. As the eucharistic bread is prepared to be distributed, the congregation sings or recites:

Lamb of God, you take away the sins of the world:
  have mercy on us.
Lamb of God, you take away the sins of the world:
  have mercy on us.
Lamb of God, you take away the sins of the world:
  grant us peace.

The priest describes the consecrated bread itself using this image: "This is the Lamb of God, who takes away the sins of the world." As in the Exodus, we are liberated, or given a new life, every time we share in the Eucharist. In that sharing we also unite ourselves with Jesus in his death so that we may be one with him in his risen life. That is the great truth we call the Paschal Mystery.

Jesus is present with us today, carrying us through suffering and troubles even when we are not aware of his presence.
Student art: Untitled, oil painting by Regina Kwan, Bellarmine Jefferson High School, Burbank, California

Jesus, Present in a New Way

The Resurrection of Jesus, and especially the accounts of his appearances to his disciples after the Resurrection, tell us a great deal about the presence of Jesus in our life today. An awareness of that presence is an important part of the development of Christian faith.

Jesus' resurrected body was not simply his physical body recovered to health. His body was *resurrected,* not *resuscitated.* It was a glorified body. Only people with faith or at least an openness to faith recognized him. Jesus had entered into an entirely new form of existence. He was still definitely Jesus, but at the same time, he was different from the physical Jesus who had walked among the people during his life. For instance, he was able to move through locked doors to be in the presence of his disciples.

The post-Resurrection appearances of Jesus are important because they are transitional moments. That is, the appearances reveal the change from Jesus' earthly physical presence two thousand years ago to his presence as we experience it today. Today Jesus is no longer present among us in a physical way—we can no longer see or touch him. Nevertheless, Jesus is truly present among us. As he promised, Jesus is present through his Spirit, a Spirit who continually brings back to our mind all that Jesus taught us and who gives us the courage and insight to live out that message.

The appearances offer another, related insight about Jesus' risen life: Present through his Spirit in our midst, Jesus can only be recognized with eyes of faith. Even the disciples who experienced the appearances had to have faith. You may recall the story of Doubting Thomas, the Apostle who refused to believe that Jesus had been raised from the dead until he could put his finger into the nail holes in Jesus' hands and put his hand into Jesus' pierced side.

The encouraging fact here is that even Jesus' disciples sometimes had difficulty recognizing and accepting him in his risen state. Today we often seem to think that if only we could see Jesus, just like his followers could two thousand years ago when he literally walked among them, faith would then follow. The appearances demonstrate that faith was required even of those who were present at those marvelous moments, that only in faith were they able to recognize Jesus in their midst. We, too, can recognize him clearly through the eyes of faith.

For Review

1. What is the meaning of the Paschal Mystery?
2. How is Jesus' death on the cross and his Resurrection like an exodus for us?
3. • In Christian symbolism, why is Jesus known as the Lamb of God?
4. • In the appearances after the Resurrection, how was the Risen Jesus different from how he had been before he died?

Jesus Is with Us Today

One of the most touching stories in the Gospels is the account of Jesus' appearance to two of his followers in the evening after the Resurrection, as they walked along on the road from Jerusalem to Emmaus. The disciples were depressed and afraid; all they could think about was the terrible event that had just taken place in Jerusalem: the Crucifixion of their leader, Jesus. Their hopes were crushed. It appeared that everything they had believed in was crumbling. So preoccupied were they that when this stranger (the Risen Jesus) came along to walk with them, they did not recognize him. Seeing the disciples' sadness, Jesus talked with them along the way, encouraging them by showing them that all that had happened was not really a defeat—that it was the fulfillment of the Hebrew Scriptures. The awful suffering their leader had endured was not meaningless. Wasn't his suffering necessary to fulfill all that had been prophesied by Isaiah about a suffering servant who would give his life for the people and thus save them?

Still the two disciples did not recognize that this man who accompanied them on their journey was Jesus. But their hearts were filled with joy as they talked with him. Finally, as evening came on and they reached the village, they invited their companion to come in and eat supper with them. Here is how Luke tells the rest of the story:

> When he was at the table with them, he took bread, blessed and broke it, and gave it to them. Then their eyes were opened, and they recognized him; and he vanished from their sight. They said to each other, "Were not our hearts burning within us while he was talking with us on the road, while he was opening the scriptures to us?" That same hour they got up and returned to Jerusalem; and they found the eleven and their companions gathered together. They were saying, "The Lord has risen indeed, and he has appeared to Simon [Peter]!" Then they told what had happened on the road, and how he had been made known to them in the breaking of the bread. (24:30–35)

We, too, have our own discouragements and preoccupations as we walk along on our journey of life. But we are gifted in having the Risen Jesus with us—in the Eucharist and in all those moments of sharing the bread of our everyday lives with one another. We have only to open our eyes to see him "in the breaking of the bread."

12
Think about an experience you have had that you did not really understand until after it was over. Then your eyes were opened to see something you had not recognized while in the situation. Write a letter to yourself about what you discovered.

6

The Church:

Gathering in the Spirit of Jesus

The Spirit Is Poured Out

Imagine how Jesus' followers felt after the Resurrection, as they walked and talked with the **Risen Jesus.** All their fears were swept away, for by raising Jesus, God had triumphed over death itself. Jesus' presence with the disciples gave them the deepest sense of joy and peace.

Jesus Promises His Spirit

The Risen Jesus, however, did not stay with his followers in a physical way for long. In John's Gospel account, before Jesus' death he had told his friends that he would soon be leaving them to return to the Father. But he also promised them, "'I will not leave you orphaned'" (John 14:18). He told them, "'The Holy Spirit, whom the Father will send in my name, will teach you everything, and remind you of all that I have said to you'" (14:26). His Spirit would be with them and dwell among them forever, guiding them in the way of truth and giving them courage and strength to do things they never dreamed possible.

The Ascension: Returning to the Father

The **Acts of the Apostles,** also referred to as Acts, is an account of the early church written by Luke. Acts tells the story of the early Christian communities and their spread from Jerusalem to the larger world.

As the Acts of the Apostles tells it, forty days after the Resurrection, Jesus did return to his Father. But first he left in the Apostles' hands the mission of spreading the Good News of God's Kingdom to every corner of the world. They would not have to take on this task alone, for the Spirit of Jesus would fill them with power:

"But you will receive power when the Holy Spirit has come upon you; and you will be my witnesses in Jerusalem, in all Judea and Samaria, and to the ends of the earth." When he had said this, as they were watching, he was lifted up, and a cloud took him out of their sight. While he was going and they were gazing up toward heaven, suddenly two men in white robes stood by them. They said, "Men of Galilee, why do you stand looking up toward heaven? This Jesus, who has been taken up from you into heaven, will come in the same way as you saw him go into heaven." (Acts 1:8–11)

Christians call Jesus' return to the Father the **Ascension** (based on the word *ascend,* or "go up"). Its feast is celebrated by Catholics each year on **Ascension Thursday**, forty days after Easter Sunday.

In calling this reality the Ascension, we need to be careful that we do not misunderstand its meaning. It is not really about Jesus "going up there." When we say the word *heaven,* we automatically tend to think of a place "up there." In the meaning it seems to have in the Scriptures, however, heaven is more than a place; it is a state of being in the presence of God—who exists everywhere, not just "up there." During our earthly life we can experience glimpses of heaven (which, for our purposes, really means "with God"). After death we can be *fully* with God. So "in heaven" Jesus is no longer tied to one place, to one era, to talking about one thing at a time to one particular group of people. He is freed

from the physical limitations of earthly existence—freed to be everywhere, with everyone, for all time, loving and caring and calling us back to God.

Jesus' physical presence, as he walked and talked on earth with people, was only one kind of presence. We may wish we could know Jesus in that way, but the presence of Jesus we can experience today is even more than that. It is the personal presence of God with us, loving us totally, perfectly, and without limits of time and space.

Pentecost: The Gift of the Holy Spirit

As Jesus had promised, the way that he would remain with his followers was through the power of the Holy Spirit poured out among them. The Acts of the Apostles describes the coming of the Holy Spirit as a dramatic, marvelous event that took place several days after the Ascension, on the Jewish feast of Pentecost. The Apostles and some of the female disciples, including Jesus' mother, Mary, were gathered in a room in Jerusalem. Here is how the event is told:

> And suddenly from heaven there came a sound like the rush of a violent wind, and it filled the entire house where they were sitting. Divided tongues, as of fire, appeared among them, and a tongue rested on each of them. All of them were filled with the Holy Spirit and began to speak in other languages, as the Spirit gave them ability.

1

Imagine you are trying to explain heaven to a seven-year-old child. Write the child a letter, using words and ideas he or she would understand.

Now there were devout Jews from every nation under heaven living in Jerusalem. And at this sound the crowd gathered and was bewildered, because each one heard them speaking in the native language of each. Amazed and astonished, they asked, "Are not all these who are speaking Galileans? And how is it that we hear, each of us, in our own native language? . . . In our own languages we hear them speaking about God's deeds of power." All were amazed and perplexed, saying to one another, "What does this mean?" But others sneered and said, "They are filled with new wine." (Acts 2:2–13)

The immediate result of the presence of the Spirit was total, uninhibited joy, so much so that bystanders thought the Apostles must be drunk. Peter, the leader of the Apostles, assured the crowd that this was not the case, then delivered a powerful proclamation of the Good News to the gathered crowd.

Notice the images used to describe the power of the Spirit—the rush of a mighty wind, "tongues" of fire resting on each person, the ability to speak in languages they did not even know. These are strong images, and they symbolize the effect that the disciples of Jesus must have felt: It was like a forceful wind came through out the old fears and clouds of doubt, brin new, fresh air of confidence and clear Apostles' hearts, souls, and minds with love, zeal, and courage. The speak boldly to anyone, even foreigners, about Jesus as the Lord and Messiah who had been raised from the dead. They felt completely transformed, made new. Jesus' Spirit indeed had been poured out among them, and they would never, ever be the same.

Christians call this coming of the Holy Spirit **Pentecost**. They celebrate this feast every year on **Pentecost Sunday**, fifty days after Easter. When Jesus walked the earth, he had gathered together the beginnings of the church by announcing the Reign of God and calling others to join in it. But the church did not really take off until Jesus left to go to the Father and sent his Spirit to his followers. Then the church was in their hands. For this reason Pentecost is sometimes called the birthday of the church.

2
Have you ever felt like a new person, as if your life was transformed in a good way? In writing, describe what you experienced, using one or more of the images in the Pentecost story: a mighty wind, fire, or the ability to communicate in ways you did not realize you could.

The Spirit at Work
in the Early Christian Communities

In Jerusalem

That amazing outpouring of Jesus' Spirit kept on flowing in the early community of followers in Jerusalem. The Acts of the Apostles reports that three thousand Jews were baptized in the name of Jesus after Peter preached to them on Pentecost. Here is how Acts describes the joyful new community:

> They devoted themselves to the apostles' teaching and fellowship, to the breaking of bread and the prayers.
>
> Awe came upon everyone, because many wonders and signs were being done by the apostles. All who believed were together and had all things in common; they would sell their possessions and goods and distribute the proceeds to all, as any had need. Day by day, as they spent much time together in the temple, they broke bread at home and ate their food with glad and generous hearts, praising God and having the goodwill of all the people. And day by day the Lord added to their number those who were being saved. (2:42–47)

The early Christians shared what they had with all who were in need. Today, members of a parish bring groceries to church for a food drive to help people who are poor.

The followers of the **Way** (an early name for Christianity), with their generous, grateful spirit, were so attractive to those around them that people flocked to join them. They still considered themselves good Jews—notice that they went to the Temple in Jerusalem every day. As followers of

the Jesus movement, they also "broke bread" in their homes, that is, they shared the Eucharist in memory of Jesus, along with their meals. No one, not even the poorest among them, had to go without, for they put all their money and possessions together and shared them.

Beyond Jerusalem

Before long the Spirit of Jesus flowed beyond the Jerusalem church into new communities of followers—local churches the Apostles started in towns in the region of Palestine. Inevitably the young movement began attracting non-Jews, or **Gentiles**, as converts. The first community that included both Jewish *and* Gentile followers of Jesus was established in the city of **Antioch.** The Acts of the Apostles tells us that "it was in Antioch that the disciples were first called 'Christians'" (11:26), because they were followers of **Jesus the Christ** (*Christ* is the Greek word for "messiah").

With so many Gentiles being baptized, the Apostles, who were Jewish followers of Jesus, had an important decision to make: Would the Gentiles who joined the Jesus movement have to become Jewish first and keep the whole Jewish Law, including the practice of circumcision for males? At a meeting known as the **Council of Jerusalem**, the Apostles decided to open the doors to Gentiles without requiring them to become Jews first. After this, the movement of Jesus' followers spread like wildfire throughout the Roman Empire.

Paul, Apostle to the Gentiles

The man most responsible for spreading the Gospel beyond Jerusalem and to the Gentiles was **Paul**, a Jew and zealous Pharisee who had once persecuted the followers of Jesus. Paul (at the time called Saul) had been dedicated to putting an end to this new movement. He had never met Jesus during Jesus' earthly life, but one day Saul had a life-changing encounter with the Risen Lord. He was never the same again after this encounter. Now Paul was zealous for Christ, starting up new churches of Jesus' followers in cities and towns all over the empire. Paul is known as the **Apostle to the Gentiles.**

3
Imagine you are one of the early followers of the Way of Jesus in the Jerusalem community. Pretend you are trying to describe what it is like to be part of this community to a friend who has not yet joined but is curious about it. Write up a dialog between you and your friend.

After beginning or visiting a church in a city—for instance, **Corinth**, **Ephesus**, or **Philippi**—Paul would write letters to the community from a distance, even from prison, where he was held a number of times for stirring people up about the Christian faith. Passionate, tender, and sometimes scolding, these letters, also called the **Epistles**, nurtured the faith of the new churches. They were the first written documents in what would become the Christian Testament (traditionally called the New Testament).

Paul and Peter eventually made their way to Rome, where Peter led the local church there and Paul was kept under house arrest by the Romans. Both of these great Apostles were martyred—killed for their faith—in about the year 64, during a Roman persecution of the Christians.

The Separation from Judaism

Once the Christians became open to Gentile converts without insisting they follow the Jewish Law, the rift between the Christians and the leaders of Judaism widened. Then, after the Temple was destroyed by the Romans in 70 and the Jews were scattered from their center in Jerusalem, the leaders of Judaism became even more concerned that the Jewish practices be kept strictly. Before long, Jewish Christians were no longer allowed by the Jewish leaders to worship in the town synagogues with their fellow Jews. At that point the Christian movement separated from Judaism and became a religion of its own—**Christianity.** Even so, Christians knew their faith was built on Judaism, and they continued to read and pray the Hebrew Scriptures (traditionally called the Old Testament), as we still do today in Christian worship.

For Review

- What is meant by the Ascension of Jesus? When do Catholics celebrate the feast of the Ascension?
- What happened at Pentecost? When do Christians celebrate the feast of Pentecost?
- Describe the meaning of the three images of the Spirit's power at Pentecost.
- What was Paul's important role in the early church?
- Why and when did the Christian movement separate from Judaism?

4
Write a letter to someone you know who needs encouragement, hope, and friendly advice. After you have written the letter, consider whether you want to mail it or perhaps talk to the person to convey the same message as in the letter.

What Is the Church?

The early church, the followers of Jesus who experienced the outpouring of the Holy Spirit in the first decades after Pentecost, is the root and foundation of the contemporary church we experience today. In fact, today's church is the continuation of that same early Christian community, but with some two thousand years of history behind it. It has grown and developed through the almost twenty centuries of its existence, and has spread to every continent on earth. Today about one-third of the world's population is Christian, and more than half of those Christians, nearly one billion people, are Catholic.

The Gathering of Believers Who Carry on Christ's Mission

Whether we are talking about the church of the year 70 or the church of the year 2000, the essence of the church is the same. The **Christian church** is the gathering of those who profess belief in Jesus Christ and are baptized into that faith. But it is more than that. The church is also the active presence of Jesus in the world, carrying on his mission through the power of the Holy Spirit. And what was Jesus' mission? As we have seen in earlier chapters, Jesus' mission was to proclaim and bring about the Kingdom of God through his life, sacrificial death, and Resurrection. Jesus was sent by God to unite humanity with God and begin God's Reign of justice and peace in the world. He came to bring salvation to the world. Thus the church, carrying out the mission of Jesus, is meant to be God's instrument of salvation in history.

So the church does not exist simply for itself as an institution, to give its members comfort and support, or to educate them or help them lead holy lives. It certainly should and does do those things, but the church is intended to do more than that. It exists *for the world,* to be a beacon of light and hope, a source of healing and unity in a world troubled by division, sin, and injustice.

"Christ Will Come Again"

CHRISTIAN belief is that one day, "in the fullness of time" (at the end of time), Christ will come to earth again in the **Second Coming**. He will pronounce the **Last Judgment** of the living and the dead, in which evil will be overcome once and for all, and good will be victorious. Christ will bring God's Reign to fulfillment, and suffering and sorrow will come to an end. You may recall in the Mass the words the worshipers often proclaim or sing after the consecration of the bread and wine: "Christ has died. Christ is risen. Christ will come again." This expresses the hope and longing that one day God's justice and peace will finally fill the whole world.

During the first decades of the early church, the Christians believed that Jesus' return would be very soon, within their lifetime. But when decades passed and Jesus did not come back, they had to readjust their hopes, recognizing that the end of time was probably not as near as they had once believed. They had to dig in and commit themselves to a church that would probably be around for a long time. Almost two thousand years later we can agree that it was a good idea for the early Christians to change their expectations.

The turn of a century is typically a time when many people wonder if the end of the world is at hand. Whenever a new century approaches, many preachers claim that Jesus is about to return for the Second Coming. Because the millennium, the year 2000, is almost upon us, we will probably hear a steady stream of dire predictions that the world is about to end.

It is best to put such ideas into perspective, recognizing that God's time is not human time, that God does not follow the calendar of human civilization. Christians also need to remember that they must always be ready for the coming of Christ in their life, whether in the person of a stranger looking for food and shelter, in the beauty of a friendship, or in the sudden end of their life.

The church is meant to bring all humanity—and even all creation—together as one, living in union with one another and God, as God intended from the beginning of the world.

Mary: Model of the Church, Mother of the Church

Mary, the mother of Jesus, who carried Jesus into the world by letting God's Spirit work wonders in her, has a special place among Catholics as the **Model of the Church**.

5
Write a letter to Mary asking her about her life and what it was like to be Jesus' mother. Write an imaginary reply from Mary to you.

Mary was "full of grace." She was completely open to the Spirit. Though she did not understand exactly how God was at work in her, nevertheless she agreed to bring the Son of God into the world. So Mary is a model of how the church can be open to God in every age and thus bring the healing, loving presence of Jesus Christ into the world.

Through Mary, humanity and divinity were brought together in Jesus. In the church, humanity and divinity come together as its members try to *be* Christ in the world through the power of the Holy Spirit. Being the mother of Christ, Mary is also the **Mother of the Church.**

Catholic Tradition holds that because of Mary's unique role among all human beings, at the end of her life on earth she was united with God without going through the corruption of death. This is called the doctrine of the **Assumption** (because Mary was taken up, or "assumed" into heaven). In a way unlike any other human being, Mary shares in the glory of Jesus' Resurrection. She gives us hope that one day we, too, will share in that Resurrection.

Being the mother of Christ, Mary is also the Mother of the Church.
Student art: "Holy Family," pencil drawing by Lisa Huebner, Notre Dame Academy, Toledo, Ohio

"Church" at Different Levels

The church is the assembly, or gathering, of believers, but it exists at different levels—from a small group of Christians to the whole worldwide church. The church can mean any of these:

- a group of Christians gathered for liturgy, the **liturgical assembly**
- a specific **parish** or congregation, such as Saint Mary's Church
- a local **diocese**, which is a group of many parishes led by a bishop, such as the Diocese of San Antonio or the Archdiocese of Philadelphia
- the whole **worldwide church**

Images of the Church

We can think of the church, whether at a small-group or worldwide level, by using three images from the Scriptures:

- the church as the **People of God**
- the church as the **Body of Christ**
- the church as the **Temple of the Holy Spirit**

   These images show how the church is the work of the Trinity in us human beings—the work of God the Father, Jesus Christ the Son, and the Holy Spirit. (The meaning of the Trinity is covered in more depth in chapter 8.)

If one of us hurts, we all do.
Student art: "Frustration," linocut print by Lainie Tiscia, Saint Agnes Academy, Memphis, Tennessee

People of God

Saint Peter expressed the image of the church as the People of God in his first epistle to several Christian communities:

> But you are a chosen race, a royal priesthood, a holy nation, God's own people, in order that you may proclaim the mighty acts of him who called you out of darkness into his marvelous light. (1 Peter 2:9)

Like the Israelites, chosen long ago by God to be the ones through whom God would save the world, the church is the People of God. Also like the Israelites, the church is a "pilgrim" people, on the way to the "Promised Land"—the Kingdom of God—but not there yet. Like the Israelites, the church is a chosen people but not a perfect people. It is made up of imperfect persons who sin and lose their way, and who at times even disgrace the religion of Christianity. But the church is beloved by God and ultimately guided by God, who will never abandon it.

Body of Christ

In his first letter to the Christian community at Corinth, Saint Paul wrote about the church as Christ's own body:

> For just as the body is one and has many members, and all the members of the body, though many, are one body, so it is with Christ. For in the one Spirit we were all baptized into one body—Jews or Greeks, slaves or free—and we were all made to drink of one Spirit. (12:12–13)
>
> . . . If one member suffers, all suffer together with it; if one member is honored, all rejoice together with it.
>
> Now you are the body of Christ and individually members of it. (1 Corinthians 12:26–27)

Paul was telling us that we are the hands and feet, the heart, mind, and soul of Christ in the world. We are Christ, now living in history. And though we have many different talents or contributions to make (like hands and feet do), we are all needed and are all united as one. If one of us hurts, we all do. If one of us is glad, we all are. We are meant to care for one another as members of one Body and to care for the world as Christ does, to *be* Christ in the world. The sharing in the Eucharist expresses and brings about this unity with Christ and one another.

Temple of the Holy Spirit

The Spirit of God was poured out, and continues to dwell, not in a *building* called *a* church but among a *people*

called *the* church. Paul made this clear to the Christians of Corinth and of Ephesus:

> Do you not know that you are God's temple and that God's Spirit dwells in you? . . . God's temple is holy, and you are that temple. (1 Corinthians 3:16–17)

> In [Christ Jesus] the whole structure is joined together and grows into a holy temple in the Lord; in whom you also are built together spiritually into a dwelling place for God. (Ephesians 2:21–22)

Remember that before Paul became a Christian, he was devoted to the Jewish Temple in Jerusalem, the focus of so many dreams and hopes for the Israelite people. For him it must have been a great insight to realize that the Temple of the Lord is not a building but a *community of people*. The people are the place where God dwells, where the Holy Spirit is alive and active. Whenever we are inclined to think of the church as simply the building where we worship, we can recall Paul's teaching.

A church is not simply a building for worship but a community of people.

6
Of the three images of the church given here—People of God, Body of Christ, and Temple of the Holy Spirit—choose the one that most appeals to you. In a paragraph, describe what appeals to you about it.

Small Christian Communities: The Past and the Future

ROM the writings of Saint Paul and the Acts of the Apostles we learn that the early Christians gathered to worship and celebrate the Eucharist in people's homes. This idea may seem strange to Catholics accustomed to worshiping in churches and standing in long lines to receive Communion. But over the last few decades, more and more Catholics have begun gathering in small groups, like the Jews and the early Christians, to pray, read the Bible, and learn more deeply how to live as Christians in the modern world.

Such groups today are most commonly referred to as **base communities,** or **small Christian communities.** These communities form for a number of reasons: a group from a parish with an interest in Scripture study begins to meet informally; a group interested in social justice meets to explore faith-based strategies against injustice; a pastor promotes the development of small communities to enrich the life of a large parish. Whatever the motivation, the groups are usually small—up to twenty people. They meet regularly—two or four times a month—often in one another's homes. They read the Scriptures and try to relate them to their individual and community lives. They pray together, grow as a community, and develop a sense of service to one another and to the wider world.

These small Christian communities flourish among people of all races, classes, and ages. Here are a few comments of small Christian community members throughout the United States, taken from an article in *U.S. Catholic* magazine:

Alfredo Diaz: Through my base community, I began discovering I was part of an Hispanic family.

I also discovered that I was part of the Catholic community, which was much richer than I had been led to believe. . . .

Before I got involved in a base community, my faith was simple—naive. Now it's more conscious and critical, a more authentic kind of faith.

Phyllis Jepson: Reading and talking about Scripture as a group makes me much more attentive to what I'm being asked to do as a Christian. When I was growing up, I had the idea that if I went to church on Sunday . . . I was doing all that I was called to do by God. Now I see my responsibility to the hungry, the imprisoned, those who mourn, and all other people in need.

Teresa Barajas: When we get together and share, I feel so happy. When we talk and work together for a good cause, it makes me feel good—that God is there. . . . The closer I get to people, the more I find God in the people.

Don Curtis: It's given me a feeling of inner peace, a different outlook on life. It has allowed my faith to grow, to become adult. I've spoken out more about my faith and have strengthened my beliefs. I'm more aware now of other people's problems. I have no reservations about small faith communities. I think they are the wave of the future for the Catholic Church.

The Splits in Christianity

It is a painful reality that Christians today are divided, not united under one organized church. What should be the one Body of Christ is fragmented. As you are no doubt aware, a variety of Christian **denominations**, which usually call themselves churches, exist today. This is because over the centuries many groups have "branched off" from the "main trunk" of Christianity, which is the **Catholic church.** The Catholic church is the "main trunk" because it traces its history back to the church of the Apostles through an unbroken line of bishops, who are the successors of the Apostles. It is led by the **pope,** who as bishop of Rome is the successor of Saint Peter, first among the Apostles. (In chapter 8 we will consider the role of the pope in Catholicism.)

The splits in Christianity occurred for many reasons—sometimes over disputes about rituals, at times over differences in beliefs. Sometimes the reasons were more senseless, having to do with political or military conflict, personal power struggles, or hurts and misunderstandings. Often a combination of all these reasons was involved.

Christian churches today include Catholics, **Orthodox Christians, Protestant Christians** (which include many denominations), and other small denominations. Although the Christian churches are not now officially united under one leadership, much more unites them than divides them, principally their love for Jesus Christ. In recent decades Catholics, Protestants, and Orthodox Christians have been working with one another to build mutual understanding and respect—a movement called **ecumenism.** As a result, some Christians are discovering just how much their faith traditions have in common. However, differences still prevent them from being united as Jesus hoped all his followers would be. John's Gospel tells of Jesus' prayer for unity to his Father at the Last Supper, a prayer that the movement to bring about Christian unity echoes today:

> "I ask not only on behalf of [the Apostles], but also on behalf of those who will believe in me through their word, that they may all be one. As you, Father, are in me and I am in you, may they also be in us, so that the world may believe that you have sent me." (John 17:20–21)

Beyond the Christian Religion

Beyond the worldwide church of Christian believers are billions of people who are not Christian—Jews, Muslims, Hindus, Buddhists, Confucians, Shintoists, members of native

Distinctive onion-domed buildings of the Russian Orthodox church, one of the denominations of Christianity
Student art: "Moscow and Miss Hoffman," ink drawing by Christine Grier, Mercy High School, Omaha, Nebraska

and tribal religions, and so on. Do they have the truth or not? How does Christianity relate to them? Are they considered saved by God?

The Catholic answer to those questions, as expressed in church documents over the last several decades, is that God is certainly (though incompletely) revealed in non-Christian religions—especially in Judaism and in Islam, the other major monotheistic religion—and aspects of God's truth are also revealed in the other religious traditions as well. In fact, many of the moral concerns and principles of Christianity are shared by all the great religions of the world.

However, Catholics believe that the fullest revelation of God and God's truth has been given to humankind in Jesus Christ. It is through the church of Jesus that all humankind will ultimately be saved, though we do not know now in just what way that will happen. But those who are convinced of the truth of other religions besides Christianity can also be saved because of their sincere search for God. The Catholic belief that non-Christians can be saved is rooted in the conviction that Christ died for all, and that all human beings, regardless of religion or any other differences, are sons and daughters of the God who loves us all without boundaries. As Saint Paul said in a letter to his friend Timothy:

> I urge that supplications, prayers, intercessions, and thanksgivings be made for everyone. . . . This is right and acceptable in the sight of God our Savior, who desires everyone to be saved and to come to the knowledge of the truth. (1 Timothy 2:1–4)

Within the Catholic Church

States of Life

The Catholic church is composed of people in these states of life:

- the laypeople, or laity
- the religious—those consecrated to religious life by vows
- the ordained clergy—that is, priests, deacons, and bishops

Most Catholics are **laypeople**, or **laity**—single or married, divorced or widowed, young or old. In whatever occupations or roles they have in life, they are called to share fully in the mission of the church, bringing the Reign of God to the world.

7
Interview a non-Christian who is convinced of the truth and wisdom of her or his faith. Find out what is important to this person about her or his faith, and write a page-long description of it.

Another group within the Catholic church are **religious**, those who take **vows** that dedicate them in a special way to God—usually, they take the vows of **poverty, chastity,** and **obedience.** Religious sisters, brothers, or religious order priests belong to any of hundreds of religious orders or congregations in the church, such as the Franciscans, the Dominicans, the Sisters of Mercy, or the Marist Brothers. They are involved in a variety of ministries—teaching, hospital work, parish leadership, social work, retreat work, and so on.

The **ordained clergy—priests, deacons,** and **bishops—** give a distinct kind of leadership and service to the church. Priests and bishops preside in the celebrations of the sacraments (which we will consider in chapter 9). In Catholicism the sacraments, especially the Eucharist, are central to the

Facing page: **A Muslim man prays at the Dome of the Rock, an Islamic shrine in Jerusalem.**
Below: **In Catholicism the ordained clergy have the special role of presiding in the celebration of the Mass.**

life of faith, so the role of the clergy is very significant. Clergy, too, have a variety of occupations: pastors, teachers, chaplains, campus ministers, administrators of church offices, and so on. Some clergy are members of religious orders in addition to being ordained. Single or married men may become permanent deacons, dedicated to works of charity, preaching, and assisting in the celebration of the sacraments.

At a certain point in their development to maturity, all Catholics need to consider which state of life God is calling them to, and how they can best use the talents and interests God has given them to contribute to Jesus' mission of salvation for the world.

8
List questions you have about any of these states of life in the Catholic church.

Meet the Saints

The church is its people. The ideal way to understand the church is to meet a few of its greatest, best-known people and to discover through them how the Spirit of God has been working in the church all through history.

Perpetua: Wife, Mother, Convert, and Martyr

Meet **Perpetua**, a young woman in the early church of North Africa, which was part of the Roman Empire. While preparing to join the church, she was arrested by Roman authorities with other **catechumens** (those preparing for baptism through a long process of initiation into the church) and thrown in prison. The Roman empire inflicted periodic **persecutions** on the early Christians. We know about Perpetua through the diary she kept in prison and through the eyewitness testimony of other Christians who kept diaries.

Perpetua was of noble background, and she had a servant girl, **Felicity**. Felicity was pregnant and had also been imprisoned for being a catechumen. Perpetua, too, was a mother; her infant son meant everything to her. When she was finally allowed to keep him with her in prison, that "dungeon" became a "palace," in her words. And although Perpetua and Felicity were mistress and servant, in prison these two young women became like sisters.

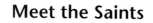

Another group within the Catholic church are **religious**, those who take **vows** that dedicate them in a special way to God—usually, they take the vows of **poverty**, **chastity**, and **obedience**. Religious sisters, brothers, or religious order priests belong to any of hundreds of religious orders or congregations in the church, such as the Franciscans, the Dominicans, the Sisters of Mercy, or the Marist Brothers. They are involved in a variety of ministries—teaching, hospital work, parish leadership, social work, retreat work, and so on.

The **ordained clergy—priests, deacons**, and **bishops**—give a distinct kind of leadership and service to the church. Priests and bishops preside in the celebrations of the sacraments (which we will consider in chapter 9). In Catholicism the sacraments, especially the Eucharist, are central to the

Facing page: **A Muslim man prays at the Dome of the Rock, an Islamic shrine in Jerusalem.**
Below: **In Catholicism the ordained clergy have the special role of presiding in the celebration of the Mass.**

life of faith, so the role of the clergy is very significant. Clergy, too, have a variety of occupations: pastors, teachers, chaplains, campus ministers, administrators of church offices, and so on. Some clergy are members of religious orders in addition to being ordained. Single or married men may become permanent deacons, dedicated to works of charity, preaching, and assisting in the celebration of the sacraments.

At a certain point in their development to maturity, all Catholics need to consider which state of life God is calling them to, and how they can best use the talents and interests God has given them to contribute to Jesus' mission of salvation for the world.

8
List questions you have about any of these states of life in the Catholic church.

What About Young People?

If you are Catholic or belong to another Christian denomination, perhaps you are wondering, "What about me? What's in the church for people my age?" You do not have to be an adult to participate in the church. In fact, the church very much needs you at this stage in your life, because you have particular gifts and a youthful, searching spirit to offer. You can be a channel of God's love and joy in the world in a way that adults cannot—maybe through your musical talent, your sincere questioning of things that do not make sense to you, your enthusiasm in a parish youth group, your hospitality to newcomers at your school, or the special presence you bring to lonely shut-ins or people in nursing homes. It is a good idea to consider what you might have to give and then go ahead and give it. That is a significant way to be part of the church.

Something else besides what you can give, though, is also important to consider: You, and anyone who wants to discover the meaning of the church, need to find a place where you experience a welcoming church community. After all, we get to know the church not in the abstract but in the flesh, through real people who invite us into a loving community. That is how we come to experience God's love for us, and we begin to feel a part of something that is wonderfully beyond us and that calls us to live in a new way. That welcoming community may be in your parish youth group or Confirmation program. It may be right here in a high school religion class or a campus ministry group. Sometimes when you volunteer to do service you discover that sense of community with the other volunteers.

Young people can be a channel of God's love and joy in the world.
Student art: "Friends," color photo by Brant Roshau, Trinity High School, Dickinson, North Dakota

You may be wondering if you can find such a welcoming experience of church; perhaps your parish does not have a program or group for young people, and that makes it hard. If you are in that situation, talk with any young people or adults who might be interested in doing something with you to make a welcoming experience of church happen. No doubt others feel as you do. Your pastor, a teacher, or a youth minister would probably love to hear from you. Even just talking with others about your hopes and disappointments can be the start of building community, whether it is with other young people or with a trusted adult.

9
Have you experienced a welcoming church community in your parish, school, or service group? If so, describe it in writing. If not, reflect in writing on how you might find such a community.

For Review

- Give a definition of the church, including its mission.
- In what sense is Mary the Model of the Church?
- What is meant by the Assumption of Mary?
- At what different levels does the church exist?
- Describe the meaning of the images of the church as People of God, Body of Christ, and Temple of the Holy Spirit.
- How did Christianity become divided?
- What are the three main groups of Christians?
- What is Catholic teaching about how humankind will be saved? According to Catholic belief, can non-Christians be saved?
- What are the three states of life in the Catholic church?
- How can young people participate in the church?

The Spirit in the Church Through History

The Spirit that was poured out on the followers of Jesus at Pentecost is the same Spirit that is with the church today, almost two thousand years later.

Throughout the church's history, the Spirit has been at work in the life of the church, in good times and in bad. The Spirit has been guiding its leaders, raising up new voices when the church most needed to hear them, and inspiring men and women to acts of great courage and sacrifice. The heroic lives of Christians through the ages are perhaps the best evidence we have that God has been with the church all along and is with the church today.

Meet the Saints

The church is its people. The ideal way to understand the church is to meet a few of its greatest, best-known people and to discover through them how the Spirit of God has been working in the church all through history.

Perpetua: Wife, Mother, Convert, and Martyr

Meet **Perpetua**, a young woman in the early church of North Africa, which was part of the Roman Empire. While preparing to join the church, she was arrested by Roman authorities with other **catechumens** (those preparing for baptism through a long process of initiation into the church) and thrown in prison. The Roman empire inflicted periodic **persecutions** on the early Christians. We know about Perpetua through the diary she kept in prison and through the eyewitness testimony of other Christians who kept diaries.

Perpetua was of noble background, and she had a servant girl, **Felicity**. Felicity was pregnant and had also been imprisoned for being a catechumen. Perpetua, too, was a mother; her infant son meant everything to her. When she was finally allowed to keep him with her in prison, that "dungeon" became a "palace," in her words. And although Perpetua and Felicity were mistress and servant, in prison these two young women became like sisters.

Before long, though, Perpetua had to give her son back to her parents to raise—she and Felicity were about to be executed for refusing to sacrifice to the Roman gods. Felicity gave birth just two days before the execution, and a Christian woman came forward and agreed to raise the baby as her own.

The Christian prisoners went to their torture and execution, which was held in an amphitheater as public entertainment. Perpetua, although wounded by wild animals, ran to Felicity to help her when she was attacked by the beasts. Perpetua's love and serenity in facing death inspired the early church to be courageous in the face of persecution. The two women were martyred in the year 203. The names of Perpetua and Felicity have been included in the prayers of the Eucharist since the earliest centuries of the church.

10
Have an imaginary talk with Perpetua about why she was willing to go to death for her Christian beliefs. Write up your dialog with her.

Benedict and Scholastica: A New Way of Living

Meet **Benedict** and **Scholastica**, related to each other as brother and sister, who together founded a monastic way of life in sixth-century Italy. They lived in a decadent society that was crumbling around them. In the monastic lifestyle men and women move away from the concerns of the world and seek holiness alone, as hermits, or in small communities. To help people lead holy lives in community, Benedict and Scholastica began monasteries where manual work was combined with prayer and study, and where the great heritage of Christianity could be kept alive and passed on by copying the sacred books by hand.

The pattern, or rule, of life that Benedict and Scholastica developed became the basis for **Western monasticism.** The monastic way of life was one of the most significant developments in the history of the church and of Western civilization because it created harmony and order in the midst of chaos, encouraged growth in holiness, and ensured that knowledge would be passed on. **Benedictine** sisters, brothers, and priests today remind us of the great gift to the church and the world given by Benedict and Scholastica.

Francis and Clare: A Return to the Gospel

Meet **Francis** and **Clare of Assisi**, Italy, who lived about 1200, a time when the church had become very wealthy. Wars among Christians were common, and Christians were on a rampage of military Crusades against Muslims in the Holy Land.

Into this time of challenge for the church came Francis, a young man who had fought in wars but had experienced a conversion of heart. He seemed to see through all the corruption, excessive wealth, and violence around him to the

11

Look into either *(a)* a group of Benedictines today or *(b)* a group of Franciscans or Poor Clares today. Try to find some members to talk to about the work they do and the lifestyle they lead. Write a report on what you discover.

heart of the Gospel—the poverty, humility, and nonviolence of Jesus. This led to some drastic changes in his life, much to his father's dismay. Francis began living a life of total simplicity, trusting in God's providence to care for his needs. He wandered about the countryside, preaching the love of God and serving the poor and the sick. Soon he was gathering other men around him to live this kind of life. His followers became a religious order, later called the **Franciscans.**

A rich young woman of Assisi, Clare, was inspired by Francis to start a similar movement of women. The **Poor Clares,** as they later became known, followed a life of simplicity and total trust in God, but they did not leave their convent walls because of the customs of the time.

Francis and Clare, in their quiet and joyful way, inspired many in the church to take a good, hard look at their values. They called the church to be true to its own origins in Jesus. Francis is one of the most popular saints of all time because people see in him a figure who seems most like the Jesus of the Gospels—poor, trusting, nonviolent, serving, and completely in love with God.

Catherine of Siena: Strong Advice for the Pope

Meet **Catherine of Siena**, Italy, a young woman of remarkable intellect, generosity, and courage who is perhaps best known for telling the pope what he should do.

In the fourteenth century the church was beset with a scandal involving a series of popes who moved the center of the church from Rome to Avignon, France. Now, on the face of it, that does not sound like such a terrible thing to do. But the **Avignon Papacy,** as that period of almost seventy years is called, was a corrupt time in the church for several reasons—excessive wealth in the Avignon palace and court, political control of the pope by the French kings, and a loss of the tradition of Peter, who died in Rome as its bishop. At the age of thirty, Catherine went to Avignon to see the pope and exhort him strongly to move the center of the church back to Rome. In a letter she pleaded with him to return the church to its early condition of being poor, humble, and meek. The following year the pope brought the papacy back to Rome.

Young Catherine had been a member of a lay branch of the Dominican religious order since her teenage years. As a youth she had a contemplative heart and stayed in her room praying much of the time. When she emerged at the age of twenty-one, it was to serve people in an incredibly active life. She cared for sick and dying people in the streets of Siena during the terrible bubonic plague, or Black Death, which wiped out one-third of the population of Europe in a few years. Recognized as an uncommonly holy person with great conviction and a forceful personality, Catherine became known for her ability to mediate conflicts among powerful Italian cities called city-states. Nobles and generals looked to her for advice. Her wisdom, her strong persuasion skills, and her deep holiness accompanied her as well on that momentous visit to the pope in Avignon. She died of illness at age thirty-three.

Facing page: **Saint Clare and Saint Francis of Assisi, by Robert Lentz**
Below: **Saint Catherine of Siena, by Ade Bethune**

Ignatius of Loyola: "Soldier for Christ"

Meet **Ignatius of Loyola**, Spain, a spiritual leader in the reform of the church in the sixteenth century and the founder of the **Society of Jesus**, or the **Jesuits**.

In Ignatius's lifetime the Catholic church was being torn apart. The **Protestant Reformation**, which had started as a reform of the Catholic church, resulted in the breakaway of large groups to form new denominations of Christians. The Catholic church badly needed to have new life breathed into it. So it undertook its own reform to correct the abuses that had started the Protestants' conflicts with the church.

In the midst of that crisis in the Catholic church, Ignatius of Loyola and the Jesuits came on the scene, ushering in a deep spiritual renewal when it was so badly needed. Ignatius had been a soldier, and he was used to war. But after his leg was severely injured in battle, he had a conversion experience. He vowed to become a "soldier for Christ," using only the weapons of prayer, learning, teaching, and preaching to convert people to the Gospel.

Soon Ignatius was gathering other university students around him. He led them in a process he developed called the **Spiritual Exercises.** To this day, Catholics and others use these well-known exercises of prayer and meditation to deepen their conversion to Christ.

This little band became the Society of Jesus, and they grew quickly. Ignatius gave them intense training, and the seminaries and universities founded by the Jesuits to train others raised the level of education among the clergy as a whole. The Jesuits were scholars and writers, too, and their work was significant in the reform of the Catholic church. The Jesuits also became missionaries to the continents where Christianity had not gone before, carrying the Good News to the far corners of the earth.

Today the Jesuits are known for the excellence of their Catholic universities and high schools.

Elizabeth Ann Seton: First American-Born Saint

Meet **Elizabeth Ann Seton**, a woman who lived an amazingly varied life. Born in New York in 1774, just before the Revolutionary War, she became a wife and the mother of five children. But when she was widowed at the age of thirty, she began to be attracted to the Catholic church, especially to its devotion to the Eucharist. Her relatives, members of the Anglican church, were appalled that she would want to be part of a church of poor immigrants.

Courageously Elizabeth left her family supports behind and became a convert to Catholicism. She took her children to Baltimore and began a small school there. Soon, with the

Facing page: Angelo Roncalli walks in the streets of Rome just before his election as Pope John XXIII.
Below: A sculpture of Saint Elizabeth Ann Seton with students, by Margaret Beaudette, SC

encouragement of a bishop, she decided to begin a religious community of sisters in Emmitsburg, Maryland, to run a school and an orphanage. The **Sisters of Charity**, founded in 1809, was the first religious order to spring up in the United States. Elizabeth's school, which served poor children as well as those who could afford to pay, set the pattern for the **parochial Catholic school system** that would later grow and flourish. Catholic parish schools served the primarily poor immigrant church of the United States, and today we are the inheritors of that school system.

Mother Seton, as her sisters called her, was declared a saint by the church in 1975, the first person born in what became the United States to be named a saint.

Pope John XXIII: Bringing in Fresh Air

Meet **Pope John XXIII**, born to an Italian peasant family as Angelo Roncalli. In 1959 he was seventy-six years old and happily ready to retire from his duties as an archbishop, when he was amazed to be elected pope—a position he certainly had not been looking for. No one expected much of the papacy of such an old man. He was warm, charming, and funny, and people loved him. But they expected he would just serve the church quietly for a few years until he died and the next pope replaced him.

But Pope John was listening to God, not the press or even those who worked in the Vatican. Everyone was shocked when he announced that he was calling an ecumenical council (a worldwide council) of bishops to look at developments in the Catholic church and the world in a new light. As he explained it, he wanted to open the windows of the church and let in some fresh air.

Most Catholics did not see the need for such a council; they were fairly content with the church as it was. But Pope John knew better. He recognized that the church had become locked into the patterns it had established at an earlier council, the **Council of Trent**, in the sixteenth century. That was when the church, in an effort to respond to the Protestant Reformation, had tried to standardize church practices. What had been good for the sixteenth century was no longer good for the twentieth century. The church needed to look at itself and the world anew.

The results of the **Second Vatican Council**, which lasted from 1962 to 1965, have had an enormous impact on the worldwide Catholic church. Every aspect of church life has been examined and renewed, with special emphasis on rediscovering the spirit and practices of the early church. Pope John, who died in 1963, did not live to see the whole Council through, but his spirit of joy and openness was with the

12
List the qualities you admire in either *(a)* Catherine of Siena, *(b)* Ignatius of Loyola, or *(c)* Elizabeth Ann Seton. Write about how you would like to develop those qualities in your own life.

13
Talk with someone who grew up in the Catholic church before 1965. Ask that person how the church changed after the Second Vatican Council and how he or she reacted to those changes. Write a page-long essay about what you discover.

world's bishops as they prayed and discerned new directions for the church. Pope John XXIII is beloved by many Catholics as the pope of Vatican Council II.

A Youth Group in Guatemala: Church of the Future

Meet a group of **Guatemalan young people,** teenagers from that Central American country. Shirley Kelter was a religion teacher at a Catholic high school in Wisconsin when she visited Guatemala in 1991. She wants to introduce these young people to you:

I spent part of a summer in Guatemala, working in a community of missionaries. It was a chance to see the church of Latin America in action, and especially to find out about the lives of young people there.

An opportunity arose to participate in a youth group gathering of teenagers who came into town a long distance, many on foot, from their native villages in the mountains. The leader led an icebreaker with them, much like the kind of activities we do in our youth groups in the United States to get people warmed up to one another. What impressed me was that these kids were so similar to the kids I know here in the United States. Some were shy and needed a lot of coaxing to talk. Some were outgoing and funny. Some were sensitive, listening so carefully to others. Some were fidgety. It was just like home!

Following some small-group activities and discussions, it came time for them to express their concerns to the group and to God in prayer.

Guatemalan teenagers at a youth group gathering

One young person talked about how the military soldiers were everywhere in the villages, striking fear in everyone. He asked God for an end to the terror of war they were living in. A girl talked about how sad it was to see orphans on the streets; she prayed that they might have homes and families.

Another girl brought up her concern that the old religious customs were being left behind by the people, that the young were not interested in the religious processions as much anymore or in honoring the saints. She feared that religion would die out if they did not keep up their customs. A boy talked about the terrible poverty that people in Guatemala suffer, and how he believed that only a revolution would change it.

All the young people spoke so intently as they brought these concerns to God and one another. Their faith was deep and hope-filled in response to the oppression they experienced.

Next, because they loved to sing, I taught them some Spanish songs that we sing in the United States with our youth groups: "Envía Tu Espíritu" and "Digo Sí, Señor" (translated in English as "Send Out Your Spirit" and "I Say Yes, My Lord"). They thought I would only teach them English songs, and they were delighted that I knew some Spanish ones that they didn't know!

I told them about the teenagers I teach in Wisconsin, and some of the kids said, "Give our love to your students," "Write us letters," and "Send pictures of snow."

That day they were getting ready for a national convention of Guatemalan youth, entitled (in English) Youth with Christ Building a New Latin America. To prepare for it, they composed a song to bring to the convention.

I will never forget the day I spent with them; it was a powerful experience for me to get to know these young people who represent the future of the church.

The Catholic church today is growing most rapidly in poor regions, mainly in the southern parts of the world—places like Central America, South America, and especially Africa. As members of a global church, the Body of Christ, we in North America need to reach out to our brothers and sisters who represent by their growing numbers the future of the church on earth.

The Catholic church is growing most rapidly in Central America, South America, and Africa.
Student art: "Steeple," by Lisa Munzenrider, Benilde–Saint Margaret High School, Saint Louis Park, Minnesota

14
If you could ask three questions of the Guatemalan young people in the youth group, what would they be?

The Communion of Saints

You may be wondering why a group of teenagers from Guatemala was included with the lineup of great church figures that preceded them. The great figures described in that lineup are in fact canonized saints—officially declared to be saints by the Catholic church—except for Pope John XXIII, who many people believe will be canonized someday.

So why is a group of contemporary teenagers included under a topic called "Meet the Saints"? In Catholic tradition "the saints" can mean officially recognized, canonized saints. But the term also has a much broader meaning, as broad as the whole church itself. "The saints" are all of us who are trying to live the Gospel of Jesus, and all the faithful persons who have gone before us and died, and are now united with God in eternal life. A special bond holds all the saints together, creating the **Communion of Saints.** That bond is God's life of love itself. The church is the Body of Christ—across time, across space, across the barrier that separates the living from the dead.

You do not have to be well known to be a saint. Your faithful grandmother or grandfather who loved you and died, leaving an empty place in your heart, is a saint. A peasant who lived an obscure life in tenth-century Europe trying to take care of his family and be faithful to the Gospel is a saint. And you may be a saint as well.

Catholics have a special love for the saints who have gone before us in the worldwide Christian church. They believe that these people who have died are still involved with us, still care about us, rejoice with us when we are glad, and pull for us when we are in trouble. Just because they have died does not mean they are not part of the church anymore. So Catholic devotion to the saints is a way of saying, "We are not alone in this journey of life. Others have made the journey, and they can help us along if we let them."

15
Do you know someone who has died whom you would consider a saint (that is, someone faithful to the Gospel of Jesus during her or his life and now united with God forever)? If so, write a letter to the person expressing what you think and feel about her or him.

For Review

- Give one significant fact about each of the following persons or pairs of persons in church history: Perpetua and Felicity, Benedict and Scholastica, Francis and Clare, Catherine of Siena, Ignatius of Loyola, Elizabeth Ann Seton, Pope John XXIII.
- Where is Catholicism growing most rapidly today?
- What is the Communion of Saints?

Together, We Will Make It

Monarch butterflies have an amazing life of journeying. The story of their journey is a kind of parable of what the church is like, the communion of Jesus' followers across time and space.

Every year monarch butterflies take part
in a journey of five thousand miles,
from their ancestral home
    in the mountains of central Mexico
to places in Canada and the United States,
and then back home again to Mexico.

No one monarch can complete
the whole round-trip journey.
It takes several generations of butterflies
to migrate north from Mexico in spring
and then back south to their special home in fall.

How do the monarchs transmit
    the instructions and route
to their children and grandchildren
that will have to carry on and finish the journey?
No one has discovered the process of cooperation
and communication that makes this happen.

But without fail, each year
    hundreds of millions of monarchs
find the distant home in Mexico
    that they had never known.

And we can find our way home too.

Joined across time and space in the Communion of Saints that is the church, we who long for "home" will find our way to the home we were created for—the Reign of God.

7

The Scriptures:
Hearing the Inspired Word of God

The Power of God's Word

Picture this scene: Large crowds are following Jesus as he preaches in the towns and villages of Galilee. People are fascinated by this man who proclaims a God whose love is so wide and deep that it embraces everyone, including the lost and forsaken, the rejects of society—*everyone.*

A few of those rejects—some tax collectors and sinners—come near Jesus to better hear this good news. Several Pharisees and scribes, who disapprove of such "riffraff," grumble about this fellow Jesus, who insists on welcoming, and even eating with, losers and outcasts. What business does he have letting "those people" think they are so important?

Hearing their grumbling, Jesus tells this story:

> "There was a man who had two sons. The younger of them said to his father, 'Father, give me the share of the property that will belong to me.' So he divided his property between them. A few days later the younger son gathered all he had and traveled to a distant country, and there he squandered his property in dissolute living. When he had spent everything, a severe famine took place throughout that country, and he began to be in need. So he went and hired himself out to one of the citizens of that country, who sent him to his fields to feed the pigs. He would gladly have filled himself with the pods that the pigs were eating; and no one gave him anything. But when he came to himself he said, 'How many of my father's hired hands have bread enough and

to spare, but here I am dying of hunger! I will get up and go to my father, and I will say to him, "Father, I have sinned against heaven and before you; I am no longer worthy to be called your son; treat me like one of your hired hands."' So he set off and went to his father. But while he was still far off, his father saw him and was filled with compassion; he ran and put his arms around him and kissed him. Then the son said to him, 'Father, I have sinned against heaven and before you; I am no longer worthy to be called your son.' But the father said to his slaves, 'Quickly, bring out a robe—the best one—and put it on him; put a ring on his finger and sandals on his feet. And get the fatted calf and kill it, and let us eat and celebrate; for this son of mine was dead and is alive again; he was lost and is found!' And they began to celebrate.

Homecoming, by Marion C. Honors, CSJ
Facing page: A first-century statue of Ulysses, the central figure in Homer's Greek epic *The Odyssey.* Such stories can be powerful, but the source of the Bible's power is different: the Bible contains God's own Word.

"Now his elder son was in the field; and when he came and approached the house, he heard music and dancing. He called one of the slaves and asked what was going on. He replied, 'Your brother has come, and your father has killed the fatted calf, because he has got him back safe and sound.' Then [the elder son] became angry and refused to go in. His father came out and began to plead with him. But he answered his father, 'Listen! For all these years I have been working like a slave for you, and I have never disobeyed your command; yet you have never given me even a young goat so that I might celebrate with my friends. But when this son of yours came back, who has devoured your property with prostitutes, you killed the fatted calf for him!' Then the father said to him, 'Son, you are always with me, and all that is mine is yours. But we had to celebrate and rejoice, because this brother of yours was dead and has come to life; he was lost and has been found.'" (Luke 15:11–32)

- Who do you think the father in the story is meant to represent?
- Which character do you think the outcasts in Jesus' audience identified with? How do you think the story affected them?
- Which character do you think the Pharisees and scribes in Jesus' audience identified with? How do you think the story affected them?
- Which character did you identify with in the story? How did the story affect you?

Jesus knew the power of stories, like this one that we know as the **parable of the prodigal son.** That is why he used stories so often in his preaching and teaching. Stories touch us; they draw us in and stir up something in us—especially if we find someone in the story that we can identify with. Stories have the power to change us, or at least unsettle us, because they affect our heart as well as our head.

Our Story, the Word of God

The **Bible,** the Scriptures of the Christian faith, is full of stories meant to touch people and make a difference in their life. And even more, the Bible as a whole is *our* Story, the Story of God's people—who we are, how our God has loved us and saved us, and where we are going. It is not just *a* story but *the* Story (capital *S*) that Christians live by and know themselves by.

So the Bible is the powerful Story of a people. But many stories are powerful—the *Star Wars* movies tell a powerful story, as does the classical Greek epic *The Odyssey,* by Homer. What is the difference between the powerful Story told in

1
Write up a one-page account of how the story that Jesus told affected you, including which character you identified with.

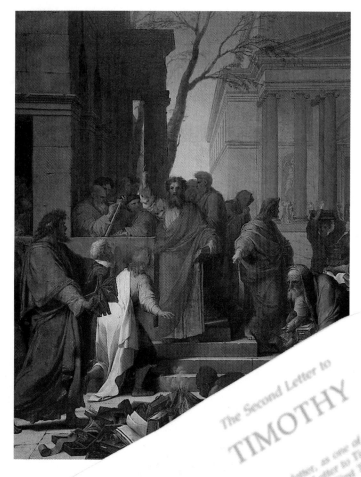

Saint Paul preaching at Ephesus, by a seventeenth-century artist

2
When you hear someone say that the Bible is the Word of God, what do you think they mean? Answer in a paragraph.

the Bible and the many other powerful stories that have been told throughout history?

Christians believe that the power of the Bible has a deeper origin than the power of a story like *The Odyssey*. The Scriptures contain God's own Word, the gift of God's truth revealed to us; this is the source of their power. The Bible was written over many centuries by human beings who used their own means of expression, but the Bible's truth is inspired by God. (We will take up the meaning of "inspired by God" later in this chapter.) As **God's Word**, the Scriptures have a power beyond any other story we can imagine.

No Chaining the Word of God

While in prison for spreading the Gospel, Saint Paul once wrote to his friend and fellow Christian Timothy about the power of God's Word:

> Remember Jesus Christ, raised from the dead, a descendant of David—that is my gospel, for which I suffer hardship, even to the point of being chained like a criminal. But the word of God is not chained. (2 Timothy 2:8–9)

The Scriptures are not dead words on a page. They are alive and active, full of God's power. They make a difference in people's lives. Paul says, "They may put *me* in chains, but *nobody* can chain up the Word of God!"

This chapter offers several examples of how the Scriptures can make a difference in a person's life. Several passages from the Bible are highlighted in color sections, and with each one is a prayer written like an imaginary letter to God. The "Dear God" prayer shows how that scriptural passage might affect a young person today.

For Review

- Why do stories have the power to affect people's lives?
- What is the Christian belief about the power of the Scriptures? Where does this power come from?

What Is in the Scriptures?

This course so far has quoted various parts of the Bible to illustrate aspects of the Catholic Christian faith. Now it is time to step back and look at the Scriptures as a whole.

Sacred Writings

The word *scriptures* means "writings." Nearly every religion has its own set of writings that members of that religion regard as sacred and authoritative because of the connection of these writings with the divine. For instance, Muslims revere the Qur'an (also spelled Koran) as their sacred scriptures, which they believe were revealed by God to the founder of Islam, Muhammad. Hindus look to the Bhagavad Gita as a sacred book, and Confucians hold the Analects, or the teachings of Confucius, in the highest regard.

The Bible: Jewish and Christian

Jews look to the Hebrew Scriptures with the greatest reverence. They call these Scriptures the Bible (from a word meaning "book"). Christians, too, call their sacred Scriptures the Bible. But the Jewish Bible corresponds closely to what Christians know as the Old Testament in their own Bible. In addition to the Old Testament, the Christian Bible includes the New Testament, that is, the sacred, authoritative writings from the early Christian communities led by the Apostles.

Testament is another word for *covenant.* In the Hebrew Scriptures, *Covenant* refers to the bond between God and the Israelites. In the Christian Testament, this bond is renewed and extended to all humankind. This Covenant is established by Christ's shedding his blood for us.

Unfortunately the words *old* and *new* may imply that the Scriptures of the Jewish people are old-fashioned or no longer relevant, and that the Scriptures of the Christian era are a replacement for the old. This is a serious misunderstanding of these terms. The Catholic church emphatically opposes the idea that the Hebrew Scriptures are "out of date." From the days of the early Christian communities to the present, Christians have had a great reverence for the Hebrew Scriptures, reading them as the Word of God at eucharistic worship, and using them as a source for understanding God and humankind. In prayer, too, Christians often turn to the great writings of the Hebrew Scriptures to address God.

Muhammad being protected by four archangels who have brought him a message from God. Muhammad was the prophet to whom Muslims believe God revealed their sacred scriptures, the Qur'an.

The Hebrew Scriptures

Catholic Christians have adopted the following forty-six books from the Hebrew Scriptures:

The Pentateuch	The Historical Books	The Wisdom Books	The Prophetic Books
Genesis	Joshua	Job	Isaiah
Exodus	Judges	Psalms	Jeremiah
Leviticus	Ruth	Proverbs	Lamentations
Numbers	1 Samuel	Ecclesiastes	Baruch
Deuteronomy	2 Samuel	Song of Songs	Ezekiel
	1 Kings	Wisdom	Daniel
	2 Kings	Ecclesiasticus	Hosea
	1 Chronicles		Joel
	2 Chronicles		Amos
	Ezra		Obadiah
	Nehemiah		Jonah
	Tobit		Micah
	Judith		Nahum
	Esther		Habakkuk
	1 Maccabees		Zephaniah
	2 Maccabees		Haggai
			Zechariah
			Malachi

The Books of the Bible

The Christian Testament

The twenty-seven books of the Christian Testament are listed here in the order they appear in the Bible:

The Gospels	The Acts of the Apostles	The Epistles	The Book of Revelation
Matthew *Easy*		Romans *Easy*	
Mark *Easy*		1 Corinthians	
Luke *Easy*		2 Corinthians	
John *Easy*		Galatians	
		Ephesians	
		Philippians	
		Colossians	
		1 Thessalonians	
		2 Thessalonians	
		1 Timothy	
		2 Timothy	
		Titus	
		Philemon	
		Hebrews	
		James *Easy*	
		1 Peter	
		2 Peter	
		1 John	
		2 John	
		3 John	
		Jude	

Out of respect for Jewish people, whose faith is so closely related to that of Christianity, in this course we are using the terms *Hebrew Scriptures* and *Christian Testament* instead of *Old Testament* and *New Testament.*

Getting Free

Dear God,

I am so glad this week is over. It's been the most awful week of my life, but in the end, kind of the most wonderful week, too.

How did all those lies get started? It seemed like a little thing at first, telling Liza I couldn't go to the movies with her Sunday night because I had to study for a test. Well, I did have to study, but actually I was going to her friend Maura's, and Maura didn't want Liza there because she's tired of her. Maura seems so neat, and I really wanted her friendship. So I told this white lie to Liza about having to study.

But it all got so crazy and complicated. Liza heard I was at Maura's, and then I had to tell Liza a lie about Maura to cover up the first lie. Then Maura found out and got furious with me and wouldn't speak to me, and she started telling people what I did. I couldn't stand to have people think bad about me, so I started making up stuff about Maura.

By the middle of the week I thought I was going to die; I felt so nervous and trapped by all these lies. The only way to deal with them seemed to be to make up more lies. I was drowning in lies!

But somewhere in the back of my head came this little voice, "Why don't you just get free of all these lies?" It seemed like maybe it was you, God, reaching out a hand to pull me out of the ocean of lies I was drowning in.

I don't know how I ever got the nerve to sit down with Liza and then with Maura and tell them the whole truth and ask for their forgiveness. You must have been there with me through the whole thing. They were really hurt and mad. But I think maybe we have the chance to be true friends, not phony friends, after this. And I feel SO FREE.

Today in religion class I picked up my Bible, and it flopped open to the part about how you saved the Israelites by taking them through the sea on dry land and drowning Pharaoh's army instead of the Israelites. And then this woman Miriam gets up with her tambourine and gets all her women friends to dance and sing with her for joy! And I thought, "Wow, cool, that's sort of like me." And I guess all those lies are like Pharaoh's army that got drowned, instead of me.

Thanks for being with me through it all.

Love,
Tracy

When the horses of Pharaoh with his chariots and his chariot drivers went into the sea, the LORD brought back the waters of the sea upon them; but the Israelites walked through the sea on dry ground.

Then the prophet Miriam, Aaron's sister, took a tambourine in her hand; and all the women went out after her with tambourines and with dancing. And Miriam sang to them:

"Sing to the LORD, for he has triumphed gloriously;
horse and rider he has thrown into the sea."

Then Moses ordered Israel to set out from the Red Sea, and they went into the wilderness of Shur. (Exodus 15:19–22)

Like a Library

You may have the impression that the Bible is basically one book, composed from beginning to end as a single continuous account. If that is your image, it would not be surprising, because from childhood on we see the Bible as a big, thick book on the shelf.

In fact, the Bible is not simply *a* book, nor is it just two books—the Hebrew Scriptures and the Christian Testament. It is a collection of dozens of books, long and short, filled with many different kinds of writing. Stories abound, of course, but there are also poems, conversations, rituals, speeches, legends, letters, biographies, historical records and accounts, laws, family trees, songs and hymns, prayers, and bits and pieces of wisdom, like proverbs. So we can think of the Bible as being more like a library than a single book. For Christians, what is special about this library of literature is that all of it was written under God's guidance, as the inspired account of God's people and God's relationship with them. Thus the Bible has a power and authority that goes way beyond that of ordinary literature.

Each of the two divisions of the Christian Bible—the Hebrew Scriptures and the Christian Testament—has major sections within it. Let's briefly look at those sections within the Hebrew Scriptures and the Christian Testament. The full list of books in the Bible can be found on page 170–171.

3
Find an example of each of the following kinds of writing in the Bible. For each passage, write down the book it is in, the chapter number, and the verse numbers.
- a song, poem, or prayer
- a greeting in a letter
- a historical account of an event
- a legend
- a law
- a piece of wisdom, like a proverb

The Hebrew Scriptures

Catholics group the forty-six books of the Hebrew Scriptures into four major sections, in this order:
- the Pentateuch
- the historical books
- the wisdom books
- the prophetic books

While reading this material on the Hebrew Scriptures, it may be helpful to refer to the timeline of biblical Jewish history on page 63.

The Pentateuch

Christians refer to the first five books of the Bible as the **Pentateuch** (meaning "five books"). Jews call these books the Torah, which means "instruction" and "law." These books are the heart of the story of Israel and the most significant

The Book of Genesis includes the stories of Creation, with their message that everything good comes from God as a gift.
Student art: Untitled, oil painting by Carina Mo, Bishop Kearney High School, Brooklyn, New York

writings for Jews. Among these books are the accounts of the origins of the Jews as a people. In fact, Genesis, the first book, means "origin." Genesis includes the stories of Creation, of Adam and Eve, and of Noah and the flood. In addition, Genesis covers stories about the call of Abraham (about 1850 B.C.E.) and the other patriarchs and matriarchs.

The Pentateuch also contains the Book of Exodus, which includes the amazing stories of Israel's liberation from slavery and exodus from Egypt; of Moses and the Sinai Covenant between God and the Israelites (around 1250 B.C.E.); and of the giving of the Law, the people's part of keeping the Covenant. The Pentateuch ends with the Israelites just about to enter the Promised Land, Canaan.

The Historical Books

The **historical books** begin with the Israelites entering Canaan around 1200 B.C.E. and proceeding to take over the land by force. Although the books are called historical, this does not mean they are all equally factual. In Joshua and Judges, for instance, a good deal of legend is mixed in with history.

This historical section of the Bible tells of the monarchy and of Israel's kings—like Saul, David, and Solomon, around the year 1000 B.C.E. It recounts the breakup of the kingdom of the Israelites into the two kingdoms of Israel and Judah, which was followed by centuries of corrupt kings and occasional reformer kings. The period of exile for Judah (587–537 B.C.E.) and the developments in Judaism after the Exile are also covered in the historical books.

The Wisdom Books

Some of the most beautiful literature the world has ever known can be found in the **wisdom books.** We have already read passages from several psalms in this course. The **Book of Psalms** contains 150 songs, expressing a wide range of heartfelt sentiments—gratitude and praise, anger with God, rage at enemies, grief, repentance, desperation, fear, trust, joy, and so on.

Other wisdom books focus on themes such as the meaning of life and suffering, how to be good and upright in everyday life, and the joys of married love.

4
Choose a psalm from the Bible that expresses a feeling similar to what you have felt at one time or feel now. Rewrite the psalm in your own words, reflecting on your own experience.

Walking in the Valley of Death

God or whoever's out there,

Here I am at the Juvenile Study Center. "Study Center"—yeah, sure. It's really just a jail for kids.

How did I get here this time? It was a dumb thing—me and my friends got drunk last night and picked off this car and took it for a ride. I don't remember much else, except the crash and all the broken glass. Then the emergency room. My head is still pounding, but I guess I'm okay.

God, I hate this place. All this screaming, and the guards are rough. Now they're talking about maybe sending me away to the juvenile corrections place to do some serious time, because this was my third offense. That's got me really scared.

But this weird thing happened when they brought me in. I had to walk down this long, dark hallway from the police desk to the lockup rooms. Every time I've gotten put in here I feel like I'm going to my death when I walk down that hallway. I'm in handcuffs. I feel lower than dirt. And I think my life is over.

Last night, though, when they took me down that dark hallway, I had this line going through my head from something they prayed at Grandpa's funeral. I don't know why; it just stuck with me.

Even though I walk through the valley of
the shadow of death,
I fear no evil;
for you are with me.

I'm real scared this time. I screwed up so bad again. It seems like everything's been going bad ever since Grandpa died last year. He cared about me. He was all I had. I wish I could just start over, start a new life. But maybe I can, you never know. Even though I feel like I'm walking through that death valley, maybe you're with me, and maybe Grandpa is too, and we're going to come out on the other side okay. It's the only thing that's getting me through right now.

Mike

The LORD is my shepherd, I shall
not want.
He makes me lie down in green
pastures;
he leads me beside still waters;
he restores my soul.
He leads me in right paths
for his name's sake.

Even though I walk through the valley of
the shadow of death,
I fear no evil;
for you are with me;
your rod and your staff—
they comfort me.

(Psalm 23:1–4)

The Prophetic Books

We have heard already from three of Israel's prophets in this course: Isaiah, Amos, and Jeremiah. Remember that prophets were not so much predictors of future events as confronters of present evil situations. So when the Israelite kings corrupted the practice of the faith by worshiping idols and depriving the poor of what was due to them, the prophets went into action. Sometimes the prophets leveled blistering accusations at the wealthy and the proud. But other times they consoled the people in periods of great trial and distress, reminding them of God's great promises to Israel, and assuring them that God would never abandon them. The **prophetic books** are the records of their writings.

Let's turn now to the Christian Testament.

Up on Eagles' Wings

God,

Okay, I'm about to either explode or collapse. I just can't take it anymore! I've got midterm exams this week. I've gotten two of them over with, but I still have the worst four to go. That's enough all by itself, but then Wednesday night my mother's having this dinner in her honor for her twenty-fifth anniversary of working at the bank, and of course I have to be there for that. And the coach still expects us to be at basketball practice three times this week.

Then I found out that my aunt Eileen, my most favorite person in the whole world, has cancer, and they're doing surgery right away. She needs help with little Danny and Molly after school while she's in the hospital. I really want to help her right now, but I don't know how I'll be able to. Besides, I've been breaking down in tears every time I think about her. Oh, God, please help!

Even just telling you this helps me a little. When I tell you, I feel like you're on my side and you'll help me figure it out. I need to calm down and think straight and decide what's really the most important and what I can skip or put off. Maybe I can talk to some teachers and my coach, and Mom, too.

Something from the Bible just popped into my head. Aunt Eileen loves to quote this when she's all worn out and discouraged:

> Those who wait for the LORD shall renew
>   their strength,
>   they shall mount up with wings like
>   eagles,
> they shall run and not be weary,
>   they shall walk and not faint.

Oh, God, help me with feeling so wiped out and panicky. And take care of Aunt Eileen and make her strong. Let us both fly like eagles!

Tiredly,
Brigid

The Christian Testament

Twenty-seven books make up the Christian Testament, grouped in these major sections:
- the Gospels
- the Acts of the Apostles
- the Epistles
- the Book of Revelation

The Gospels

The accounts of Jesus' life, death, and Resurrection are found in the four **Gospels**—the books of **Matthew**, **Mark**, **Luke**, and **John**, which are probably the most familiar parts of the Bible to Christians. Matthew, Mark,

Have you not known? Have you not heard?
The LORD is the everlasting God,
    the Creator of the ends of the
    earth.
He does not faint or grow weary;
    his understanding is unsearchable.
He gives power to the faint,
    and strengthens the powerless.
Even youths will faint and be weary,
    and the young will fall exhausted;
but those who wait for the LORD
        shall renew their strength,
    they shall mount up with wings like
    eagles,
they shall run and not be weary,
    they shall walk and not faint.
                        (Isaiah 40:28–31)

Below and facing page: **Each evangelist is identified with a symbol. Matthew's symbol is a winged man; Mark's, a winged lion; Luke's, a winged ox; and John's, an eagle.**

Luke, and John—the four **Evangelists**—are traditionally accepted as the writers of the Gospels, but parts of the Gospels may have been written by other disciples in the name of the Evangelist whose name is on the Gospel. (The word *evangelist* comes from a Greek word meaning "good news" or "gospel.")

Each Gospel, or proclamation of the Good News, offers a distinctive portrait of Jesus and a different emphasis on his message. The Gospels are not biographies in the sense of providing exact dates, locations, and factual details about Jesus' life. Because each of the Gospels was written within a certain Christian community and with a particular audience in mind, each gives a somewhat different angle on Jesus and his message. A comparison may help: In trying to photograph a mountain, it takes many different views to get a full picture of the mountain on film—from each side, from the top, from the bottom, and so on. With six or eight camera angles, we get a sense of the whole mountain. The Gospels are somewhat like that. Each portrait adds to the understanding we have of the mystery of Jesus and the Good News he preached.

Briefly, here are the different portraits we have of Jesus and his message in the four Gospels:

Matthew. Matthew, a tax collector, was one of Jesus' Apostles, a Jew whose Gospel was written for a primarily Jewish audience. It emphasized to the Jews that Jesus was clearly the Messiah they had been waiting for, and that Jesus' whole life was the fulfillment of all the ancient promises made by God to Israel. Matthew's Gospel shows Jesus as a great teacher, the "New Moses." This is the Gospel containing the **Sermon on the Mount**, which is a collection of many of Jesus' sayings and teachings, including the Beatitudes. Matthew's Gospel was written between the years 80 and 100.

5

In one of the Gospels, find a teaching of Jesus that seems puzzling or hard for you to accept. Write a letter to God expressing how you react to that teaching.

6

If you were a Gospel writer today, writing to an audience of young people in our society, what aspect of Jesus and his message would you focus on?

Mark. Mark was the first Gospel written (in about the years 65 to 70) and the shortest. It was apparently addressed primarily to Gentile (non-Jewish) Christians in Rome. The church was undergoing severe persecution in Rome; Saints Peter and Paul were probably martyred during this persecution. Mark's Gospel is full of references to the trials and persecution that Jesus' followers might expect, and it highlights the suffering and death of Jesus. This theme encouraged the Roman Christians by letting them know they were suffering in union with Christ and would one day be glorified with him.

Jesus comes through as very human, full of strong emotion, in Mark's Gospel. Reading it is a good introduction to the story of Jesus.

Luke. The Gospel of Luke, written about the year 85, is actually the first volume of Luke's two-volume history of early Christianity. His second volume is the Acts of the Apostles.

A portrait of Jesus as compassionate Savior and Healer emerges from Luke's Gospel. Luke, supposedly a physician and the only Evangelist who was a Gentile Christian, showed Jesus working many healing miracles. Luke addressed his Gospel primarily to Gentile Christians, many of whom were well educated and wealthy. This Gospel emphasizes the image of Jesus embracing poor people and outcasts of society. As Luke conveyed it, the Christian message is for *everyone*—rich and poor, men and women, Jews and Gentiles.

The Gospels of Matthew, Mark, and Luke are often referred to as the **synoptic** Gospels. This means that when they are read side by side, parallels in structure and content can easily be seen. According to scholars, these parallels came about because the writers of Matthew and Luke used Mark, the earliest Gospel, as a source.

John. John's Gospel comes out of a Jewish Christian community led by John. It offers a distinct picture of Jesus that emphasizes his divine Sonship. This Gospel reflects a deepened understanding of Jesus as divine, perhaps because it was the last Gospel to be written (between the years 90 and 100). It is full of symbolic language and reflections on the nature of God. Its beautiful discourses and teachings of Jesus make it a wonderful source for personal and communal prayer.

Giving to the "Least Ones," Giving to God?

God—

All right, am I totally dense or what? They just read over the P.A. system this Scripture quote for the day, about how you're supposed to treat everybody who asks you for something like they're God, because they sort of are God.

Now I just don't see it. I know there are poor people out there, and homeless people and prisoners. But is it my fault they're that way? And even if it isn't my fault (which it isn't!), how can somebody who's homeless really be like God asking for help? A lot of those homeless people got that way from doing drugs or not being willing to work, and that's not being like God. And the people in prison—they're put there for all the crimes they did. Am I really supposed to treat them like they're God? Caring for sick people I can see, but criminals?

That thing about, "As long as you did it to one of these least ones, you did it to me" sounds really good and idealistic. But it's hard to see how it would work in the real world. Help me get what you're talking about. I really want to get it, but it just doesn't make sense to me. I don't know what to do with it.

Your friend,
Sherry

Jesus spoke this parable:] "When the Son of Man comes in his glory, and all the angels with him, then he will sit on the throne of his glory. All the nations will be gathered before him, and he will separate people one from another as a shepherd separates the sheep from the goats, and he will put the sheep at his right hand and the goats at the left. Then the king will say to those at his right hand, 'Come, you that are blessed by my Father, inherit the kingdom prepared for you from the foundation of the world; for I was hungry and you gave me food, I was thirsty and you gave me something to drink, I was a stranger and you welcomed me, I was naked and you gave me clothing, I was sick and you took care of me, I was in prison and you visited me.' Then the righteous will answer him, 'Lord, when was it that we saw you hungry and gave you food, or thirsty and gave you something to drink? And when was it that we saw you a stranger and welcomed you, or naked and gave you clothing? And when was it that we saw you sick or in prison and visited you?' And the king will answer them, 'Truly I tell you, just as you did it to one of the least of these who are members of my family, you did it to me.' Then he will say to those at his left hand, 'You that are accursed, depart from me into the eternal fire prepared for the devil and his angels; for I was hungry and you gave me no food, I was thirsty and you gave me nothing to drink, I was a stranger and you did not welcome me, naked and you did not give me clothing, sick and in prison and you did not visit me.' Then they also will answer, 'Lord, when was it that we saw you hungry or thirsty or a stranger or naked or sick or in prison, and did not take care of you?' Then he will answer them, 'Truly I tell you, just as you did not do it to one of the least of these, you did not do it to me.' And these will go away into eternal punishment, but the righteous into eternal life." (Matthew 25:31–46)

The Acts of the Apostles

The continuation of Luke's Gospel is the Acts of the Apostles, or simply, Acts. Luke wanted to show how the Holy Spirit was alive and active in the early church after Jesus' departure from earthly life. Thus Acts is sometimes called the **Gospel of the Holy Spirit.**

The first half of Acts tells the story of the early church community in Jerusalem from the time of the Ascension and Pentecost. Peter figures prominently in the first half of the book. The second half follows Paul's journeys as he converts the Gentile world to the Gospel. Acts is full of high drama and action-packed stories of courage and faith in the early church.

The Epistles

The twenty-one letters collected as the Epistles were written to various Christian communities or individuals in the early church. The letters respond to a wide variety of problems and needs, but they also teach and encourage the communities of believers. Some of the letters offer deep, profound reflections on the Christian message. The best known epistles are those of Paul, a few of which you have heard from in this course.

Paul's thirteen epistles were written between the years 50 and 65, whereas the other epistles were written after the year 80. The letters are organized in the Bible in the following order and are traditionally assumed to have been written by the following authors (although in some cases their disciples may have written the epistles in their name):

- thirteen epistles written by Paul to various communities
- one epistle, the Letter to the Hebrews, whose author is unknown
- one epistle by James
- two epistles by Peter
- three epistles by John
- one epistle by Jude

The Book of Revelation

The last book of the Christian Testament is **Revelation**, also called the **Apocalypse** (the Greek word for "revelation"). Its author is identified in the book as John, but he was most likely not the Evangelist John, the man associated with the Gospel of John.

7
In one of the Epistles, find a piece of advice or a teaching that if followed you think would help make your school a better community.

Paul's conversion to Christ on the road to Damascus, by sixteenth-century artist Raphael. Paul went on to write many letters to Christians that became part of the Christian Testament.

The Book of Revelation is full of strange and powerful symbols of the end time. This is when Christ will come again and bring to the world the final victory of God over sin and death. Probably written at the end of the first century, Revelation was meant to give hope and courage to Christians who were enduring another ruthless persecution by the Roman authorities.

Catholic Scripture scholars today agree that Revelation's symbolic language is not to be taken literally. Its repetition of certain numbers, its strange beasts, and even its image of Christ as a lamb with seven horns and seven eyes can be very confusing to the typical reader. Christians of some denominations try to use the images in Revelation to predict when the end of the world will come. They even see signs from the book that the end is very near. In Catholic teaching, however, careful attention is paid to the symbolic meanings of the images and numbers to discover the real intent of the book. Revelation's underlying message, according to Catholic interpretation, is a call to Christians to be faithful even in the face of persecution, and to trust that God will finally be victorious.

Why *These* Books?

Why did any particular piece of writing become part of the Bible? In any religion, many writings are circulated that could be seen as conveying beliefs or teachings about that religion. This was certainly true with the Jews and the early Christians, who had many sources from which to select in composing their official, authoritative list, or **canon**, of sacred Scriptures. Why then are some books canonical (that is, included in the canon), and some books are not?

The answer to that question is complex and incomplete. Many of the choices were made in the earliest centuries of the church, and we do not have enough information about the reasons behind the choices to understand them fully. The faith answer, however, is that God guided the leaders who made the decisions about which books belonged in the canon. They believed that certain books expressed the truth of God's message in a way that others did not—that these

A medieval artist's depiction of strange imagery in the Book of Revelation
Top: The Fifth Trumpet of the Apocalypse
Bottom: Fall of the Star of Satan

books were inspired by God and that others lacked such divine authority. Other human factors and motives no doubt entered in, but even those can be seen as part of God's way of guiding the process of selection.

All Christians—Protestant, Catholic, and Orthodox—agree on the canon of the Christian Testament, the twenty-seven books listed on page 171, which were basically settled on by the year 400.

However, Catholics and Protestants differ in what they include in the canon of the Hebrew Scriptures. Catholics include the forty-six books listed on page 170. Protestants, following the canon set by Jewish authorities in the year 90, include just thirty-nine. The seven books or parts of books in the Catholic canon that are not in the Protestant or Jewish canons were written late in Jewish history, in the two hundred years before Christ. They were also preserved in Greek, not in the original Jewish languages of Hebrew and Aramaic. (In some Protestant Bibles, the seven noncanonical books are given at the end of the Hebrew Scriptures, under the section Apocrypha, meaning "unknown" or "of doubtful origin.")

Now that we have an overview of what is included in the Scriptures, let's consider how to understand the truth conveyed in them.

The oldest known scrolls of the Hebrew Scriptures were discovered in 1947, in caves at Qumran in Jordan, near the Dead Sea.

For Review

- Name the scriptures that are held as sacred by each of the following groups: Muslims, Hindus, Confucians, Jews, and Christians.
- In what sense is the Bible like a library? How many books are in each of the two major divisions of the Catholic Bible?
- List the four major sections of the Hebrew Scriptures and briefly describe what is in each.
- List the four major sections of the Christian Testament and briefly describe what is in each.
- Explain a distinctive characteristic about each of the four Gospels: Matthew, Mark, Luke, and John.
- What is meant by the canon of the Bible? Why were certain books chosen to be part of the canon?

Understanding God's Truth in the Scriptures

As previously mentioned, the Bible was not composed from front to back as a single book, or even as two books—the Hebrew Scriptures and the Christian Testament. Rather, it is a library of many kinds of books and literature developed over a span of more than a thousand years.

The Development of the Scriptures

To appreciate how God's truth lies within the Scriptures, it will help to gain a sense of how the books of the Bible were developed.

The Process

In general, the development of the Scriptures—both the Hebrew Scriptures and the Christian Testament—followed a five-step process:

1. Events. People have concrete experiences in which they somehow encounter Sacred Mystery. God reveals God's own self through the people's experiences, and they meet God, even though at the time they might not understand the full meaning of the events. An example of such a concrete experience is the Israelites escaping from slavery in Egypt, led by a great leader, Moses; or the Apostles following Jesus in his ministry for three years and witnessing his death and then his risen glory.

2. Oral tradition. Over a period of years (sometimes centuries, sometimes decades), people talk about their experiences. They come to see how God was present in those events. They tell stories about the events and pass them on from one generation to the next. Different communities may develop their own versions of the same events.

8
Recall an event in your life or your family's life that was very significant to you and your development. It may have happened years ago. Reflecting now on that event, can you see how God may have been present in the event? Write up your thoughts in a one-page reflection.

A Healing Touch

Dear God,

On Friday our high school went to see the AIDS quilt, which is on display for a few days at the college here. I didn't know what to expect. I only knew it was hundreds of cloth panels, each one representing someone who died of AIDS.

Me and my friends were kind of nervous. What would it be like to look at stuff all about gay people? On the way over, some kids were snickering about catching AIDS from the quilt. A few kids refused to go. They said they didn't want to have anything to do with homosexuals.

Then we walked into the gym where they had the panels all over the walls and on the floor. Total silence. We walked up and down the rows. Each panel was put together with so much love by family and friends of the person who died. Most of the victims were probably gay, but some were children and also people who got it from regular sex, or bad blood transfusions, or infected needles.

The panels had souvenirs of happy memories on them, photos of the person with their friends, and symbols of their favorite things, like music and sports and pets. Some panels had messages written on them about what a great person this was. Nieces and nephews wrote love notes like, "See you in heaven," and "We miss you playing baseball with us."

Lots of people were crying. Even I got kind of choked up. It was hitting us how good and fun these people who died had been, and how they were someone's kid, or brother or sister, or lover or friend. They didn't seem like outcasts anymore—people to be feared and avoided and, least of all, snickered at. I was thinking about all the love their families and friends had for them, and about how my friends and I were now feeling understanding for people who used to be strangers to us, who made us nervous just thinking about them. It seemed like a kind of healing for everybody, those who died and those of us still alive.

At Mass today, when I heard that Gospel about Jesus curing the leper, it meant something new to me. The priest said that lepers were feared and had to live away from everyone else because people were terrified of catching the disease. And everybody thought the disease was God's punishment for a terrible sin. It makes me wonder if maybe the most important thing for that leper wasn't just that Jesus healed his leprosy, but that Jesus loved him and touched him, which no one else was willing to do. He made him feel like a human being again.

God, please help me to see into things, beyond the surface, to love those who nobody else wants to be around. And bless all those people who have died of AIDS and the people who loved them. And I'm thinking of all the people with AIDS who are still alive and have no one to love them. Take special care of them.

Love,
Matt

Once, when [Jesus] was in one of the cities, there was a man covered with leprosy. When he saw Jesus, he bowed with his face to the ground and begged him, "Lord, if you choose, you can make me clean." Then Jesus stretched out his hand, touched him, and said, "I do choose. Be made clean." Immediately the leprosy left him. (Luke 5:12–13)

A manuscript of the Book of Isaiah from the Dead Sea Scrolls, which may date to around the time of Jesus

3. Written pieces. Parts of the oral tradition about an event are gradually written down—like songs, riddles, stories about heroes. For instance, the Song of Miriam is a beautiful song of joy about how God freed the Israelites from slavery. It appears in the Book of Exodus, after the Israelites have crossed the sea on dry land to escape Pharaoh's army. Miriam's Song is perhaps the oldest piece of writing in the Hebrew Scriptures, written down long before the full story of the escape was recorded. Writings usually evolve over time. Matthew's and Luke's Gospels provide other examples. As noted earlier, both of them had Mark's Gospel as a source. But it is likely that both also drew from an earlier written collection of Jesus' sayings. This collection, based on the oral tradition among the early Christians, has never been found.

4. Edited books. At some point people collected and put together in one written piece the various oral and written traditions about a particular event like the escape from slavery. The pieces were edited, but sometimes several versions of the same event were kept, even if there were differences among the accounts. For example, two versions of Miriam's Song appear in Exodus, one long and one short. (The ancients were not as concerned about being consistent as we are today!) These edited pieces came together in what we call a book. But of course people of ancient times did not have books with pages as we know them. Their "books" were scrolls of parchment or animal skin.

During and after the Exile in Babylon, the Jews edited many of their oral and written traditions into the books we have today in the Hebrew Scriptures. The Jewish people were refugees in a strange land that was hostile to their religion. Imagine how important it was for them while in exile to have these sacred writings collected and preserved. They passed them around and treasured them like letters from their ancestors. They read, studied, and prayed over them to remind themselves of who they were and how to stay faithful to their God.

An editing process also took place with the Gospels in the Christian Testament. A community—say, of the Evangelist John's disciples—put together all the materials they had from their teacher and edited them into the Gospel of John.

9
Have you ever treasured a certain book, song, poem, or letter from someone because it reminded you of who you are and what is important in life? If so, describe the book, song, poem, or letter and what it means or meant to you.

5. Canonical status. Certain of the edited works are recognized by the community of faith as inspired by God, revealing God's truth, because these pieces faithfully reflect the people's experience and belief. These books then enter the official canon of the Scriptures. Not all the written and edited works of the early Christians achieved canonical status, however. Works such as the Gospel of Thomas, the Gospel of Peter, and the Apocalypse of Peter were widely used among the early Christians, but for a variety of reasons they were not added to the official canon of the Christian Testament.

Not all the books of the Scriptures followed this exact process of development. For example, the Creation stories in Genesis are not based on people's memories of actual events; they are more like legends or myths. And the epistles known to be written or dictated by Paul did not pass through a stage of oral tradition. They were written, possibly edited to a degree, and sent as letters. They became so well known and loved that it was obvious to the early church that they belonged in the canon of the Scriptures.

God's Role in the Process

If we reflect on this rather complex process, we may marvel at how the Bible came to be. Rather than God "dictating" words or truths to one or a few writers, God entered into a long communal process with thousands of people over centuries, being present in their storytelling around campfires, their gathering around teachers, their passing the Word from father and mother to daughter and son.

Rejoicing Always

Dear God,

I don't know how to explain this, I just feel so different, not like my usual kind of bored self. We just had the freshmen retreat. We went away for an overnight, and the seniors led it. I thought it would be pretty, you know, boring, but everybody had to go so I went.

Well, it wasn't boring at all; it was great! We did all these group things that were really neat. Some of the talks the seniors gave were so funny, but then they got pretty serious about their own life, and everyone was like hanging on to every word they were saying. Then

> **R**ejoice in the Lord always; again I will say, Rejoice. Let your gentleness be known to everyone. The Lord is near. Do not worry about anything, but in everything by prayer and supplication with thanksgiving let your requests be made known to God. And the peace of God, which surpasses all understanding, will guard your hearts and your minds in Christ Jesus. (Philippians 4:4–7)

we'd talk with each other in small groups. I said stuff I'd never said out loud before, and what was so cool was that people listened to what I said; they really respected me. So then I listened real hard to what they said. We all found out a lot about each other, and there was this feeling of caring we had for each other. It sounds funny for me to be talking this way, but I'm telling you, something different happened there.

At the prayer service at the end, we listened to a song, "Rejoice in the Lord always, again I say rejoice." Everybody was smiling a lot, and the song really fit how we were feeling. Then we all had a chance to say things we liked about the retreat, and lots of people remembered different things they were thankful for. Someone even mentioned that something I said helped him. Wow, that got to me. The things people were happy about just piled up and up, and everybody wanted to hear more and more.

I feel real peaceful tonight—excited but peaceful inside, in a way I have never felt. And I'm definitely not bored! Thank you, God, for all that happened.

Love,
Darrell

The process was not neat; it was "messy," with all kinds of human factors influencing what was told, what was kept, what was discarded or changed a bit to suit an audience's needs. But God breathed life into and guided the whole process. In that sense we can say the Scriptures were *inspired* by God (a word that means "to breathe into"). And we can understand the Bible as a work truly of both divine and human origins.

Religious Truth in the Scriptures: The Catholic Insight

By now it must be fairly clear that we cannot look to the Scriptures for scientific explanations or historical accounts that are accurate and factual in all respects. The Bible gives us something much greater and more profound than scientific or historical facts. It gives us religious truth, the inner truth of God. For example, the Genesis stories are not meant to be a diary of Creation but, rather, the assurance that all Creation comes from God and is good.

The Catholic insight into interpreting the Scriptures is that we can find that religious truth by first of all understanding what the writer of any given passage intended to communicate. Who was the audience? What problems or concerns of the community influenced what was written or edited into the passage? What type of literature was the passage written in? (Some writings were intended as fiction pieces or as exaggerated heroic tales; others were meant to be more historical, factual accounts.) If there are two versions of a story in the Bible, we need not be troubled over differing details in them. Rather, we need to try to understand the inner truth behind the story, and it is often the differing details that can shed light on that truth for us.

For instance, Matthew's version of the Nativity of Jesus has astrologers, also called wise men or magi, coming from the East (indicating they were Gentiles, not Jews) to see the newborn child. Luke's version makes no mention of the wise men but depicts shepherds coming from the neighboring hillside to adore Jesus. Matthew, writing for a Jewish audience, wanted to make the religious point that Jesus came not only for the Jews but for the whole world, the Gentile world as well as the Jewish world. And Luke, writing for a fairly well-to-do Gentile audience, wanted to make a religious truth clear to them—that Jesus came not simply for privileged people like themselves but for poor and outcast people, like the shepherds, who were close to the bottom rung of society. The differing details are not contradictory; in fact, the very differences between the Nativity stories tell us more about what Jesus means for the world than either version alone.

Noel! Noel! by Edmundo Arburola, a Nicaraguan-style depiction of the Nativity

This brief look at the Nativity stories can help us make another significant point about the Scriptures: It is best to study the Scriptures with guidance. To understand the differences between Matthew's and Luke's versions we need to know about the Christian communities for whom they were writing. Were they primarily Jews or Gentiles? Were they poor or rich? Were they under persecution? The answers to such questions are important in the study of the Scriptures, but the answers cannot always be found within the Scriptures themselves. For a rich, full understanding of the Scriptures, guidance is necessary.

10

Find the Bible passages listed below and read them. Then select one whose meaning you are curious about and discuss it with someone who has a good background in the Scriptures (such as a religion teacher, or a pastor or priest). From your discussion, write up your understanding of what the inner truth, or religious truth, of the passage might be.

- Genesis 22:1–19 (Abraham's test)
- 1 Kings 19:4–13 (Elijah's journey)
- Ezekiel 37:1–14 (Vision of the dry bones)
- Matthew 20:1–16 (Parable of the laborers in the vineyard)
- Luke 14:16–24 (Parable of the great dinner)
- John 15:1–11 (Vine and the branches)

Inspired by God

Christians believe that the Bible is **inspired by God**, just as Jews view the Hebrew Scriptures as being inspired by God. God's inspiration does not mean that every word in the Bible is factually correct. Rather, it means that God inspired and guided the whole process of developing the Scriptures. Thus the sacred writers included every truth needed for our salvation, and all the books that contained that truth were chosen for the canon. The writers communicated the truth using their own powers and abilities, even their cultural limitations and at times their narrow images of God. (These images broadened over centuries of experiencing God's love for all people. But we may be shocked to read some of the deeds or attitudes attributed to God by the early writers of the Hebrew Scriptures!)

God entrusted the communication of truth to limited human beings who expressed that truth in their own way, using the tools and concepts available to them at the time. We have to be amazed at a God who trusts human beings so much and works so intimately with them to reveal divine truth.

The Heart of the Bible's Message

What is the underlying truth that God has revealed to us in the Scriptures? No one can fully capture that truth in words, but here are a few statements that attempt to summarize the Bible's underlying message:

- God is the source of all goodness, all life, and all creation.
- God made us in the divine image, out of love, and God wants to be in loving relationship with us.
- By giving us freedom, God gave us the ability to choose between good and evil. Sin and its terrible effects on relationships came into the world when human beings first chose evil.
- God will never abandon us. When we sin and fail, God is ready to forgive us. When we are oppressed, God wants us to be free.
- The whole purpose and meaning of life is to love—to love God, our neighbor, ourselves, and creation.
- By proclaiming and living out the Reign of God, Jesus, the Son of God made flesh as a human, showed us the way to live in God's love. He called his followers to a new life centered on love of God and neighbor.
- In Jesus' death and Resurrection, we are saved. His dying and rising become the pattern for our own life. If we give our life in love to others and to God, we find new life and growth.

- Through the power of the Holy Spirit, the church of Jesus Christ carries on Jesus' mission to bring about the Reign of God in the world. God's Spirit will be with the church for all time, until Jesus returns to bring all creation to fulfillment.

The Word of God cannot be chained up or controlled; it has been speaking powerfully to human beings and making a difference in their lives for thousands of years.

For Review

- What is the five-step process of development that most of the books of the Bible went through? Describe each step in a sentence or two.
- What was God's role in the process of development of the Scriptures?
- What is the Catholic approach to finding the religious truth in any given biblical passage? Offer an example from the versions of the Nativity given by Matthew and by Luke.
- What does it mean to say that the Bible is inspired by God?

The Fullness of Revelation

Christians believe that the fullness of God's Revelation of self has been given to humankind in Jesus Christ. Jesus is the one source of Divine Revelation, the truth that God wants to communicate to us.

The Catholic faith holds that we come to know the one truth revealed in and by Jesus, God's Revelation, through two means: the Scriptures (both the Hebrew Scriptures and the Christian Testament) and what is called the church's Tradition. We will explore Tradition in the next chapter.

8

Tradition:

Handing On a Living Faith

"We Are One Body"

The whole world was watching as Catholic young people from all over the globe came together to share thoughts and experiences; to learn; to be inspired by the leader of the worldwide Catholic church, **Pope John Paul II**; and to celebrate their faith. World Youth Day 1993 drew almost two hundred thousand youth from more than seventy nations to Denver, Colorado, for five days of living the reality of a global church.

A Celebration of Belonging

As the helicopter carrying Pope John Paul II touched down in Denver's Mile High Stadium, the crowd that had been cheering, stomping, chanting, and singing for over an hour let loose with a joyous roar. Journalist Jerry Daoust gives this account:

> He ascends the steps to the massive stage. The young people haven't let up; the stadium scoreboard shakes with the thunder of their greeting. Some become emotional; one young woman holds her hands up to her mouth as tears run down her cheeks. The Spanish pilgrims chant *¡Juan Pablo, segundo, te quiere todo el mundo!* —"John Paul II, the whole world loves you!"
>
>   Even God gets in on the banner-waving, it seems, when a brief rainstorm is followed by a double rainbow that arcs over the stadium. . . .

[In the evening in the streets of Denver] passing groups of pilgrims whooped and gave each other high fives, shouting over and over, "Where're you from? Where're you from?" The answers represented every part of the country, from Honolulu, Hawaii, to North Pole, Alaska; and every part of the globe: Uganda, Russia, Egypt, Israel, Australia, China, Vietnam, Nicaragua, France, Ireland, and even the warring regions of Bosnia and Serbia. Thousands of friendships spanning the globe were made in Denver during World Youth Day as participants swapped addresses on scraps of paper and t-shirts.

The event at times resembled the ultimate slumber party: 250,000 pilgrims [youth and adults] formed a multi-colored carpet of sleeping bags and blankets at Cherry Creek State Park for the all-night vigil before Sunday's Mass.

But perhaps the event's most moving scenes were quiet moments that demonstrated the deep faith of the pilgrims, such as the long lines for the Sacrament of Reconciliation at makeshift outdoor confessionals. Or the opening Mass, which some 150,000 young people attended, standing shoulder-to-shoulder for two hours at Celebration Plaza. Others attended local churches for evening prayer services, packing them so full that some had to kneel in the aisles. Most attended catechesis sessions, and it was not uncommon to see large groups of pilgrims sitting on the grass somewhere praying the rosary or studying the Bible. . . .

During a candlelight procession carrying the Holy Year Cross through downtown Denver one night, thousands of pilgrims sang the World Youth Day theme song,

The Pope Speaks to Youth, and Youth to the Pope

Pope John Paul II

During the 1993 World Youth Day events in Denver, Colorado, the pope addressed these words to the young pilgrims, and through them to all the youth of the church:

Take courage in the face of life's difficulties and injustices. Commit yourselves to the struggle for justice, solidarity and peace in the world. Offer your youthful energies and your talents to building a civilization of Christian love. Be witnesses of God's love for the weak, for the poor and the oppressed. . . . . (Address to youth after the Way of the Cross)

Young pilgrims, Christ needs you to enlighten the world and to show it the path to life. . . . At this stage of history, the liberating message of the Gospel of Life has been put into your hands, and the mission of proclaiming it to the ends of the earth is now passing to your generation. . . . This is no time to be ashamed of the Gospel. It is the time to preach it from the rooftops. Do not be afraid to break out of comfortable and routine modes of living, in order to take up the challenge of making Christ known in the modern metropolis. It is you who must go out into the byroads and invite everyone you meet to the banquet which God has prepared for His people. (Message to youth during Mass at Cherry Creek State Park)

The Young Delegates

For their part, delegates from among the two hundred thousand or so youth at World Youth Day worked on a message that was given to the pope and read at the concluding Mass:

We wish to speak to the youth of the world not about problems, despair, and hatred, but about possibilities, hope, and love. We recognize that, united with our brothers and sisters, we are the Church of today and the Church of tomorrow. . . . We strive to develop our personal gifts to the best of our ability so as to better serve society. We strive to serve in particular the weakest, the poorest, and the most vulnerable among us. To make this a reality we need to walk together, hand in hand, with all the youth and all the people of the world who love life.

> "We are one body, one body in Christ, and we do not stand alone."

a gentle melody with the lyrics, "We are one body, one body in Christ, and we do not stand alone; we are one body, one body in Christ, and He came that we might have life."

A group of young people from the Hong Kong Catholic Pastoral Association for the Deaf sang, "We are one body . . ." in the sign language with which they communicate. For them, the sense of isolation they usually feel in a crowd of hearing people vanished, as sign language was just one more variety of language amid dozens from all over the world. The big smiles and the joy of being together in such beautiful diversity made everyone feel that they belonged.

Facing page, left: Pope John Paul II greets a participant at World Youth Day 1993 in Denver.
Facing page, right: Young people hail the arrival of the pope at Mile High Stadium in Denver.

One of the emcees for the Youth Day ceremonies, Mev Puleo, herself a photojournalist and a student in theology, commented on the sense of oneness in diversity:

"The international presence is what 'made' World Youth Day. . . . Looking at the crowd, a rainbow of faces from every nation, waving banners and flags, cheering, singing, doing the 'wave' made me feel I was at an Olympics for God."

1
Do you know anyone, youth or adult, who went to World Youth Day in Denver in 1993? If so, interview the person about her or his experience, and write up the results of your interview.

Unity in Diversity

The pilgrims who went to Denver for World Youth Day were lifted up by their experience of the global Catholic church. They found in that global church a unity in the midst of their diversity. They shared a **unity of faith**—same beliefs, same sacraments, same sense of meaning in their lives. And they found this faith affirmed and expressed by a leader they could look to for wisdom and guidance—John Paul II, who as pope is a symbol and guarantor of the church's unity.

The youthful pilgrims knew they held that unity of faith in the context of many diverse cultures and languages, each using the customs and practices of its own country or re-

2
Is your school culturally diverse? List all the different cultural backgrounds of Catholicism at your school that you can think of.

gion. The pilgrims also held a common faith in the midst of an array of different problems. For instance, some came from war-torn countries; some came from desperate poverty and famine; some came from affluent countries where spiritual poverty, not material poverty, is the main challenge. Some were from urban centers where poverty and violence are growing; others came from rural and peasant environments where people are increasingly being driven off the land by huge corporations. Some came from European countries where the church has been in existence for more than a thousand years, such as Italy, France, Germany, Poland, and Ireland. Others were from places where the church is a relative newcomer, such as some Asian and African countries. In some of the pilgrims' countries, the church is being persecuted; in others it is an established part of the dominant culture. Each situation presents unique challenges for the young people who are trying to live the Gospel faithfully.

The Catholic church embraces an amazing variety of cultures, races, languages, philosophies, patterns of thinking, customs, and ways of expressing the faith. It is wonderful to recognize and affirm that variety, which can enrich Catholicism, and to see it united in one church that holds the same faith, under one leadership. This unity in diversity can bring a great sense of joy, belonging, and even awe to people when it is experienced firsthand, as the pilgrims to World Youth Day discovered.

For Review

- What is meant by saying that Catholics share a unity of faith? Who symbolizes and guarantees the church's unity?
- Give five examples of the diverse situations from which the pilgrims to World Youth Day came.

Student art: "Dancing Hammers," chalk art by Mikki Parker, Mercy Academy, Louisville, Kentucky

The Scriptures and Tradition are like the intertwined strands of a weaving.

also given us the wisdom that comes from years and even centuries of living with and reflecting on the mysteries that have been revealed to us in Jesus Christ. God honors the capacity of human beings to reason, reflect, and learn over time. Because the Holy Spirit is present in the church, guiding it in the path of truth, Catholics believe that the experiences and reflections of the church over time, throughout its history, are inspired just as surely as the Scriptures were inspired by God.

Tradition Came First

Christians and Christian Tradition were around before the Christian Testament. Think about how the Christian Testament developed in the early church. As we discussed in chapter 7, first came the community's experience of certain events like Jesus' life or the coming of the Holy Spirit at Pentecost. Then followed a period of reflecting on and talking about the experience, and sharing stories in an oral tradition. Only later were the stories written down as pieces, edited into larger works like the Gospels, and finally accepted officially as the books that we know as the Christian Testament. The church did not grow out of the Scriptures; rather, the Scriptures grew out of the Tradition of the early church. Tradition has always been essential to the church.

gion. The pilgrims also held a common faith in the midst of an array of different problems. For instance, some came from war-torn countries; some came from desperate poverty and famine; some came from affluent countries where spiritual poverty, not material poverty, is the main challenge. Some were from urban centers where poverty and violence are growing; others came from rural and peasant environments where people are increasingly being driven off the land by huge corporations. Some came from European countries where the church has been in existence for more than a thousand years, such as Italy, France, Germany, Poland, and Ireland. Others were from places where the church is a relative newcomer, such as some Asian and African countries. In some of the pilgrims' countries, the church is being persecuted; in others it is an established part of the dominant culture. Each situation presents unique challenges for the young people who are trying to live the Gospel faithfully.

The Catholic church embraces an amazing variety of cultures, races, languages, philosophies, patterns of thinking, customs, and ways of expressing the faith. It is wonderful to recognize and affirm that variety, which can enrich Catholicism, and to see it united in one church that holds the same faith, under one leadership. This unity in diversity can bring a great sense of joy, belonging, and even awe to people when it is experienced firsthand, as the pilgrims to World Youth Day discovered.

For Review

- What is meant by saying that Catholics share a unity of faith? Who symbolizes and guarantees the church's unity?
- Give five examples of the diverse situations from which the pilgrims to World Youth Day came.

Student art: "Dancing Hammers," chalk art by Mikki Parker, Mercy Academy, Louisville, Kentucky

Tradition: The One Faith Handed On as a Living Reality

How does the Catholic church hold in unity such a diverse membership? The answer lies at least partly in the Catholic belief that the truth of Christ is passed on to us not only through the Scriptures but also through Tradition. To understand how this is so, let's first look at what Tradition means.

Tradition Versus *traditions*

Right away we need to note that we are talking about Tradition with a capital *T.* That is different from the ordinary meaning of the word *tradition* (lowercase *t*), which is a customary practice, like having a turkey dinner for the whole family on Thanksgiving, opening presents on Christmas eve, or lighting the menorah during Hanukkah.

The Catholic church has many **traditions** (lowercase *t*)— like blessing oneself with holy water, genuflecting in front of the tabernacle, or making the stations of the cross. These traditional practices are valuable and important in their own time and place, but they are not essential parts of the faith. In other words, they can be changed without losing something essential to Catholic identity. Different cultures within Catholicism may have particular traditions that other cultures do not have. For instance, countries like Italy, Mexico, Spain, and El Salvador have processions in the streets to honor certain saints; and in Kenya or South Africa, Mass may include native dancing and drumming. Such traditions are part of the diversity that is so enriching to the whole Catholic church; in no way do they harm the unity of the church.

That meaning of tradition is not the same as Tradition with a capital *T.* In the Catholic understanding, **Tradition** is the process by which the church reflects on, deepens its understanding of, cherishes, and hands on to every generation everything it believes is essential to the faith, indeed, everything it *is.* (The word *tradition* comes from a Latin word meaning "to hand over.") The process of handing on the faith includes teaching and worshiping, but also *living* the faith in everyday life. That faith is understood and lived in every age, taking into account new insights into the changing world, new conditions that did not exist before, and new challenges to the truth of God's Word.

God's truth, which has been given to us in the person of Jesus Christ, does not change. But human beings, who make up the church, are limited creatures who do not understand

The church in Latin America has many of its own traditions that enrich the Catholic church as a whole.

3

Talk with someone who has experienced Catholicism in a culture different from your own—for instance, in a Mexican, Filipino, Nigerian, or Vietnamese culture. Find out about one tradition of that culture that is not part of Catholicism in the dominant U.S. or Canadian culture. Describe the tradition in writing.

God's truth perfectly or express it perfectly. So over many centuries, the church has come to a deeper understanding of God's truth under the guidance of the Holy Spirit. In the process of living out the faith from the time of the Apostles until now, the church has gathered a whole body of wisdom—the Tradition of the church.

Tradition is like the household treasures of a family that has been living and growing for generations, rather than the artifacts of an ancient culture enshrined in a museum and marveled at by visitors. As one theologian put it, "Tradition is the living faith of the dead; [not] the dead faith of the living."

God's truth is understood over the centuries through the long, patient process of Tradition.
Student art: "Waiting," photo by Lisa Munzenrider, Benilde–Saint Margaret High School, Saint Louis Park, Minnesota

A "Scriptures *and* Tradition" Approach

Many other Christian denominations do not have the same belief in church Tradition that Catholics do. They see the Scriptures as the *one* way God has revealed sacred truth. Catholics, however, see both the Scriptures *and* Tradition as the ways of handing on God's Revelation in Christ.

A "Scriptures Only" Approach

A **"Scriptures only" approach,** held by some Christians, is that God has given us divine truth in the Bible alone. Christians with this perspective believe they will find in the Bible whatever they need to know about life, about God, and about how to be a follower of Jesus. In thinking about any moral or religious question, they believe the best answer will be found by going directly to the Scriptures alone for insight.

Why the Scriptures *and* Tradition?

However, a **"Scriptures and Tradition" approach,** which is the Catholic approach, says that God has made divine truth available to us not only in the Scriptures. God has

4
Agree or disagree with this statement and, in a paragraph, explain why: *I would rather believe in the living faith of the dead than the dead faith of the living.*

The Scriptures and Tradition are like the intertwined strands of a weaving.

also given us the wisdom that comes from years and even centuries of living with and reflecting on the mysteries that have been revealed to us in Jesus Christ. God honors the capacity of human beings to reason, reflect, and learn over time. Because the Holy Spirit is present in the church, guiding it in the path of truth, Catholics believe that the experiences and reflections of the church over time, throughout its history, are inspired just as surely as the Scriptures were inspired by God.

Tradition Came First

Christians and Christian Tradition were around before the Christian Testament. Think about how the Christian Testament developed in the early church. As we discussed in chapter 7, first came the community's experience of certain events like Jesus' life or the coming of the Holy Spirit at Pentecost. Then followed a period of reflecting on and talking about the experience, and sharing stories in an oral tradition. Only later were the stories written down as pieces, edited into larger works like the Gospels, and finally accepted officially as the books that we know as the Christian Testament. The church did not grow out of the Scriptures; rather, the Scriptures grew out of the Tradition of the early church. Tradition has always been essential to the church.

An Interwoven Process

Ever since the beginning of the church and the forming of the Christian Testament, the Scriptures and Tradition have been woven together. They are not two separate sources of God's truth. Rather, they are two interwoven means that God uses to communicate the truth to us. After all, Tradition is always a reflection on the church's learning and experience in light of the Scriptures. The Holy Spirit acts within that whole process to inspire the church to arrive at a deeper understanding of Jesus Christ and his message. Tradition can never be developed independently of the Scriptures.

Signs of a Living Faith:
Vietnamese Refugees at Sea with God

At the end of the war in Vietnam in 1975, when the Communists from North Vietnam were taking over the capital of South Vietnam, Saigon, a group of young Catholic seminarians of a Vietnamese religious order had to flee for their lives. They drifted for a week on the open sea in a small boat with other refugees, afraid they could die at any moment in the dangerous sea. One of those seminarians, Nhuan Nguyen, did eventually make it to the United States. Eighteen years after escaping Vietnam, following a long process of spiritual searching, he was ordained a priest in the Maryknoll religious order in 1993.

The day after his ordination, in a voice filled with emotion, Nguyen recalled the war that forced him and thousands of others to flee their homeland: "'I smelled the stench of burning villages and the stench of burning bodies.'" He told of how he and his seminary companions from Saigon, including a priest, had to make the perilous escape by sea, without even hazarding to bid farewell to their families:

"As we drifted helplessly, we had Mass. Like Jesus coming to his disciples, walking on the water, Jesus came to us in our little boat. We thought we might become food for the sharks, but instead God became food for us. From that moment on, our spirit became strong and we were able to trust in God's love more than we trusted in our boat."

"We are one body, one body in Christ, and we do not stand alone."

The Church's Teaching Voice

Obviously the process of formulating and expressing the church's Tradition is much more involved than simply going to the Scriptures for answers to life's questions. It takes time, prayerful discernment, and patience with the complex process, for the church to arrive at the teachings it embraces as part of its Tradition. And further, think of what would happen if everyone as an individual had the authority and power to determine what the church's Tradition is—what is essential to the faith. A great deal of confusion and probably complete lack of unity would result. We would have millions of versions of "the truth." If the "one body in Christ" is to have any unity of faith, the task of discerning what is true cannot simply be left to individuals to decide for themselves.

So who has the job of bringing together and interpreting the experience and reflections of the church's members into the essential Tradition of the church? Catholics see this authority as belonging to the official teaching voice of the church, called the **Magisterium** (from a Latin word meaning "to teach"). The Magisterium consists of the pope, believed by Catholics to be the successor of Saint Peter, and the Catholic bishops of the world, the successors of the Apostles. The pope and the bishops are responsible for discerning what is essential to the faith based on the experience of the church's members and on the work of theologians and Scripture scholars, all under the guidance of the Holy Spirit.

5
Do you think that deciding what is true should be left up to each individual, or do people need the guidance of the church to know what is true? Write a one-page reflection on this question.

The National Conference of Catholic Bishops, part of the church's Magisterium, in a 1983 session at which they released a historic pastoral letter on peace and war in the modern world

Forms of Church Teaching

Church teaching may be expressed by the Magisterium in any of the following forms:

- pastoral letters written by bishops for their own dioceses
- statements or pastoral letters by national or regional conferences of bishops—such as, in the United States, the National Conference of Catholic Bishops or, in Canada, the Canadian Bishops' Conference
- a major teaching document prepared with the advice of the world's bishops—such as the *Catechism of the Catholic Church,* issued in English by the Vatican in 1994
- documents written by a gathering of all the world's bishops (called an ecumenical, or worldwide, council, like Vatican Council II, which took place from 1962 to 1965); or by a representative group of the world's bishops who meet about a particular topic, like global justice or the role of the laity in the church (this is called a worldwide synod)
- a papal encyclical—that is, a letter from the pope to the worldwide church—or an official declaration from the pope

Doctrines and Dogmas

Official church teachings, expressed by the Magisterium, are called **doctrines.** Official Catholic teaching on Original Sin is an example of a doctrine. Although the fundamental truth of a given doctrine does not change over time, the church's understanding of the doctrine can always grow and develop.

Doctrines taught under the fullest solemnity and authority of the church are identified by a distinctive name—**dogmas.** Examples of dogmas are the Trinity (God is Father, Son, and Holy Spirit), the Incarnation (God became human in Jesus), and the Resurrection (Jesus was raised from the

6
If you were going to write a letter to the whole world about something you thought everyone needed to hear, what would you write about? State the topic you would choose, begin the letter "Dear Fellow Human Beings of the Earth," and write the first two sentences of your letter.

dead and lives in glory). Virtually all Christians believe in these dogmas. Two doctrines about Mary, held by Catholics and defined as dogma by papal declarations, were discussed earlier in this course: the Immaculate Conception (Mary was conceived free from Original Sin) and the Assumption (Mary was assumed body and soul into glory with God). All dogmas are doctrines and may be correctly referred to by either name; however, not all doctrines are dogmas.

Infallibility

An important doctrine related to the teaching voice of the Catholic church is **infallibility**. According to this Catholic doctrine, when the church makes a solemn definition on matters of faith and morals, the church is free from the possibility of error. Infallibility is not a human characteristic, like intelligence; rather, it is seen as a gift of the Holy Spirit that protects the church from error.

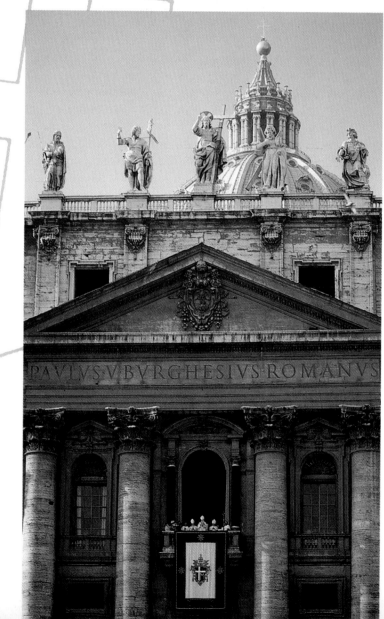

The pope greets the crowds in Saint Peter's Square, Vatican City, Rome.

Infallibility can be exercised in only two ways. When the pope defines a matter regarding faith or morals, and speaks as the head of the Catholic church with the clear purpose of uniting the church, he is empowered by the Holy Spirit to speak infallibly. Also, the world's bishops, as a group, can teach infallibly in communion with the pope under certain circumstances. In neither case are the human beings involved considered to be infallible; it is Christ's infallibility that is given to the church.

Dogmas that have been defined infallibly do not necessarily express the truth perfectly for all eras. After all, human statements like doctrines and dogmas are always subject to the limitations of the time period or culture in which they were framed. We can always grow in our understanding of the mysterious truth these statements seek to express. So throughout the life of the church, even infallibly pronounced statements can be refined and communicated in new ways so that the truth behind them can be more deeply grasped.

The teaching authority of the pope with the bishops is one important way that the church has been able to keep unity in the midst of diverse conditions, customs, and ways of thinking among Catholic people around the world. The young pilgrims who traveled to Denver for World Youth Day seemed to sense how powerful it is to belong to a church that is united in its faith yet diverse in its ways of expression. They seemed hungry for a clear vision and a firm purpose in their life, and eager to look to their world leader to unify them around that vision and purpose.

7
Describe in writing a situation in which you felt great unity in a gathering of friends, team members, schoolmates, youth group or parish members, or in a big public gathering. Explain why the gathering had a great spirit of unity, and describe what it felt like to be part of that unity.

For Review

- What is the meaning of church *Tradition?* How does it differ from *traditions* in the church?
- What is the Catholic understanding of a "Scriptures and Tradition" approach to knowing God's truth?
- What is the church's Magisterium? Why is it needed?
- Give three examples of ways that church teaching may be expressed by the Magisterium.
- What are doctrines? What are dogmas? Give three examples of dogmas from the text.
- What is meant by infallibility?

What All Christians Believe

The three major divisions of Christianity—Catholic, Protestant, and Orthodox—share essential beliefs that are at the core of their faith. Let's look at beliefs they generally hold in common before we consider some characteristics or gifts that the Tradition of Catholicism in particular has to offer.

The Apostles' Creed

A **creed** is a profession, or statement, of faith. The Latin word *credo* (meaning "I believe") is the source of the word *creed*. *Credo* is the combination of two other Latin words, meaning "heart" and "set," so the root meaning of *credo* is, "I set my heart on." Thus a creed is best understood as a statement of heartfelt, active belief that is more than just intellectual acceptance.

The **Apostles' Creed** is a very early statement of the Christian faith. It is based on a creed used in the second century, close to the era of the Apostles themselves. All Christians can claim faith in the beliefs expressed in the Apostles' Creed, although they may differ slightly in their interpretations of those beliefs.

This course has sought to introduce, or more deeply explain, the Catholic Christian faith to you. While reading the Apostles' Creed, take note of the chapters of this book that deal with the contents of the creed. (The chapter numbers and titles are given across from the section of the creed they pertain to. Chapter 7, on the Scriptures, pertains to the whole creed.) As you will notice, you have already been studying in this course much of what is contained in the Apostles' Creed, and other sections of the creed will be the focus of later chapters.

I believe in God, the Father almighty, creator of heaven and earth.	chapters 1, Identity and Development; 2, Faith; and 3, Judaism
I believe in Jesus Christ, his only Son, our Lord. He was conceived by the power of the Holy Spirit and born of the Virgin Mary.	chapter 4, Jesus
He suffered under Pontius Pilate, was crucified, died, and was buried. He descended into hell. On the third day he rose again.	chapter 5, Jesus and the Paschal Mystery
He ascended into heaven and is seated at the right hand of the Father. He will come again to judge the living and the dead.	chapter 6, The Church
I believe in the Holy Spirit, the holy catholic Church, the communion of saints,	chapters 6, The Church; and 8, Tradition
the forgiveness of sins,	chapter 9, The Sacraments
the resurrection of the body,	chapters 5, Jesus and the Paschal Mystery; 6, The Church; and 12, Christian Morality
and the life everlasting.	chapters 5, Jesus and the Paschal Mystery; and 12, Christian Morality
Amen.	

Notice that the Apostles' Creed follows a structure that highlights belief in the Trinity—in God as Father, Son, and Holy Spirit. The Nicene Creed, the creed recited at Mass on most Sundays, follows this same trinitarian structure, but with somewhat more complex language. Both of these creeds represent the essence of the Christian faith, which above all is a faith in the Trinity.

8
Choose one of the statements in the Apostles' Creed and write a list of questions you may have about it. Discuss these questions with your teacher, pastor, or youth minister. Write down the answers you arrive at.

The Trinity: Bringing Us into the Divine Life of Love

Every belief in the Christian faith goes back to the **Trinity.** Everything else in Christianity is related to this truth of who God is and how God relates to us.

The Father, Son, and Holy Spirit
The "simple" explanation of the Trinity is that there are **three divine Persons**—the Father, the Son, and the Holy Spirit—in **one God.** There is one divine nature, but three

Persons. This is simple to state, perhaps, but not so simple for us to understand.

The understanding of God as Trinity is rooted in the Christian Testament, where God is revealed as Father, Son, and Holy Spirit. God is one; there is only one God. But God is at the same time a loving union of Persons—the Father, the Son, and the Holy Spirit. This is puzzling, so do not be surprised if you feel confused. When theologians and church leaders formulated this understanding of God into the dogma of the Trinity back in the fourth century, they knew they were trying to put into words a reality that is beyond human beings' limited abilities of understanding and expression.

You may be wondering what the dogma of the Trinity has to do with us human beings and our lives. Let's consider how God relates to us as Trinity.

God Is Personal and Relational

The first lesson we learn for our own life from the doctrine of the Trinity is that God is **personal**, and being personal, God is also **relational**. The Persons of the Trinity are in loving relationship, or communion, with one another. But they are also in relationship with *us*. God is not alone—an abstract, isolated being floating out there somewhere. No, God reaches out to us, calling us to share in God's own life of love in the Trinity. As human beings, we have a built-in longing for God. We are made in God's image, and so we, like God, are yearning for loving relationships. Our salvation, our fulfillment and deepest joy, is to participate in the life of God's love.

The Trinity Saves

Salvation, the new life of grace lived in union with God, is brought about by the whole Trinity, not just one Person of the Trinity. For Catholics it is not enough to say, "Jesus saves," because it is believed that *God* saves, *through* Jesus, *in* the Holy Spirit. A more detailed explanation would be: God the Father, the source of all love, pours out that love into the Son, who became one with humanity as a human, Jesus Christ, and who died and rose from the dead for us. The love of the Father and the Son flows out to all through the power of the Holy Spirit. The Spirit—God present and active everywhere—transforms humanity and all creation and unites human beings with the Source of love so that they can live, now and forever, in God's life of love. This understanding of how the Trinity saves is evident in the way Catholics pray in their public worship—to "God the Father, through Jesus Christ his Son, in the Holy Spirit," or a similar formula.

Images of the Trinity

All this may seem quite abstract to you, so we will look at a couple of metaphors, or images, of the Trinity. These come to us from a theologian, Tertullian, who wrote during the second century, in the early years of the church.

Tertullian compared God as Father, Son, and Holy Spirit to a river. Every river has a source, which we can think of as God the Father, source of all goodness. The river flowing out from its source can be likened to Jesus Christ, the Son of God, who comes forth from the Father. The river irrigates the land and helps crops and other plants to grow, which is like the Holy Spirit acting in our life to change us, renew us, and bring forth good growth.

In another image of how the Father, Son, and Holy Spirit relate to us, Tertullian said it is like the sun in the heavens (the Father), the sunbeam coming to earth (Christ), and the point where the sun hits the earth and brings us warmth and light (the Spirit). Saint Augustine used a similar metaphor, relating the Trinity to a fire source (the Father), shining its rays (the Son) into the darkness, and making everything around it warm (the Holy Spirit).

All these images of the Trinity include a source (the Father), a way that source is communicated or given out (the Son), and a means by which the source brings forth good effects (the Holy Spirit). God is saving us every day, trying to bring us into loving communion with God, one another, and all creation. God saves us through the loving activity of the Trinity, reaching out to us, transforming us, and uniting us with our divine source.

9
Come up with another image of the Trinity besides the three given in the text. Draw a picture of it and explain the image in writing.

For Review

- Write the Apostles' Creed.
- Give the "simple" explanation of the Trinity.
- Describe the first lesson we learn from the doctrine of the Trinity.
- Offer one image or metaphor of the Trinity from the text and tell how it corresponds with the Father, the Son, and the Holy Spirit.

Baptism in a South African Village

South Africa is a new democracy. Until the early 1990s, under the minority white-ruled government, black South Africans had few rights and could not even vote. They were in a state of virtual slavery. After a long process of struggle and negotiation, finally blacks were freed and allowed to vote in a national election in 1994. The whole country elected Nelson Mandela as the first black president of *all* South Africa's people. For decades before that, the Catholic church had been playing a crucial role in educating blacks for eventual freedom, and it continues to do so today.

Catholics in a small village in the northern part of South Africa have built a church—a church building, yes, but even more important, a church community that is vibrant with faith and love.

A Franciscan sister from Minnesota, Ramona Miller, gives this account of that community and of the day she visited them for a grand celebration of baptisms:

Like most village churches in South Africa, this community does not have a resident priest. They are led by a layman, Benedict Moilia, who is their catechist, or teacher. During the week, he lives and works away from the village to support his family. On the weekends, he comes home and volunteers as the leader of the church community. A priest assigned to this parish and several others comes in to celebrate the sacraments with the community.

The people are enormously proud that they constructed the church themselves, which took two years. They feel that their pulling together around this project shows their strength as a community. While they were building the church, they decided to hold off on having baptisms until the church was completed. Then they could celebrate in grand style, baptizing over one hundred children and adults.

Excitement grew as they realized they could build not just a modest font for the baptismal water but a huge pool that people being baptized could get into and be totally soaked with water—full immersion, as it's called.

Now you need to know that this little village had been in the midst of a drought for six years. It is not yet desert there, but it is very dry and parched. Water is guarded with great care; it is not used lightly. It must be hauled in from a precious spring-fed water source at some distance from the village.

When I arrived for the baptismal liturgy, people were scurrying about getting ready. Many plastic containers of water had been hauled in by a pickup truck to fill the great baptismal pool. People were coming in from all around, some having walked long distances to get there.

The liturgy lasted four and a half hours. I was so hungry, but the people did not even seem to notice the time passing or their own hunger.

One by one, the many candidates for baptism came forward, the children held by their parents. Benedict, the catechist, helped each one into the pool, where he or she was plunged into the refreshing, cool water three times by the priest:

I baptize you in the name of the Father (plunge),
and of the Son (plunge),
and of the Holy Spirit (plunge).
Amen.

What a sense of the lavishness of God, providing all this precious water! Nothing was held back.

After the liturgy a buffet party that lasted into the night was given at Benedict's family's simple hut. Many friends had come early to prepare the home to be the center of hospitality for the community. A group of ten men dressed in colorful shirts entertained us for seven hours straight with their unbelievably beautiful singing. It was a celebration unlike any I have witnessed before.

"We are one body, one body in Christ, and we do not stand alone."

Special Gifts
of the Catholic Tradition

The faith that unites Christians of all varieties is far greater than that which separates them. The faith of the Apostles' Creed, with its belief in the Trinity, is central to all Christianity.

With their belief in the sacredness of Tradition, however, Catholics have special gifts or qualities to offer Christianity and the world. We will look at four of these dimensions of Catholic faith:

- *A sense of the sacramental.* A sense that God and the sacred are encountered in the ordinary things and events of everyday life
- *An emphasis on the communal.* A recognition that the church, as a community, is essential to individual salvation and the life of faith
- *A commitment to both faith and reason.* A reliance on both human intelligence and faith in God to understand what God intends
- *Love for the saints.* A relationship with those who have died who were especially close to God and now are models and helpers for those still living

These dimensions are evident not only in Catholicism. Certainly other Christian denominations and the Jewish religion as well have some or all of them in different degrees.

Baptism is a joyous celebration of God's gift of the waters of new life. Here the rite is being performed in a South African village.

Yet, these are particularly Catholic gifts, and taken together they help make up the special character of Catholicism.

A Sense of the Sacramental

In the Catholic vision of reality, all of the world is sacred because it is created by God and filled with the presence of God. God is not "out there" but "with us" in every aspect of our experience. We only have to open our eyes in a new way to see how God is present in our life and in the world around us. This awareness is a **sense of the sacramental**—a sense that God and the sacred are encountered in the ordinary things and events of everyday life.

Symbols and Symbolic Actions

God can be experienced in a meal, a refreshing drink of water, a hug from a friend, and an enduring marriage. Catholics try to recognize God as "visible" by finding ways to celebrate God's presence in the ordinary material world.

That is why Catholics have traditionally appreciated symbols such as holy water, incense, candles, Rosary beads, religious medals, statues of saints and angels, and beautifully decorated churches. Catholics find God's power present in certain symbolic actions, or rituals, called sacraments. For Catholics, these material things and visible actions symbolize spiritual realities, and they offer a "window" into the sacred.

The Seven Sacraments

In the official **seven sacraments** that Catholics celebrate, certain materials and actions from everyday life are used to symbolize and actually bring about God's saving grace in people's lives—breaking and sharing bread, pouring and sharing wine, anointing with oil, pouring water, placing hands on a person's head or shoulder, making a promise, and so on. The Eucharist, one of those sacraments, is at the center of Catholic life and worship.

Chapter 9 considers in more depth the sacramental sense and the seven sacraments of the Catholic church. Chapter 10 focuses on the Catholic sense that time itself is sacramental, as expressed in the church's liturgical year, which is its annual cycle of feasts and sacred seasons.

An Emphasis on the Communal

Catholics believe that God is working in the world through communities of people, not just through individuals.

10
Think back on your day or your week. Describe one visible thing or action you experienced that can communicate God's presence.

Because human beings are relational—made for relationships and community—God saves them through community, in particular the community of Jesus Christ called the church. So the church is extremely important in the faith life of Catholics.

People need the guidance and wisdom of this community that loves God and that loves them if they are to figure out what is right and true. And they need all the grace and support that the church can give them through the sacraments. This is one reason the Catholic church requires that where possible, its members participate in the Eucharist each weekend on Saturday evening or Sunday in order to stay connected with the community's life of faith and be nourished by it and also build it up.

11
Write how you would respond if a friend asked you this question: *Why can't I just relate to God one-to-one? Why is the church needed in my relationship with God?*

Signs of a Living Faith:

Students Advocate for the Homeless

Students at Cathedral High School in Saint Cloud, Minnesota, take a course in social justice as part of their religion requirements. In the course, they learn, among other things, about Catholic social teaching and its strong advocacy for poor people and those most vulnerable in society. The young people study society's tendency to shove those who seem unlike us—the "strangers"—to the margins of society, where they will not be "a bother" to people. They examine how this tendency might be evident in their own community.

The students' teacher, Kevin LaNave, gives this account of an action that some of the students took as a response to what they were learning in their social-justice course:

The student approached the podium at the City Council meeting. "My name is Kara," she began, "and I'm with a group of students concerned about this issue." Coordinators of a local emergency shelter, unable to house an expanding population of homeless families, were proposing a site for a new shelter; and neighbors to the site were raising objections. Kara read the letter the group had written. It spoke of their interactions with the shelter's residents ("we have learned they are people—just like us"), and how their desire to respond was rooted in their faith ("we want to do more than just talk about 'being good Christians'; we want to act on it").

Watching, I recalled Jesus standing up in His hometown synagogue to share His convictions about God's call to live justly. I have often seen Christ's prophetic spirit emerge in the actions of youth.

"We are one body, one body in Christ, and we do not stand alone."

Catholic social teaching affirms the need for justice among human beings.
Student art: "Homeless in America," linocut print by Amy Cooper, Saint Agnes Academy, Memphis, Tennessee

The **emphasis on the communal** in Catholicism means that there is a strong tendency to keep the faith of the church united, rather than allowing groups within the church to hold different beliefs. The pope and the bishops are servants of the whole Catholic church who are responsible for guarding and keeping the faith so that the community is united around its shared beliefs.

At times the pope and the bishops speak out on behalf of poor and oppressed people in the world, explaining how the Scriptures and Tradition can be applied to social issues of the time. Taken as a whole, these teachings that promote justice are called **Catholic social teaching.** The concern for justice in the world community is one more sign of Catholicism's emphasis on the communal. Chapter 12 looks at Catholic social teaching as an important theme of Catholic moral teaching.

A Commitment to Both Faith and Reason

In learning about God, the meaning of life, and how to live, should we trust our own intelligence, our power of reasoning? Or should we have faith, trusting that God will enlighten us as to what we need to know? The Catholic answer is that we need both faith and reason. In other words, we can use our own intelligence to look for evidence of God's existence in the world and in our own life, and to determine what is right and wrong. But we also need faith in Christ to know God fully and understand how God wants us to live.

One example of the **commitment to both faith and reason** can be found in the Catholic approach to the Scriptures. To understand what God is communicating to us in the Scriptures, we need to have faith that they are God's Word, God's message to us. But we also need to use intelligence to interpret the Scriptures. Scripture scholars use the tools of science and archeology, knowledge of history and ancient languages, and appreciation of the many forms of literature in which the authors of the Bible wrote. These tools enable scholars to figure out the intent behind what was written in a given passage. For Catholics, no contradiction exists between what can be known by intelligence and what can be known by faith. Faith sheds light on what our reason tells us, and reason helps us understand and articulate our faith more clearly.

The school you are attending is another example of Catholic respect for both faith and reason. Catholicism has put much emphasis on education. It has a long tradition of support for study (did you know that the first universities were part of the cathedrals of the Middle Ages?). Faith and reason are highly valued in your school and in the great Catholic high schools, colleges, and universities around the world. Some of the greatest intellectuals in history have been saints of the church, like Augustine, **Thomas Aquinas**, and **Teresa of Ávila**. In them we can see the union of reason and faith at its best.

Love for the Saints

In chapter 6 we met a number of saints from the Catholic church's history, and we discussed the Communion of Saints, the bond among all faithful Christians, both living and dead.

This focus on the saints and the Communion of Saints is characteristic of Catholicism. Sometimes it is misunderstood as an attempt to substitute the saints for God, giving honor and glory to human beings that should be given to God alone. At some points in history, Catholic devotion to the saints has been excessive, but when that happens, it usually gets corrected and becomes more balanced in time.

A healthy **love for the saints** is a beautiful and consoling part of Catholicism that does not at all threaten the love that is due to God. The devotion to saints is really just an aspect of two other dimensions of Catholicism already discussed—the sacramental sense and the communal sense. Saints are like sacraments of God; they were flesh-and-blood people who today are still pointing us to God through the example of their lives. They are full of God's love. We can honor them for that. And we can treat them like family, recognizing they are still part of the Body of Christ; they care about us and want to help us. The Letter to the Hebrews speaks of all those brave and faithful men and women who have gone before us in the faith: "We are surrounded by so great a cloud of witnesses" (12:1). For Catholics, who are so aware of the presence of the saints, the "great cloud of witnesses" can seem very near and very strengthening.

Mary, the Mother of God, deserves special honor. Many people around the world are devoted to Mary, as they are to their own mother. They relate to Mary as their protector and advocate. She is the focus of festivals, pilgrimages to shrines, special holy days, and processions. One of the most beloved prayers in Catholicism is the Rosary, the prayer in which the "Hail Mary" is repeated many times while a person meditates on mysteries of Jesus' and Mary's lives.

12
List examples of how both faith and reason are valued at your school.

Pilgrims to the Guadalupe Shrine

For over four centuries, millions of pilgrims have made their way to Tepeyac, a hill in Mexico City. They come to the site where, in 1531, the Blessed Virgin Mary is said to have appeared as an Aztec native woman to Juan Diego, a poor peasant, and to have spoken to him in an Aztec language.

In one of her appearances, the Virgin sent Juan Diego off with amazing winter-blooming roses wrapped up in his cloak. This was to be a sign to the disbelieving Spanish bishop that the Virgin Mary wished a temple to be built on that spot. When Juan Diego arrived to show the roses to the bishop, they tumbled out of his cloak. But there on the rough cloak was an even more miraculous sign—an image of Mary herself, the **Virgin of Guadalupe.**

The poor people of the Americas have interpreted this visit to a poor native by the Virgin of Guadalupe as a sign that God is with them, that the Reign of God is theirs.

In a great church shrine called a basilica, the miraculous image of the Virgin on Juan Diego's cloak is on display for all to see. In more than 450 years, this image and the rough cloth it is on have not deteriorated. At the site, pilgrims raise their voices in prayer—praising the Lord, asking for Mary's help in their lives, and thanking her for favors received. For the poor of the Americas,

the Virgin of Guadalupe is their mother, and the basilica is their home.

Some of the pilgrims' reasons for coming to the shrine were recorded in an issue of Maryknoll magazine:

Jesús Herrera, from Mexico City. I have brought my son Rodrigo to dedicate him to the Virgin of Guadalupe. We came to give thanks for the good health of my son and my wife, Candelaria, who had a long and difficult delivery. The Virgin Mary knows a lot about birth and babies.

Altagracia Bautista, from La Paz, Mexico. The doctor told me I had cancer, so I came on this long pilgrimage to conform myself to the will of God.

Hernán Pujupat Masonía, from Cuenca, Ecuador. As a Native American, I have always wanted to visit Guadalupe. Here you feel the solidarity of the Virgin with poor and marginated people.

José Cervantes Vásquez and his wife María de Lourdes García with their daughter Lucía, from Coahuila, Mexico. Here the Virgin Mary became one with us. In these difficult times it helps to remember that she is on our side. Knowing this helps us not to feel so alone.

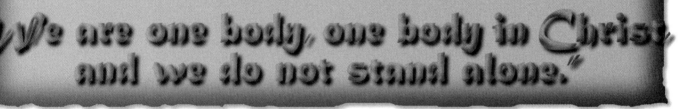

"We are one body, one body in Christ, and we do not stand alone."

13
Research the life of one saint who interests you. Write a report of that person's life, including questions you would want to ask that saint and things you most admire in him or her.

Catholics approach the saints as special friends who can be our heroes and role models, and they reach out to the saints for help in prayers called intercessions. Catholics are confident that the saints' love for God also reaches back to them through the ups and downs of life.

Sacramental, communal, committed to reason as well as faith, and devoted to the saints—these characteristics represent the special gift that Catholicism offers to all of Christianity and to the whole world.

For Review

- What is meant by a sense of the sacramental?
- What is meant by the church's emphasis on the communal? Name three ways that this emphasis is shown in Catholicism.
- Describe the Catholic understanding of how reason and faith are both needed to know God, the meaning of life, and how to live.
- Briefly explain why Catholicism includes devotion to the saints.

"We Do Not Stand Alone"

The Catholic faith is a great heritage handed on from generation to generation, lived out in new ways in every era. In that process, the faith is understood and expressed according to the needs and challenges of every age. Thus a body of wisdom, the church's Tradition, is built up and passed on.

The process of building up the Tradition of the church over centuries has not always been smooth. There have been great and noble moments; heroic leaders; and courageous, good, ordinary people living the faith from day to day. But sin has also entered into the process. The church's history has been marked by occasional violent disagreements, even wars, over theological issues. Human factors such as greed, lust for power, and pride have sometimes played a role in the process. At times, leaders of the church, even popes, have acted in shameful and unchristian ways. To say that the Spirit is with the church, protecting it from error, does not mean that the church's members are free from sin. And there have been, and continue to be, legitimate disagreements in the church over various issues. Even in the midst of disagreements, the Spirit is certainly at work in people's sincere attempts to resolve conflicts and arrive at the truth peacefully, with charity toward one another.

Despite the "messiness" of the process, Catholics believe that the Spirit of Jesus has been with the church all along. The Holy Spirit has been guiding the church in the path of truth through all the dangers along the way. The Spirit will never abandon the church. Through God's grace, the unity of faith has been and will be preserved until the end of time.

> "We are one body, one body in Christ,
> and we do not stand alone."

Pilgrims to the shrine of Our Lady of Guadalupe bring the deepest concerns of their lives to the care of the Virgin Mary.

14
Give an example from your experience of a disagreement that was resolved peacefully, and a disagreement that led to violence, hurt, or resentment. Compare what the people involved did or said in each case to lead to a peaceful or not peaceful result.

9

The Sacraments:

A Sacramental Faith

Catholicism includes a certain way of looking at the world that we have called, in chapter 8, a sense of the sacramental. This sense is an awareness that the world is full of God's presence. If only we have the eyes to see, we will find God revealed in the people, places, things, and events of everyday life. The Catholic emphasis on such things as holy water, oil, incense, candles, statues of saints, and so on, reflects this sacramental sense.

Catholics take the doctrine of the Incarnation very seriously—the belief that God became one of us, a human, in Jesus. Based on their belief in the Incarnation, Catholics understand that everything human, and all creation, can reveal God to us. The world is good, therefore, not only because God created it but also because God united with the world in Jesus. And God remains with the world through Jesus' Spirit, which is poured out among us for all time.

Grace: God's Love All Around Us

Grace—God's loving, active presence in the world—is all around us, among us, and within us. God constantly offers to touch our life, trying to reach us through the people, events, and material things we experience every day:

- a special, close conversation with a friend
- a teacher's caring about how we're doing in school
- a loss or failure that causes us to think hard about what is important in life

- a meal shared with people we love
- an incident of admitting we were wrong and asking for forgiveness
- a warm hug from a loved one
- the beauty of a crisp, sunny fall day
- the falling of rain that relieves a summer hot spell

If we are open to them, such experiences are "saving moments," moments of grace. In these moments God truly comes to us, through our very humanness, and helps us grow into the person we are meant to be. Moments of grace transform us, sometimes a little, sometimes a lot. And even if we are not consciously aware of God's presence in these moments, grace can still help us grow into fullness of life.

Symbols: Snapshots of Meaning

We have already mentioned some familiar symbols in Catholicism. Let's stop and consider what any symbol, not just a sacred symbol, actually is. Here is one definition: A symbol is a tangible (able to be perceived with the senses), physical reality that represents an invisible reality. A symbol is a "snapshot of meaning." For instance, a wedding ring represents the love and faithfulness involved in the marriage covenant. A flag stands for a country's identity and can be a sign of pride in one's country. A person like Adolf Hitler stands as a symbol of great evil for many people, whereas Mother Teresa of Calcutta symbolizes compassion and goodness. To some people the state of California means "land of opportunity," and Texas stands for "bigness."

Symbols are fascinating in that any one symbol can be interpreted with several different meanings. For instance, fire may represent warmth but also destruction; an ocean may represent mystery but also loneliness. Symbols reach us at different levels of our awareness. They may touch several emotions at once and charge our imagination. They may kindle in us great dreams or a sense of defeat, hope or fear, love or emptiness. Symbols can be rich, powerful ways of expressing meaning.

Rituals: Symbolic Actions

Rituals are concrete, visible actions that have symbolic meaning for a group or community. They are done in a similar way every time they are performed. Think, for instance, of a graduation ceremony with the customary speeches and

1
List three possible meanings for each of the following symbols: *fire, water, stone, bread, oil, wine, light.*

awarding of diplomas. Consider a birthday party with the singing of "Happy Birthday," the cutting of the cake, and the opening of presents. A school pep rally before a big game is also a ritual.

All these actions communicate meaning and have real power to affect us if we put our heart into them. However, because rituals are repeated actions, those who participate in them may be tempted to do them routinely and with inattention and boredom. They may just sit back and let "the performers" do the action, instead of entering into it wholeheartedly themselves. If this is so, the participants may not be open to the effects of the ritual. Think of a pep rally in which the cheerleaders do their cheers very well and the captain of the team gives an inspiring speech, but the audience members just yawn and look away, not caring about what is going on or the outcome of the game. The intended effect of the pep rally— to charge up everyone's spirit for the game—is lost.

In the Catholic faith, symbolic actions are drawn from experiences of everyday life. The rituals that make up the seven sacraments are full of such actions. For instance, the pouring of water over us suggests refreshment or cleansing. The rubbing of oil into our skin reminds us of being healed or strengthened. The lighting and holding of a candle suggests that truth and hope will overcome the darkness of ignorance and despair. The blessing of bread reminds all of us that spiritual nourishment is as important for us as physical nourishment.

The World Is Full of God's Present

SHH, be quiet.
Sit still, and you can hear God.
Look closely,
concentrate, and you can see.
You're trying too hard.
Open your mind,
let your eyes wander,
focus on the world around you.
Let the sounds pour freely into your ears.
Do you hear the song of that bird?
That is God singing.
Do you see the children laughing?
That is God laughing.
Do you smell the spring flowers?
That is God beckoning.
God is everywhere.
When you are in despair,
God is with you.
Look outside your window,
and God will appear.
Not as an apparition,
a demon,
or a light,
but in the song of the children
skipping rope,
and those playing ball in the park,
the homeless man begging for change
down on the corner,
and the person with AIDS
struggling in the face of death.
Abstract yet present,
God is not hard to see,
a light full of color,
magnificent hues.
From black to white,
God sees no boundaries.
God is in everything,
Everything is in God.

(Michael Elmer Bulleri,
Sacred Heart Cathedral Preparatory,
San Francisco, California)

2
Think of two rituals that happen in a group or community you belong to—one ritual where people typically have their heart in it, and one where they do not. Consider what effects each ritual has on people, and write up your reflections in a one-page essay entitled "When Your Heart Is in It, and When It's Not."

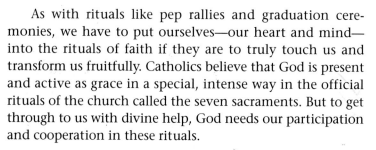

As with rituals like pep rallies and graduation ceremonies, we have to put ourselves—our heart and mind—into the rituals of faith if they are to truly touch us and transform us fruitfully. Catholics believe that God is present and active as grace in a special, intense way in the official rituals of the church called the seven sacraments. But to get through to us with divine help, God needs our participation and cooperation in these rituals.

For Review

- What is the understanding about humanness and creation that comes from the doctrine of the Incarnation?
- What is a saving moment?
- What is a symbol? Give two examples from the text of how a symbol can have different meanings.
- What is a ritual? Give two examples of ritual actions from the church's sacraments.

Being Jesus in the World: The San Miguel Center

BACK-OF-THE-YARDS, an old neighborhood in west Chicago, has always been poor, but today the needs of this now mostly Hispanic area are desperate. Poverty, drugs, gang warfare, and despair are facts of everyday life. Gunfire is common. Many young people are killed on the streets. Schools are overcrowded and unsafe; children are battered and neglected at home; and the high school dropout rate is very high—70 percent of Hispanic boys in the area drop out of school by their tenth-grade year. Young people have little to hope for.

Into the midst of this broken, hurting neighborhood, a small group of four persons—two Christian Brothers and a married couple—have come together out of heartfelt concern for the area's young people. With only five hundred dollars among them, they decided to move into a house together and begin the San Miguel Center as a healing, hopeful presence in the community. Sustained by donations, they opened a small school, serving sixth graders. It is practically tuition-free, with parents paying what they can (the highest is two hundred dollars a year). The plan is to add a grade to the school each year, up to eighth or ninth grade, and then graduate the kids to Catholic high schools on scholarship.

Besides the school, with the help of many volunteers the San Miguel Center provides after-school, evening, and summer programs for young people; collects and gives away food and clothing; educates adults about the needs of youth; and intervenes in gang problems. The center tries to offer young people alternatives to the life of gangs and drugs that is constantly held out to them.

Brother Ed Siderewicz, the principal of the school, talks about the work with gangs:

> Our house sits on the dividing line between several gangs' turfs, so we're right in the middle of things. Gene, [the married man] who is in his forties, has a passion to help kids in gangs; he's got a special calling to gang work. He's a former gang member himself and was into cocaine. One day he hit bottom and had nowhere to turn but to God. His life has never been the same since. Because of his background and his conversion, the kids have great respect for him. And he is out there on the streets at midnight, one, two in the morning, getting involved when there are problems.

> We give our lives to these kids; we spend our lives with them. You could say that we're trying to *be* the presence of Jesus to them. But we also *find* Jesus in these kids. They are amazing.

Some students from Catholic high schools stayed at San Miguel Center for a weekend to experience and help with the work being done there. One high school student reflected on the weekend's value:

> The San Miguel students really showed me "Spirit." And four [teenage] guys came down and talked about their environment. This was very important because it shows me that kids in these bad neighborhoods still can have faith and believe.

The San Miguel Center makes Jesus visible and touchable in the world today. If Jesus were walking the earth now, he would very likely be spending his time in just such a place. 🔲

Moments of grace in everyday life are celebrated in the seven sacraments.
Student art: "Transformation," watercolor painting by T. J. Meeks, Holy Cross High School, Louisville, Kentucky

3
Write an imaginary letter of advice to someone who tells you he or she wants to find Jesus in the world but cannot. Give suggestions to the person about where to look for Jesus.

The Sacraments: Celebrations of the Paschal Mystery

Before we consider the seven sacraments, let's look at how Jesus and the church can be understood as sacraments.

Jesus and the Church as Sacraments

Jesus is the means by which God has communicated everything God is to us humans in a concrete, tangible way. Through his life and death, Jesus gave himself in sacrificial love for the world. Then God raised him from the dead, showing that life and love and goodness, not death, triumph in the end. In his life of love poured out for all people, Jesus showed humanity what God is like and how God wants us to be. In that sense, we can say that Jesus is the fundamental sacrament of God.

Today Jesus is not walking around on the earth in physical form, as the flesh-and-blood man from Nazareth. He has returned to his Father, and he has sent his Spirit to be with us in the world until the end of time. Now Jesus is present in the world through the Holy Spirit. As we have seen, Catholic belief is that the Spirit dwells with us in the church, sustaining us, making us holy, and enabling us to *be* Jesus in the world. This is what it means to say that the members of the church are the Body of Christ and the Temple of the Holy Spirit.

As a worldwide community of believers, the church is meant to be Jesus Christ "walking around in the flesh." The church's members embody Jesus' sacrificial love by announcing God's love for all, welcoming the lost and forsaken, feeding the hungry in body and soul, forgiving the sinner, healing the sick and brokenhearted, teaching and preaching, challenging the powerful, and uniting people in love. In this way the church is the continuation of Jesus on earth. Its members are not perfect at showing Christ to the world, but with the Spirit's help, they continually strive to be Jesus for others.

If Jesus is the sacrament of God, then the church is the sacrament of Jesus. The church is the way that people can see and touch and experience Jesus concretely in the world today. For members of the church, being Jesus as a community is an awesome responsibility.

The Seven Sacraments

You may be wondering how the seven sacraments of the Catholic church fit in. First, let's identify them:

The Sacraments of Initiation	The Sacraments of Healing	The Sacraments in Service of Communion
• Baptism • Confirmation • Eucharist	• Penance (or Reconciliation) • Anointing of the Sick	• Holy Orders • Marriage

Baptism, Confirmation, and the Eucharist are called **sacraments of initiation** because they bring Catholic Christians into the life of Christ. Penance and the Anointing of the Sick are called **sacraments of healing** because they bring healing, comfort, and strength when people need forgiveness or when they are ill. Holy Orders and Marriage are called **sacraments in service of communion** because they bring people into particular ministries in the church, as ordained clergy or as married people.

The seven sacraments are powerful ways the church carries on the life of Christ in the world. They are communal rituals that celebrate the saving moments of grace that occur for people in everyday life. Jesus' living, dying, and rising—the Paschal Mystery—is celebrated in the lives of believers. The sacraments are special, intense moments when God's grace, the loving life of the Trinity, is particularly focused and given to people, bearing fruit in them if they are open to it. For Catholics, the seven sacraments not only signify the saving change going on in the believer but also help to bring about the change they celebrate.

For Review

- What does it mean to say that Jesus is the fundamental sacrament of God?
- What does it mean to say that the church is the sacrament of Jesus?
- Define a sacrament. List the seven sacraments according to the categories given in the text.

The Sacraments of Initiation: Baptism, Confirmation, and the Eucharist

In the sections that follow, we will consider the sacraments in their respective categories of initiation, healing, and service of communion. Rather than simply describe the ritual of each sacrament, the text tries to show the meaning that is "underneath" the sacrament, by way of a story of a saving moment from the life of a young person. Read the story as a kind of parable of what happens to a person in that sacrament. Each story will lead into a brief description of what the sacrament is and what it does for those who enter into it with an open spirit.

Baptism: Celebrating the Grace of New Life and Welcome into Community

Six months at Gibbons High, and Suzanne's whole life seemed changed. Getting into a totally different circle of kids in another part of town had made all the difference.

Suzanne remembered her first day at the new school. She'd been especially nervous because it seemed like so much was at stake in changing schools—like her whole future. What if it didn't work out? What if people made snide comments about her coming from Central High—or worse yet, just ignored her? She'd been so worried about whether she would fit in.

Suzanne recalled that within fifteen minutes of setting foot in Gibbons, she had met seven kids who were really friendly. A girl named Annette had been assigned to take her around to classes and introduce her to everybody. That worked out great because Suzanne didn't have to think up things to talk about; it all came easily with Annette's help. Within a few weeks, Annette was one of her best friends.

The stakes were high in changing schools because Suzanne had gotten into some bad patterns back at Central. The kids she hung around with there were into trouble—doing drugs, drinking, shoplifting, and lying to their parents about everything they did. Suzanne had picked up those behaviors, too. School, activities, and her relationship with her parents had gone rapidly downhill.

One day Suzanne was caught shoplifting clothes at a mall; she was taken off by the police in a squad car, which really scared her. Later she had to go to court and got put on probation. It was a shock to her, kind of a wake-up call that things were going in the wrong direction. It was a signal to her mom and dad, too, that Suzanne needed help to change. She and her parents struggled over how to turn things around. Finally, together they decided that Suzanne needed a fresh start with new friends who would not drag her down. A new school looked like the best answer, though it wouldn't be easy for Suzanne to make such a huge change.

Now, with six months of life in the new school behind her, Suzanne was feeling great relief. Her new friends weren't perfect, but they were headed in the right direction. She liked them. She had turned away from the trouble she'd been in, she was doing well in school, and she had a part in the school play. She felt like she really belonged at Gibbons. She was really coming into her own.

Suzanne wanted to leave behind an old life that was hurting her. But to do that she needed to be welcomed into a community that would give her a chance at a new life. She needed the support not only of her parents but also of new friends who would help her discover joy and inner freedom. Fortunately she found that at Gibbons.

The Sacrament

The story of Suzanne gives us some idea of the meaning underlying the sacrament of Baptism. **Baptism** is about being welcomed into a new life in the community of Jesus Christ. The sacrament celebrates leaving behind an old life of being a slave to sin and embracing the freedom and responsibility of

Water is the main symbol of the sacrament of Baptism.
Student art: **Untitled, color photo by Michael Caudill, Saint Xavier High School, Louisville, Kentucky**

4
Have you ever experienced a sense of new life—new hopes and possibilities that could come about only if you left something else behind? If you have had such an experience, write about it. If you have not, write about the feelings you might have if faced by such an experience.

life in the community of Christ, the church. It is "dying" to an old self so as to be raised up to a new self—somewhat like Suzanne's experience.

You are probably most familiar with Baptism for babies. But in the early centuries of the church, Baptism was mostly for adults. These adults were usually Gentiles, and by being baptized they were changing their lives in a difficult and dangerous way. They were rejecting the Roman state religion, in which political leaders were given godlike status, to follow Jesus the Christ, one who had been put to death by the Romans as a criminal and whose followers were convinced he was the Son of God. The Gentile converts joined a community of loving, joyful Christians who were even willing to be martyred for their faith.

Today when babies are baptized, their parents want to bring them into the community of Jesus Christ, and they profess their own faith on the child's behalf. Godparents, chosen by the parents, participate in the Rite of Baptism and are responsible for supporting the parents in helping the young Christian "grow into" Christian life. The entire community, too, welcomes the child and pledges to support the parents and child as they grow in the life of Christ.

The sacrament ritualizes coming into this new life by entering the waters of Baptism. The priest (or, in case of necessity, a baptized layperson) pours the water on the person being baptized three times, or the person goes down into the water three times, "in the name of the Father, and of the Son, and of the Holy Spirit." The water symbolizes and brings about the cleansing and purifying action of the Holy Spirit in the person. It also recalls how God saved the Israelites in the waters of the sea by bringing them out of slavery in Egypt to freedom on the other side of the sea—just as God is saving us today. The words of Saint Paul give a description of an important meaning of the baptismal water: In Baptism, Christians become "dead to sin and alive to God in Christ Jesus" (Romans 6:11).

Other symbolic actions—anointing with oil, lighting a candle, and wearing a new white garment—also convey meaning in the ritual. But the water rite is essential.

Adults who want to be baptized prepare and come into the community in a step-by-step process that can last a year or two. Through this process, called the **Rite of Christian Initiation of Adults (RCIA)**, candidates for Baptism, called catechumens, are accompanied by a godparent (or sponsor) as they learn about the Catholic faith. The climax of the process takes place in a beautiful ceremony at the Easter Vigil, where candidates for Baptism celebrate all three sacraments of initiation in one great community ritual—Baptism, Confirmation, and the Eucharist. Then they are full members of the church, welcomed into the new life of Christ and the Christian community. (If a candidate has been baptized previously in another Christian denomination, that Baptism is recognized by the Catholic church. Such a candidate is not baptized a second time, but is still welcomed with a ritual celebrating full membership in the Catholic church through being confirmed and sharing in the Eucharist for the first time.)

If you are baptized, then every time you participate in someone else's Baptism, you have a chance to recall the new life given in your own baptism, with the freedom and responsibility to be Christ in the world.

Confirmation:
Celebrating the Grace of the Spirit's Gifts

Every day after school, Luke went to an apartment in his building to look after nine-year-old D. J., whose parents would come home after five o'clock. It was an okay way

to make some spending money, and, he had to admit, it could even be fun. Luke got a kick out of showing D. J. the neat games and tricks he had played at that age, teaching him sports, and easily sending him into gales of laughter. And D. J. idolized Luke. It felt good to Luke to be a "big brother" to someone.

The fun came to a halt one day, though, when D. J.'s parents decided to separate. Luke found out about it from D. J., who was grimly kicking up grass in front of the apartment building when Luke arrived after school. "My stupid parents—they hate each other! My Dad's moving out tonight."

Luke murmured, "Wow, that's tough. I'm sorry." But the little boy just kept kicking up grass and scowling. Luke's attempts to be funny and suggestion of playing a game of Uno or hitting some balls fell flat. D. J. was not interested, period.

Several afternoons went by like this. D. J. just wanted to be by himself in his room or glare at some TV show with a stony, cold look on his face. No more brotherly fun. Heavy gloom hung over everything.

One night when Luke was home, stretched out on his bed listening to music, he thought about D. J. and how powerless he felt to do anything for this kid. Almost without being aware of it, he sighed a little prayer: "God, I don't know what to do. Just help me out with D. J., okay?"

The next afternoon, D. J. was waiting for Luke with his now familiar cold stare. This time, though, instead of suggesting fun things that D. J. would turn down, Luke said: "You know, D. J., you look like you've got so much going on inside you. I know if I were you right now, I'd be feeling lots of awful stuff." D. J. softened his hard expression a bit, giving Luke an opening to ask, "You want to talk about it?"

With that, D. J. burst into tears. Luke put his arm around him, and the little boy sobbed. For half an hour, D. J. poured out his heart, which was full of anger at his parents, fear for the future, self-blame (did his parents break up because of *him?*), and loss. He felt like he had lost his family, his dad, everything that made life okay.

Luke was surprised at how calm he felt during all this. He sensed deep down that this was what D. J. needed to do with his "big brother." After that flood of feelings, D. J. seemed relieved; the weight on him suddenly felt lighter. Luke took the opportunity to offer with a grin, "How 'bout hitting a few balls out back?"

This time D. J. perked up, "Yeah, I'll race ya down the stairs!" Luke realized that things would continue to be hard for D. J. But at least D. J. had started to get those bottled-up feelings out. That was a step in the right direction.

Luke remembered his prayer of the night before, thinking to himself, "Hey, I guess God helped me know what to do. Pretty amazing."

The Sacrament

The sacrament of **Confirmation** recognizes that once we have entered the new life of Baptism, our attempt to be Christ in the world has just begun. We need constant grace from God, through the power of the Holy Spirit, to be true to our new life of faith. So in Confirmation, we are "sealed in the Spirit," reminded that the Spirit given to us in Baptism is always with us to inspire us, lead us, and give us strength. We experience a new openness to how the Holy Spirit is acting in our life.

The **Gifts of the Holy Spirit**, given in Baptism, are the ways the Spirit acts within us. Confirmation makes us more ready to respond to those gifts, which are **wisdom**, **courage**, **understanding**, **right judgment**, **knowledge**, **reverence**, and **wonder and awe in God's presence.** Which of the seven Gifts of the Holy Spirit do you think Luke was responding to in the story?

In the early centuries of the church, Confirmation was part of the baptismal ceremonies, just as it is in the RCIA today. This was because most people were baptized into the new faith of Christianity as adults. Today most Catholics are baptized as infants. So Confirmation is usually celebrated later, when a young person can understand the power of the Holy Spirit and be more aware of and responsive to the Spirit's activity in her or his life.

Young people being confirmed go through a significant period of preparation so that they will understand what this full life in the Christian community means for them. The bishop usually presides at the Confirmation ritual for young people. The essential rite of the sacrament is the bishop's anointing of the candidate's forehead with sacred oil (a symbol of strengthening, cleansing, healing, and joy) while saying the words, "Be sealed with the Gift of the Holy Spirit."

5
Of the seven Gifts of the Holy Spirit, which ones seem most needed today by people your age? Beside each one you choose, write an example of a situation in which a teenager might need that gift.

Eucharist: Celebrating the Grace of Giving Ourselves

Thirteen years on the move with Mom. Tina, now seventeen years old, was weary of it all. Would she ever have friends, a school to go to, or a place to call home? It was hard spending your life in shelters, every once in a while getting into a city you think might be the answer—only to have it all fall apart for Mom in a few months, and then hitting the road again.

Now here they were in another shelter in a small midwestern city. This was different from a lot of the other shelters, though. This one was more like a home, with people living there who cared about you and called you their "guest." That sounded funny, but they said it was all part of being a Catholic Worker house.

Mom was so happy in this place that she started singing again. Pretty soon she was in the kitchen, bustling around helping out like she loved to do. Because everyone was like family in this house, people could pitch in however they wanted to. The day that Mom started baking, Tina knew things were looking up. Soon Mom's fabulous cinnamon rolls were coming out of the oven every morning, followed later by fragrant loaves of bread, and then several kinds of pies. Everyone at the house dove into the baked goodies, and when people came to visit the house, Mom would send them off smiling with a bag of cinnamon rolls. One frigid, windy, snowy night when she had to take a taxi, Mom brought a warm cinnamon roll out for the cab driver, to cheer him in such miserable weather. He was astonished.

Tina herself caught the spirit of Mom's generosity, and she began painting a mural of colorful cartoon characters on the walls of the basement, where the children who were guests would play with the house toys.

It was quite remarkable—the change in the mother and the daughter who had come to the shelter in fear and despair. Mom and Tina felt a sense of joyful hope they had not had for a long time.

Tina and her mother shared a broken, poor life. Yet they had gifts to offer. Mom had her love of baking and her great skills in the kitchen. Tina had artistic talent and a spirit of fun with children. They found a community where they could share their gifts with others, including those who were homeless like themselves. God's grace was at work in this saving moment of their stay at the Catholic Worker house, transforming Tina's and her mother's offerings into life for themselves and all those around them.

The Sacrament

The **Eucharist** is the central saving act for Catholics, the core of the church's life in Christ. To participate in it is to be fully initiated into the community of Jesus. In the Eucharist, simple gifts of bread and wine, "which earth has given . . . fruit of the vine and work of human hands," are offered to God by the priest on behalf of the people. Then those gifts are transformed by God into nourishment for the people's spirit—Jesus himself, his body and blood given back to them and shared as food and drink for the journey of life.

The **Mass,** another name for the Eucharist, recalls Jesus' sacrificial gift of himself to all humankind by dying on the cross so long ago. The sacrificial Mass also makes the power of Jesus' dying and rising present to us today. It brings Jesus' death and Resurrection right into our midst and enables us to live out this Paschal Mystery in our own life—as Tina and her mother were living it in their gifts of themselves and their talents to those at the Catholic Worker house. The

Mass celebrates all those saving moments of giving ourselves and receiving nourishment from God in the sharing of what we have.

In a full course on the sacraments, the ritual of the Eucharist would be covered in detail. Here it is enough to say that it has two essential parts: the **Liturgy of the Word** and the **Liturgy of the Eucharist.** In the Liturgy of the Word, the Scriptures are proclaimed and reflected on as spiritual nourishment. In the Liturgy of the Eucharist, with a priest as presider, the bread and wine are offered to God. Then they are transformed into the body and blood of Jesus Christ by the power of the Holy Spirit, and shared by the people as food for their life's journey. In sharing Jesus' body and blood, the people are meant to *become* Jesus—becoming hope, life, and joy for the world. Not only are the gifts of bread and wine changed in the Eucharist; those who participate are changed as well.

6

Think of an incident when, in giving something of yourself to others, you changed or grew yourself. Describe in writing what you gave and how it transformed you.

For Review

1. What does Baptism celebrate? What ritual action and words symbolize what happens to a person in Baptism?
2. When infants are baptized, who professes faith for them?
3. What is the Rite of Christian Initiation of Adults?
4. What is the meaning of Confirmation? What happens for individuals in this sacrament?
5. What is the essential rite of the sacrament of Confirmation?
6. What is the central saving act for Catholics?
7. What does the Mass, or Eucharist, recall and make present today?
8. What are the two essential parts of the Eucharist? What happens in each part?

The Sacraments of Healing: Penance and Anointing of the Sick

Penance: Celebrating the Grace of Reconciling

Tomás was bored and wanted to get out of the house. It bugged him that Greg said he would rather stay home and watch television than go to the mall with Tomás. Over the phone, Tomás let Greg know how disgusted he was with him: "If you'd get off your can once in a while, maybe you'd have some friends. I'm not gonna waste my time on you."

The next day at school, when Tomás saw Greg, Greg's face turned red, and he looked the other way. Tomás remembered the cutting remark he had made to Greg, and he felt bad about it. He wished things could be made right with Greg again. He wondered why he had said it. Maybe, Tomás reflected, it was because he was so disgusted with *himself* for being so bored all the time.

Tomás pulled his courage together, caught up with Greg down the hall, looked him in the eye, and said: "Hey, Greg. That was a dumb thing I said yesterday. I wish I hadn't said it. You think you can forgive me?"

Greg broke into a broad grin. "Yeah, if you can put up with me, I can put up with you." They went off together talking nonstop about the game the day before on television.

We need to ask forgiveness not only for the sake of the one we have hurt but also for ourselves, for we are hurt by our own sin.
Student art: Untitled, linocut print by Eleanor White, Saint Agnes Academy, Memphis, Tennessee

When we hurt someone, we need to acknowledge what we have done. It is not enough simply to let it go by and pretend it will all be forgotten. The wound of sin is real, and we need to ask forgiveness so as to heal the wound and be reconciled (brought back together) with that person. We also need to do so for ourselves, for we are hurt by our own sin. Tomás found that out in a saving moment of asking and receiving forgiveness. In doing that, Tomás, Greg, and the relationship between them were healed.

The Sacrament

The sacrament of **Penance** is also called the sacrament of **Reconciliation**, because its purpose is to bring people back to God and one another through forgiveness. In the sacrament, all the moments of forgiveness and reconciliation that happen in everyday life—like Tomás reconciling with Greg—are brought together and celebrated.

The ritual includes the confession of one's sins to a priest, the expression of one's sorrow for sin and intention to turn the behavior around, and the words of forgiveness (absolution) given by the priest. In this action the person is reconciled to God, to himself or herself, and to the whole community.

When we sin, we hurt not just ourselves or another person, we harm the whole community. So we need to be reconciled with God and the whole community. That is why Catholics confess their sins to a priest in the sacrament. When the priest raises a hand in blessing over the person or lays a hand on the person's shoulder and says the words of forgiveness, he offers that forgiveness on behalf of God and the whole Christian community. In addition, the priest usually gives some words of encouragement and spiritual advice, and suggests that the person do some action as a penance—like do certain good deeds or offer prayers —that will help the person grow in her or his life's journey.

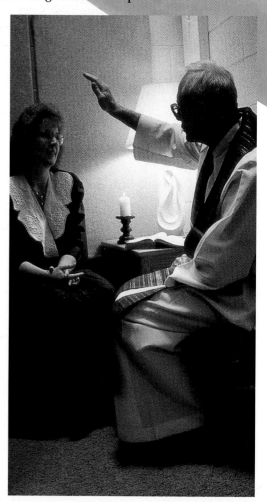

The sacrament of Penance is often celebrated nowadays as a community, in a Penance service. This highlights the reality that our sin is not just a private thing between us and God; it involves the whole community. Confession to a priest is done privately by each person, with the words of forgiveness being given individually, but other parts of the rite, such as hearing the Word of God, praying, and singing thanks to God are done as a community.

7
Does a relationship in your life need healing and reconciliation—for example, a relationship with a family member, friend, or teacher? If so, write a letter (not to send, but just to get you thinking) in which you attempt some honest communication about what has come between the two of you. Then pray for God's help for both of you.

Anointing of the Sick: Celebrating the Grace of Healing Life's Hurts

Another D on a Friday quiz gave Emmy a numb feeling. Her social studies tests were getting worse. "What a way to end the week," she thought, as she jammed the paper into her bag.

As a child, Emmy had struggled with a learning disability. She often could not recognize words or even individual letters. By fifth grade, Emmy still could not read—even though she could understand things read to her very well. Beginning that year, her visual problem cleared enough for Emmy to become an avid though slow reader. But by high school she was still a marginal student, taking twice as much time on homework and tests as her classmates. And spelling was still a mystery to her.

Ms. Totino, the social studies teacher, asked to see Emmy after Friday's class. "Why bother?" thought Emmy. She saw her education ending next year, after she graduated from high school. What lay beyond that scared her. She had friends who started working at a local fast-food joint after they graduated. Low pay, high stress, odd hours. She hung out with them because around them she didn't feel inferior, like she did with her college-bound friends—ex-friends, more likely, she thought. Emmy's best friend from grade school, Donna, seemed to be bailing out on her lately.

Emmy went to the meeting after all. Ms. Totino commented on the test briefly and then asked Emmy what she liked to do outside of school. Emmy sensed genuine interest and was soon talking excitedly about the books she loved and, more shyly, even about the journal she had kept for years. "I'd love to read it sometime," said Ms. Totino. "Yeah, you'd enjoy my creative spellings," Emmy chuckled. It felt good to be able to laugh about it.

Emmy began stopping by after class for chats. Ms. Totino talked with her like an adult, sharing her own good humor and interests, like travel to Italian cities and museums. She once told Emmy that she herself had not been a great student in school. In college she used to say that a C stood for "Celebrate!"

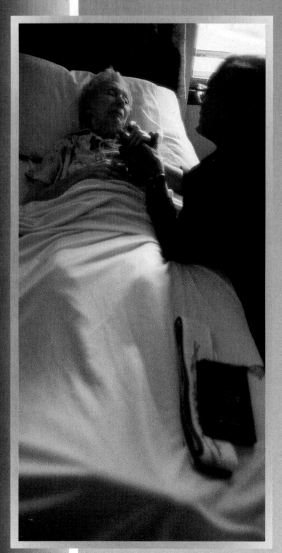

Emmy's tests never improved beyond low C's, but she began to feel better about herself. Her spirits rose, and she surprised herself by getting curious about local two-year colleges and vocational training. Ms. Totino visited Emmy's parents and talked encouragingly about Emmy's opportunities. Emmy realized too that her parents' confidence in her was solid. Best yet, Donna asked Emmy why *she* had been dropping their friendship!

At the end of the semester, Emmy sent Ms. Totino a card thanking her for "the best yeer I've had in school."

Sometimes life deals us a blow that leaves us wounded and shaky. The suffering happens not because we have done anything wrong, but simply because life inevitably brings such hurts—an illness, whether physical or psychological; an accident; a disability; or just a gradually weakened state that comes with getting older. In Emmy's situation, her learning disability affected more than her school performance. Her self-esteem and sense of hope were damaged.

When Ms. Totino took a genuine interest in Emmy, the hurt in Emmy gradually healed. She grew stronger, more confident, and more trusting about the future. She reunited with her good friend. Through the saving moment of Ms. Totino's concern, Emmy was being healed.

The Sacrament

The sacrament of the **Anointing of the Sick** is about healing the hurts of life, especially when the hurts involve physical or mental illness, an injury, or a condition that makes a person weak and vulnerable to more hurt or even death. Emmy's situation and the help given to her by her teacher are a kind of parable to show us what the sacrament basically is all about—receiving the love of God as a healing touch from our community when we are laid low by the hurts of life.

The main symbolic actions of the sacrament are the laying on of hands and anointing with oil by the priest, along with the prayers that ask for God's healing. These actions, done on behalf of the whole community, convey God's care, strengthening power, and healing. In some cases physical healing may actually take place after the sacrament. But whether or not a physical recovery happens, the sacrament brings about healing of a person's spirit at a time when that is needed as much as a physical cure.

Anyone who is seriously ill (either physically or emotionally), injured, or suffering from the increasing frailty of old age can celebrate this sacrament. It is especially important to have the wider community there to pray with those

8
Think of a time you needed the support and love of relatives or friends because you were feeling wounded and shaky. Were you able to get that support, and if so, how did it come to you?

who are suffering. When a person is near death, special prayers of comfort and of entrusting the dying person to God are included, and the person receives the Eucharist for the last time as a kind of "food for the journey" back to God.

For Review

1. What is the purpose of the sacrament of Penance, and what does it celebrate?
2. What does the ritual of Penance include?
3. Why do Catholics confess their sins to a priest instead of asking forgiveness from God privately?
4. What is the sacrament of the Anointing of the Sick concerned with?
5. What are the ritual actions of Anointing, and what do they convey?
6. Who can receive Anointing of the Sick?

The Sacraments in Service of Communion: Holy Orders and Marriage

Holy Orders: Celebrating the Grace of Leading as a Servant

Jim's job as class president was to get everyone moving on the ninth-grade class project. By March they had raised four thousand dollars, enough to give them a fabulous overnight trip to a huge theme park, with time still left to raise more money and plan the trip.

Some new students came into the school in April, kids from the migrant farmworkers' camp just outside of town. Every year in the planting and growing season, they came with their families to work for a big agricultural business, then left to go somewhere else for a few months. The students were shy and had a hard time with English—most were Mexican American—and they didn't do well in class, probably because they were always moving around from school to school. Most of Jim's classmates just let them be. The new kids preferred to keep to themselves, right?

However, Jim made friends with one of the girls, Rosaria, and before long he was visiting her family's small, box-like quarters at the camp. There Jim saw poverty like he had never seen it before. He also discovered that Rosaria's little brother and sister, like the other children in the camp, had no toys at all, nothing to play with. Some of the little ones went out to the fields with their parents. They had breathing problems from all the poisonous chemicals being used on the soil and the crops. Jim was really bothered about this.

With Rosaria's help, Jim began to dream of something wonderful. But first he would have to take it to the class to get their reaction. What would they think about taking the money they had raised that year and putting it into something great that would last? He presented his idea of a playground with sturdy, fun equipment for the farmworkers' children, constructed at the camp but a good distance from the fields.

Some students balked at this: What about their big trip? Didn't they deserve to have it? But gradually, through Jim's enthusiasm, the idea caught on. Everyone was charged up about the playground project. Guided by a couple of the students' parents and some farmworkers who knew construction, the students built the large playground—castle, maze, climbing tower and slide, elevated walkways, swings, and more—all of sturdy wood. Jim worked hardest of all.

To celebrate the completion of the playground, the students, their parents who had helped, and the camp residents shared a scrumptious Mexican feast outdoors in view of the playground. Guitar music and song filled the twilight sky as children scrambled with delight over the new equipment.

Jim realized that whenever these children would come back in future years to this camp, they would always have this playground to look forward to. They would always feel welcome in this town. Somehow the migrant worker families would never seem like outsiders again.

Through his concern about the children at the migrant farmworkers' camp, Jim sensed a calling to bring about something wonderful—a project that would bring joy to children whose lives were quite bleak. As a natural leader, Jim moved people's hearts and got them excited about the dream. And when the time came for the actual construction, he was right in there working hard alongside everyone else. He was a leader who knew how to serve, and that is the kind of leader Jesus was. The whole effort for Jim was truly a graced saving moment.

The Sacrament

The sacrament of **Holy Orders** celebrates a particular ministry, or service, in the church—the calling, or vocation, of those who are entrusted with official leadership in the church as deacons, priests, and bishops. Because the sacraments are so central to Catholicism, these ordained leaders have a crucial role in presiding at the church's sacraments.

As with Jim, ordained members of the church are called not only to lead but to serve. They hold out the dream of the Reign of God to people and attempt to get them to see its possibilities. They try to move people to bring about that dream, encouraging everyone to share their gifts and talents. Ordained persons must be community builders who take special care to ensure that outsiders are welcomed in, not left on the margins. And they have to know how to lead others in celebrating. This is the special, challenging work of those called by God and chosen by the church to be ordained deacons, priests, and bishops.

In the sacrament of Holy Orders, the rites for ordination of a priest include the laying on of hands by the bishop,

9
From your own experience, from the news, or from history, give an example of someone who has been able to lead as a servant. Be specific in writing about the behaviors that showed this person's qualities of leadership and service.

who conveys his authority from the Apostles themselves. Anointing the candidate's hands with oil is also part of the ritual, for the priest will be using his hands in many sacramental ways in his ministry—laying hands on others; using his hands to anoint others with oil; and blessing, breaking, and sharing the bread and wine of the Eucharist.

Priests of a diocese are united with their bishop as co-workers who share responsibility with him for the church of that area.

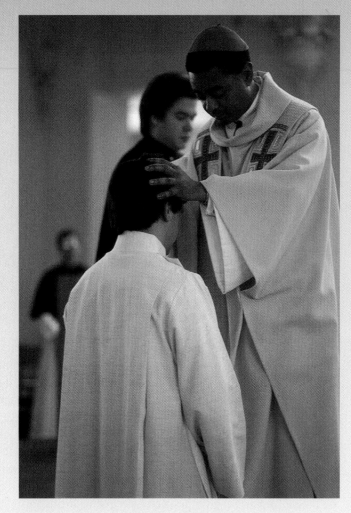

Marriage: Celebrating the Grace of a Faithful Bond

Natanya and Renée had been through a lot together. In the same school since kindergarten, they had become best friends in about third grade. From playing dolls together as little kids, to being Girl Scouts, camping together, sleeping over, and working on homework together, the girls were rarely apart.

In junior high, Renée got a bit tired of Natanya and branched out to other friends. After some hurt feelings, Natanya realized she needed to be less clingy toward Renée, so she developed some other friendships too.

Once the girls were over that challenge, their friendship truly blossomed in high school. They became best listeners to each other, best advice givers, and best encouragers. They shared all their ups and downs about their boyfriends with each other. They even knew how to have a good argument, make up, and come out of it understanding each other better. Most of all they cared about each other so much that they wanted what was best for the other one even when it didn't suit them personally.

This was becoming a deep, mature friendship. Years, geographical separations, and different life choices would never be able to destroy it. Natanya and Renée were in this friendship for life.

Friendship—especially the kind of faithful, loving friendship that Natanya and Renée had—is sacred. It demonstrates something of how God loves us. Friendship shows us this in the flesh-and-blood, walking-around-on-earth way that we human beings need so much to experience. God is forever faithful, seeing us through the hills and valleys of

Friendship is sacred. It shows something of how God loves us. *Student art:* **"Sisters," pencil drawing by Lisa Wojtowicz, Pope John XXIII High School, Sparta, New Jersey**

our life. God does not turn away from us when we make mistakes. God hangs in there for the long haul and calls us back with love when we have been distant and aloof, or just out of sorts. Friends like Natanya and Renée mirror that kind of faithful love in their lifelong relationship. For them, each moment of the friendship—and their whole lifetime of friendship—is a saving moment. It offers them God's love through each other.

The Sacrament

Marriage between a man and a woman is, above all else, a lifelong, faithful friendship. If the man and the woman are not friends, their marriage will not survive, or it will survive only as an empty shell without any meaning. The sacrament of **Marriage** celebrates the kind of friendship that mirrors God's love for us—a permanent covenant to always be there for the other in love and service.

Of course, marriage has a special dimension that Natanya and Renée's friendship did not have. The bond and commitment of marriage is expressed by a woman and a man in the most intimate physical way possible—through sexual intercourse. In the union of their bodies, a woman and a man symbolize the closeness and unity of God with us. They make God's love tangible and real to each other in their physical lovemaking.

Perhaps this is a new way for you to think about marriage and sex. But it points to just how sacred these marvelous realities are, and how important it is that the special physical relationship of the couple be cherished and never used destructively.

The ritual of the sacrament is a simple one. Essentially it consists of the exchange of vows by the couple, who promise their commitment to each other for their whole life. Often the ceremony takes place during a celebration of Mass. Ideally it is not a private ceremony, but one where the wider community of the couple's friends and family is there to witness and support the couple in their commitment.

10
Describe in writing a marriage of two people you know who relate to each other as faithful friends, partners who hang in there with each other during tough times.

The saving moment of the sacrament of Marriage really lasts for the whole life of the couple. In every moment of the two lives joined together in love, the husband and the wife meet God and are transformed by that encounter into a flesh-and-blood sign of God's love for all of us.

For Review

- What does Holy Orders celebrate?
- In what ways are ordained persons in the church intended to lead as servants?
- What rites are involved in ordination, and what do they signify?
- What does the sacrament of Marriage celebrate?
- What does the ritual of Marriage consist of?

11
Considering all the ways the sacraments relate to everyday life, which one sacrament seems to focus most on what you need in your life right now? Write about this in a one-page reflection.

Living the Sacraments

The sacraments of the church are not some "churchy" invention that is separate from the rest of life, with their importance and power confined to the walls of a church building. They are intimately connected with what is going on in our everyday life.

The sacraments bring together and celebrate the saving moments of our life—the times when we are touched by God's grace and transformed in some small or large way, even if we are not aware that it is God who is acting within us. These might be moments of finding life new and fresh again, of responding to the Spirit's gifts in us, of giving ourselves and being nourished and changed in the process, of forgiving another and being forgiven, of being healed by the love of our community, of being a faithful friend, or of leading others while serving them.

When those saving moments are celebrated in the sacraments, God comes to us in a special, intense way, transforming us more and more into the marvelous person we are meant to be. So the sacraments are the means of salvation for individuals who are open to God's power at work within them. And through those individuals, the transforming power of the sacraments can reach the whole world. The sacraments continue the saving life, death, and Resurrection of Christ in the world today.

10

The Liturgical Year: Celebrating Sacred Time

Living Is Timely

Time. We are swimming in it. We are born in time; we live and grow to maturity in time; we finally die in time. Our life has a limited span of years. As creatures, we are time bound.

Experiences of Time

People and cultures differ widely in how they experience time. Even one individual on a given day may have a variety of experiences of time, both positive and negative. For instance, here are some different senses that people have of time:

Time as a Burden

Time seems monotonous, long, and dragged out when we are bored; it is a **burden**, not an opportunity. We long for something to break the routine. Even a fire drill breaking into the midst of a long, tedious school day can make time "pick up" again.

Time as a Pressure

People in contemporary society seem particularly prone to experiencing time as a **pressure**. There is never enough time. Things have to be done "on time," and the glowing, changing digits of the clock remind us that we always seem to be behind. Hurry, hurry, our society tells us.

1

Do you sometimes experience time as a burden? as a pressure? Write an example of what you are thinking when time is either burdensome or stress-producing for you

2

Have you ever been in a state of "flow"? If so, describe in writing what that feels like.

Computers are judged by how fast they are, how little time you have to wait for them to process information or bring up graphics on the screen. People call regular mail service "snail mail" and prefer instead the instant effect of e-mail or fax. We are reminded constantly of the urgency of doing things fast.

Time as Suspended

We also have moments when it feels as though there is no time at all—that time has been **suspended** while we are totally involved in something we want to be doing. We lose track of time because we are so engrossed.

Good friends can spend hours together and not notice the time passing. So can someone immersed in assembling a model, surfing the Internet, or shooting baskets. Children especially have a talent for letting time be suspended while they play—whether it is skateboarding, playing dolls, or getting into an imaginary world of caves and tunnels made from tables, chairs, and blankets. When children play, there seems to be no time—until they are reminded it is "time to eat" or "time to go home."

Some have called this sensation in a person—child or adult—a state of "flow." The person's energy is flowing; he or she does not feel dragged down. Even work can be experienced as so absorbing and even enjoyable that it seems to take us out of time. We may be sweating and exerting ourselves, but if we are totally engrossed in it, the work becomes like play.

The sensation of time being suspended is like having a bit of the eternal, the timeless, brought right into the time-bound stream of life.

Time as Seasonal

The seasons come and go. This fact is obvious to those who live in a climate that has four distinct seasons, but it is especially felt by those who live close to the land. Spring, summer, fall, winter—the earth's **seasons** of sprouting new growth, ripening, yielding flower and fruit, and dying into the earth—all come around in the course of a year. Nothing we do can hasten their coming or going. We just have to respect their timing, knowing that it is all necessary to the process of growth and to beginning the cycle of the seasons all over again the next year.

Likewise we are aware that life has its seasons—infancy, childhood, adolescence, young adulthood, mature adulthood, old age, and finally death. A family, too, has its seasons—from the time the couple is newlywed; to the period of raising children; to the time when the children grow up, leave home, and establish their own lives and families; to the time when the couple care for each other into old age; and finally when they are parted by death.

To have a **seasonal sense of time** is to be aware of these comings and goings of life. It is to be respectful of them and patient with them even when they cause us hardship or distress. It is a calm knowledge that all things, in time, will have their season.

The Gift of Time

Cherishing the earth's seasons or the seasons of our life enables us to appreciate the rhythms of existence. We realize that life has times of light as well as darkness, of joy as well as sorrow, of birth as well as death, of peace as well as disturbance. We recognize that things take time to grow, that *we* take time to develop, that problems take time to work themselves out. What we long for does not come about instantly but requires a process of give and take, of stepping up and stepping back, of living and dying in small and large ways.

A Time for Everything

A well-known passage from the **Book of Ecclesiastes** in the Hebrew Scriptures expresses wisdom about life's seasons, and it encourages us to be patient with all that comes our way in the course of time.

For everything there is a season, and a time for every matter under heaven:
a time to be born, and a time to die;
a time to plant, and a time to pluck up what is planted;
a time to kill, and a time to heal;
a time to break down, and a time to build up;
a time to weep, and a time to laugh;
a time to mourn, and a time to dance;
a time to throw away stones, and a time to gather stones together;
a time to embrace, and a time to refrain from embracing;
a time to seek, and a time to lose;
a time to keep, and a time to throw away;
a time to tear, and a time to sew;
a time to keep silence, and a time to speak;
a time to love, and a time to hate;
a time for war, and a time for peace. (3:1–8)

Every moment of time is rich with possibilities.
Student art: "Native Skeletons," color photo by Brant Roshau, Trinity High School, Dickinson, North Dakota

3
List ten problems or difficulties you have. For each one, write whether you think you will need a short time or a long time to work it out.

When we appreciate the seasonal aspect of time, we sense that time is a gift, not something that hangs on us as a burden or something to be fought at high pressure. We see that we need time and must be patient with it. We work things out over time—whether resolving a conflict with someone, developing a talent in music or sports, dealing with the divorce of our parents, or overcoming shyness and insecurity. Time becomes our friend, our ally, and every moment of time is rich with possibilities.

A Religious Sense of Time

Rituals for the Seasons

Ancient peoples saw time as seasonal. The rhythms of growing and dying on the earth were associated with changes in the sun, the moon, and the stars. They saw the cycle of the seasons being repeated over and over, and they marked the seasons of growth and harvest and hunting with festivals and rituals. These became some of the earliest forms of religious worship, as the ancients assumed that divine powers were behind the seasons. They offered sacrifices to please and appease the gods responsible for their fortune, and to give them thanks when the harvest or the hunt produced an abundance.

Rituals as Timeless Play

For these ancient peoples, their festivals and rituals were like play, like the experience of time suspended that we discussed earlier. In these timeless, "eternal" moments, they got in touch with a source of energy that enabled them to go back to their everyday life renewed. In the celebrations of the seasons, they found the deeper meaning of their life.

Roots of Christian Feasts

Many of the Christian feasts we now celebrate have roots or parallels in festivals from pre-Christian history. For instance, ancient cultures had spring festivals to celebrate the new life coming forth from the earth and to ask the gods to bless that growth. In the history of the Israelites, the festival of spring became the Passover, which recalled the new life given to the people in the Exodus, when God freed them from slavery and brought them out of the land of Egypt. The Christian celebration of Easter occurs at about the same time in spring that Jews today have the Passover. That is no accident, because Easter, which celebrates Jesus' Resurrection and new life for all those who follow him, comes soon after Holy Thursday, when Christians commemorate the Last Supper, the Passover meal Jesus shared with his disciples on the night before he died.

Christmas has non-Christian parallels, too. Coming at the darkest time of the year in the Northern Hemisphere, it shares some similarities with the ancient festivals that marked the winter solstice, the day when the shortened daylight of winter begins to grow longer. Christians celebrate the birth of Jesus as the Light coming into the world, which echoes these pre-Christian festivals of light. And some of the Christmas traditions we think of as particularly Christian, such as the Christmas tree, also have their origins in earlier cultures.

Every major religion today has its own yearly cycle of feasts and rituals to celebrate what is important to its people. Believers who participate wholeheartedly in those rituals sense that they are in touch with something more than the everyday, that they are in contact with the timeless, the eternal, the sacred. This brush with the eternal then gives meaning to the rest of their life. This is as true for Christianity as for the other religions. But Christians, and Catholic Christians in particular, have a distinctive way of experiencing time, a way we will now consider.

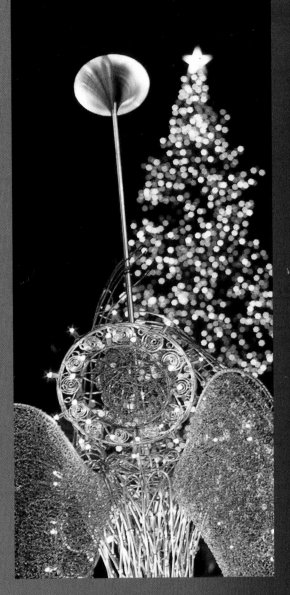

4
Look up the origin of some other custom associated with a Christian feast—like Easter eggs, the Easter bunny, or Christmas stockings. Write a brief explanation of how the custom got started.

For Review

- How does a seasonal sense of time differ from a sense of time as burdensome or stress-producing?
- What were some of the earliest forms of religious worship, and what did they mark?
- Give two examples from the text of how Christian feasts were rooted in pre-Christian festivals.

The Structure and Heart of the Liturgical Year

When you think of a year, perhaps the calendar year—January through December—comes to mind. Or maybe the academic year—September through June—pops into your head. The church's liturgical year does not follow either of those time frames. It begins in late November or early December with the start of the season of Advent, the period of four weeks before Christmas. Then it continues for a full year, until just before the next year's Advent.

In the first few centuries of the early church, the structure of the church year came to consist of two major seasons: the **Easter Season**, which begins on Easter Sunday and ends with the feast of Pentecost, and the **Christmas Season**, which begins on Christmas Day and ends with the feast of the Baptism of the Lord. Each season has its own period of preparation: Easter has Lent, and Christmas has Advent. Between those two seasons of "extraordinary time" are two periods called **Ordinary Time**. In Ordinary Time, various aspects of Jesus' life and teachings are the focus of liturgical celebrations each week.

To help us feel the differences in the seasons, each season and feast has its own characteristic color for the church environment and vestments (clothing) worn by the priest or the other liturgical ministers.

The scriptural readings selected for the liturgies of each Sunday of the liturgical year are rotated every three years so that people do not hear the same readings every year. The book of these readings is called the **lectionary**, and many Protestant churches use the same or nearly the same readings in their Sunday services as Catholics do.

Easter is the heart of the liturgical year. Easter focuses most intensely on the Paschal Mystery. All the other events in Jesus' life, from his birth to his Ascension, are important because he died and was raised from the dead. The celebration of Easter sheds its light on the whole year; every Sunday (the day of the Lord's Resurrection) is considered a "little Easter."

Because contemporary society highlights the celebration of Christmas, it may seem strange to say that Easter is the heart of the church year. But from the beginning of the church, Easter was the primary Christian feast; Christmas was not made a feast day for at least a few centuries.

Let's look more closely now at the liturgical year from the beginning to the end. It will help to follow the diagram of the year on the following page.

Roots of Christian Feasts

Many of the Christian feasts we now celebrate have roots or parallels in festivals from pre-Christian history. For instance, ancient cultures had spring festivals to celebrate the new life coming forth from the earth and to ask the gods to bless that growth. In the history of the Israelites, the festival of spring became the Passover, which recalled the new life given to the people in the Exodus, when God freed them from slavery and brought them out of the land of Egypt. The Christian celebration of Easter occurs at about the same time in spring that Jews today have the Passover. That is no accident, because Easter, which celebrates Jesus' Resurrection and new life for all those who follow him, comes soon after Holy Thursday, when Christians commemorate the Last Supper, the Passover meal Jesus shared with his disciples on the night before he died.

Christmas has non-Christian parallels, too. Coming at the darkest time of the year in the Northern Hemisphere, it shares some similarities with the ancient festivals that marked the winter solstice, the day when the shortened daylight of winter begins to grow longer. Christians celebrate the birth of Jesus as the Light coming into the world, which echoes these pre-Christian festivals of light. And some of the Christmas traditions we think of as particularly Christian, such as the Christmas tree, also have their origins in earlier cultures.

Every major religion today has its own yearly cycle of feasts and rituals to celebrate what is important to its people. Believers who participate wholeheartedly in those rituals sense that they are in touch with something more than the everyday, that they are in contact with the timeless, the eternal, the sacred. This brush with the eternal then gives meaning to the rest of their life. This is as true for Christianity as for the other religions. But Christians, and Catholic Christians in particular, have a distinctive way of experiencing time, a way we will now consider.

For Review

- How does a seasonal sense of time differ from a sense of time as burdensome or stress-producing?
- What were some of the earliest forms of religious worship, and what did they mark?
- Give two examples from the text of how Christian feasts were rooted in pre-Christian festivals.

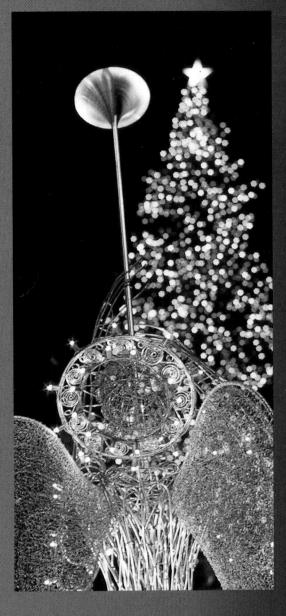

4
Look up the origin of some other custom associated with a Christian feast—like Easter eggs, the Easter bunny, or Christmas stockings. Write a brief explanation of how the custom got started.

The Liturgical Year: God's "Time" Enters Our Time

Catholic belief is that with the coming of God's Son, Jesus, into the world, all time has become holy. **God's "time,"** which is **eternal** and **timeless**, has broken through into our time.

The events of our salvation—the life, death, and Resurrection of Jesus Christ—happened in real time in the past. Yet they are not simply past events that we remember. Jesus' life, death, and Resurrection to new life are happening in us *now* and are saving us *now*. The Paschal Mystery is a past reality but also a present one. It points to that future day when all creation will finally be brought into unity in the Reign of God.

Taking in the Mystery over Time

Because we are limited human beings, we cannot grasp the whole Paschal Mystery all at once, or live it out in one moment of salvation. We need to take it in gradually and digest it a little at a time until it becomes a part of who we are. The church's liturgical year provides an opportunity, over time, to absorb the Christian story—the mystery of our salvation—and to celebrate how it is happening in our own life. Those ritual celebrations can be like "eternal moments" that give meaning to the rest of life's moments, the everyday times.

So in the **liturgical year,** we walk through twelve months of seasons and feasts that recall different aspects of Jesus' life, death, and Resurrection, his return to the Father, and his sending of the Holy Spirit. As one year ends, another is beginning, and we walk through the process again. During our life, we have the chance to make the journey of our salvation many times, as the story of the Paschal Mystery unfolds each year.

However, we are not meant to hear the same familiar stories and celebrate the same feast days in the same way each year. Every year as we grow and develop as a person, we have new challenges to face. If we are open to the presence of God in our joys and struggles, then the living, dying, and rising of Jesus *in us* will mean something different to us every year. We do not "get" the mystery of our salvation all at once. Gradually, through our ongoing celebrations of the Paschal Mystery, it seeps into us, and we are transformed at the deepest levels of our being—heart and head, body, soul, and spirit. We grow in God's grace to be the person we are meant to be. We are saved.

5
Write about a "dying and rising" experience you had in the last year—in other words, a time when you had to go through struggles or suffering to grow as a person.

Every year we have new challenges to face, new struggles in which God is present.

We are not alone in our journey, though. Salvation comes to us not just as individuals but as communities who walk through the Paschal Mystery together—in parishes, schools, small base communities, youth groups, families, and groups of friends.

The Parable of Groundhog Day

SEVERAL years ago the comedy movie *Groundhog Day* was popular. Its main character, Phil, a big city TV meteorologist played hilariously by Bill Murray, has a personality that leaves a lot to be desired. He is self-centered, rude, phony, and manipulative. Phil goes out on location to do a live broadcast of a small town's annual ritual of watching for the appearance of the groundhog on Groundhog Day on 2 February. He stays at a local hotel and awakens to an early alarm, to be ready for his coverage of the "big event." But everything seems to go wrong. A blizzard he did not predict moves in and prevents the broadcast. Besides this, Phil comes across several situations that morning in which he behaves with his characteristic insensitivity and meanness. Finally, trapped by the blizzard, he is forced to stay in town overnight and go back to the same hotel.

But strangely enough, when Phil wakes up the next morning to the alarm, the previous day seems to be repeating itself. Same radio news, same people in the hotel coffee shop, same old acquaintance he bumps into, same homeless guy on the street looking for help, same romantic interest, same blizzard, and everyone is again waiting for the appearance of the groundhog! Phil goes through the day again, and then again and again, making us wonder, just what is the point?

The movie takes us through a bizarre series of almost identical Groundhog Days, and finally we (and Phil) begin to get the point. Each day, with its challenging situations and encounters, gives Phil the opportunity to learn something about life and himself. At last he catches on and begins to act in a progressively less phony, selfish way every time he meets these situations. In a quirky warping of time (maybe it was a dream?), he has been given the chance to try and try again at life, until he "gets it right." In learning and trying, he is transformed, so that Phil at the end of the movie is quite a changed man. He has become a person of integrity and compassion. You might say he has been "saved."

The funny and strange process of transformation that our *Groundhog Day* hero experiences is not so different from the journey that Christians make as they walk through the events of Jesus' life, death, and Resurrection in every liturgical year. Like Phil, we are given the chance to experience the means of our salvation over and over again, until it finally "takes" and we "get it right."

The Structure and Heart of the Liturgical Year

When you think of a year, perhaps the calendar year—January through December—comes to mind. Or maybe the academic year—September through June—pops into your head. The church's liturgical year does not follow either of those time frames. It begins in late November or early December with the start of the season of Advent, the period of four weeks before Christmas. Then it continues for a full year, until just before the next year's Advent.

In the first few centuries of the early church, the structure of the church year came to consist of two major seasons: the **Easter Season**, which begins on Easter Sunday and ends with the feast of Pentecost, and the **Christmas Season**, which begins on Christmas Day and ends with the feast of the Baptism of the Lord. Each season has its own period of preparation: Easter has Lent, and Christmas has Advent. Between those two seasons of "extraordinary time" are two periods called **Ordinary Time.** In Ordinary Time, various aspects of Jesus' life and teachings are the focus of liturgical celebrations each week.

To help us feel the differences in the seasons, each season and feast has its own characteristic color for the church environment and vestments (clothing) worn by the priest or the other liturgical ministers.

The scriptural readings selected for the liturgies of each Sunday of the liturgical year are rotated every three years so that people do not hear the same readings every year. The book of these readings is called the **lectionary**, and many Protestant churches use the same or nearly the same readings in their Sunday services as Catholics do.

Easter is the heart of the liturgical year. Easter focuses most intensely on the Paschal Mystery. All the other events in Jesus' life, from his birth to his Ascension, are important because he died and was raised from the dead. The celebration of Easter sheds its light on the whole year; every Sunday (the day of the Lord's Resurrection) is considered a "little Easter."

Because contemporary society highlights the celebration of Christmas, it may seem strange to say that Easter is the heart of the church year. But from the beginning of the church, Easter was the primary Christian feast; Christmas was not made a feast day for at least a few centuries.

Let's look more closely now at the liturgical year from the beginning to the end. It will help to follow the diagram of the year on the following page.

For Review

- In the liturgical year, what do Christians walk through?
- In what way does the liturgical year transform us, if we are open to it?
- What are the two major seasons of the liturgical year, with their preparation periods? What are the time periods in between the two major seasons called?
- What is the heart of the liturgical year, and why is it considered the heart?

Through a Year of Grace

Advent: Longing for the Light of God

The liturgical year begins with the First Sunday of Advent. **Advent**, the four weeks of preparation before Christmas, means "coming." What or who is coming?

- The obvious answer is that Jesus has already come, in his birth in Bethlehem, and we must prepare to celebrate his birth.
- Advent anticipates Jesus' coming into our world today, into our own life, in whatever way Jesus will make an "appearance"—in the people we encounter, in our joys, and in our struggles that we try to work through.
- Advent also looks forward to the coming of Jesus at the end of time to bring God's Reign over all the world.

Thus the season of Advent is a time to reflect on the coming of Jesus in the **past**, in the **present**, and in the **future**.

Advent is a time of longing and expectation, of waiting for the deepest dreams of the human heart to be fulfilled. Its mood is one of hopeful anticipation as we make room in our life for God's coming to us. This quiet mood, unfortunately, is just the opposite of the signals given to us by our society as Christmas preparations take on increasing frenzy.

In the Northern Hemisphere, Advent sets in as the days grow shorter and the nights grow longer and longer. We feel almost surrounded by darkness (imagine how people must have felt before they had electric

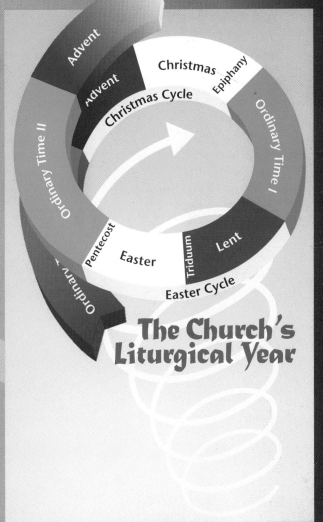

The Church's
Liturgical Year

lights to brighten the long nights). We begin to sense in our bones how much we miss and need the light of longer days. That is somewhat like the experience of waiting and yearning for God's light in our life and in our world. Faith tells us that the light of Christ will come, but we must be ready to receive Christ's light in our heart.

Los Posadas: Searching for Welcome

HISPANIC people around the world practice the popular Advent custom of **Los Posadas** (*posada* means "shelter" or "lodging"), which began in Spain. *Los Posadas* are processions that re-enact the journey of Mary and Joseph to Bethlehem, as they sought shelter for Mary to give birth to the baby Jesus. *Los Posadas* last for nine days, representing the nine months of Mary's pregnancy and the nine days the pilgrims, Joseph and Mary, spent journeying to Bethlehem.

In these nightly processions, people travel from house to house in the neighborhood (or room to room in a house). When they arrive at a house, they are divided into the "innkeepers" and the "pilgrims" (Mary and Joseph). Often two children dress up as Mary and Joseph, or carry statues of them. Singing a hymn, the pilgrims plead with the innkeepers for lodging, and they are refused at each house. After much pleading, they are finally welcomed in by the innkeepers at the last house. Here is a dialog reprinted from *Catholic Update* that might be used at the last house:

Pilgrims: In heaven's name,
    we ask for lodging.
Innkeepers: We have no room,
    you must be going.
Pilgrims: The night is cold,
    and there are dangers.

Innkeepers: Off with you now,
    for you are strangers!
Pilgrims: Please let us in,
    my wife's time is near.
Innkeepers: I know you not,
    you cannot stay here!
Pilgrims: I am Joseph,
    and Mary is my wife.
    Her child shall be
    the Word of life.
Innkeepers: Come in dear pilgrims,
    forgive me I pray.
    We welcome you and
    your child born this day!

The pilgrims are invited into the last house with great hospitality. There is time for prayer, rejoicing, and refreshments.

Los Posadas remind the participants that the strangers in our life who seek welcome and hospitality could just as well be the Holy Family seeking shelter and comfort from us. When we welcome the stranger, we are welcoming Christ into our life.

The light of the Advent wreath reminds us that Christ is coming.

The beautiful custom of the **Advent wreath** focuses on the theme of light coming into darkness. The first week, a candle is lit in anticipation of the coming of Christ. As each week passes, another candle is lit, until four candles are burning brightly just before Christmas.

Christmastime: Joy to the World!

The feast of **Christmas** on 25 December celebrates the Incarnation. God has come into the world as a human, son of Mary, Jesus, a little baby born in humble, poor circumstances. God is indeed with us, bringing hope and joy to the world by sharing our human condition. Jesus is the Light that dispels the darkness in our world and in our own heart.

The Nativity scene, or **crèche**, has been a popular custom of the Christmas Season since the Middle Ages. The crèche features the figures of Mary, Joseph, and the infant Jesus in a stable, along with shepherds and animals. Some people add the figures to the scene a few at a time as the days draw closer to Christmas. And after Christmas Day, they leave the crèche up until the feast of the Epiphany (the second Sunday after Christmas), when the figures of the three

How the Christmas Crèche Got Started

LEGENDS about Francis of Assisi—the beloved saint who lived a life of poverty, simplicity, and service to the poor during the Middle Ages—tells this story of the origins of the Christmas crèche, or Nativity scene:

Brother Francis became concerned and saddened because the peasants who lived in the hill villages of Italy were not able to read. They did not even know the story of Jesus' birth in Bethlehem because they had never read it or heard it in their language (preaching in the churches was done in Latin, a language the poor peasants did not understand). One day Francis thought up a way they could experience the story so that it would remain in their hearts, not just their heads.

He built a stable in a cave behind the village church. Then he brought real animals into the stable, giving them hay to eat in a manger or feeding trough. He asked a young village couple to be Mary and Joseph and to bring their own baby to lie in the manger and be cuddled by the parents. Other accounts say that when Francis got the Nativity scene together every year after that, he would always have a village orphan play the baby Jesus. Francis knew that from that night on, the little orphan would always be treated kindly by the villagers.

So the peasants learned the Christmas story better than they could by reading it, in a way they could never forget. For them, God became flesh among people like themselves, in circumstances like their own.

Since then the Christmas crèche has become a much loved custom around the world. The stable and figures are set up every year in churches, homes, and other places where people gather. Sometimes real people and animals participate in a "live Nativity scene," which was just the way Francis of Assisi intended it.

wise men are added. Epiphany celebrates Jesus' being revealed to the whole world, not just the Jews, through the wise men from the East who followed the star to Bethlehem.

The time after Christmas Day is often overlooked as a season of celebration. Christmastime lasts until the feast of the Baptism of the Lord, the third Sunday after Christmas. In our society, though, once gifts have been given and received, all the Christmas caroling, feasting, and excitement seem to stop and things go back to being humdrum. But for those who truly want to celebrate the coming of Jesus, the season of joy lasts for three weeks after Christmas.

Ordinary Time: Most of the Year, Most of Life

Life has its intense times. We have high peaks and low valleys, and during these times we are perhaps more open to new insights and growth than in the more even periods. But most of life is not so extraordinary; it is more ordinary. We probably could not bear to live constantly in an intense frame of mind, and it is good that we get a balance of the ordinary and the extraordinary in life.

The church's liturgical year contains that kind of balance of the extraordinary and the ordinary. The Advent-Christmas Seasons and later the Lent-Easter Seasons are intense with preparation and then great celebration. But most of the church year, like most of life, is not so extraordinary. The periods outside the Advent-Christmas and Lent-Easter Seasons are called Ordinary Time.

The use of the word *ordinary* to describe this part of the liturgical year is not meant to imply that it is a boring or useless time. The scriptural readings of Ordinary Time portray Jesus delivering his remarkable teachings and parables, and performing such miracles as changing water to wine or calming a stormy lake. In Ordinary Time the deeper meaning of the more intense seasons has a chance to sink in and truly change us.

Ordinary Time is divided into two periods (I and II). The first is between Christmastime and Lent, and the other is between Eastertime and the next Advent. Altogether, Ordinary Time covers about 60 percent of the year.

6
What is your favorite tradition of Christmastime? Describe in a paragraph why it means so much to you.

7
Choose one statement and explain your choice in writing: I would prefer to have *(a)* more time in my personal life that is ordinary rather than extraordinary, *(b)* more time that is extraordinary rather than ordinary, or *(c)* an equal mixture of both.

Lent and Holy Week:
Following the Way of the Cross

The period of preparation for Easter is **Lent.** Holy Week comes at the end of Lent, leading directly into Easter. The seasons of Lent and Easter focus on the Paschal Mystery, Jesus' passage through death to life. The focus is also on how we are living out the Paschal Mystery in our own life.

Lent

The solemn, reflective mood of Lent is apparent right at its beginning on **Ash Wednesday.** On that day, Catholics gather to receive ashes in the form of a cross on their forehead. Marked by a cross of ashes, they are reminded that earthly life is temporary, that their life and efforts sometimes seem like just a pile of ashes, and that following Jesus will lead to the cross of suffering. But this is not a depressing thought, because they know that the cross is the way to new life, to Resurrection with Jesus.

With that start, Lent goes on for a period of forty days, a number that recalls the forty days Jesus spent in the wilderness before beginning his public ministry. Throughout Lent, Catholics are challenged to renew themselves in these ways:
- **fasting**—eating small meals and skipping snacks between meals on Ash Wednesday and Good Friday—as well as

On Ash Wednesday, Catholics receive ashes in the form of a cross on their forehead.

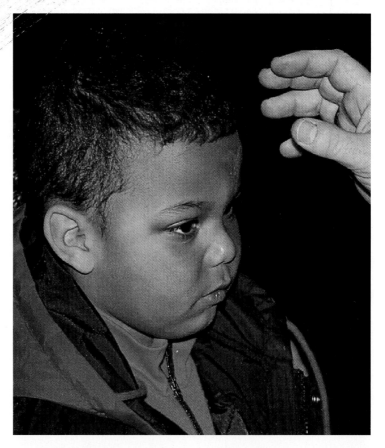

"Ashes"

SOME Catholic churches across North America sing the contemporary hymn "Ashes," by Tom Conry, every Ash Wednesday as people come forward to receive the sign of the cross in ashes on their forehead. The ashes remind them that the journey to new life travels right through the ashes of failure, weakness, and suffering.

We rise again from ashes, from the good we've
    failed to do.
We rise again from ashes, to create ourselves
    anew.
If all our world is ashes, then must our lives
    be true,
an offering of ashes, an offering to you.

We offer you our failures, we offer you
    attempts,
the gifts not fully given, the dreams not
    fully dreamt.

Give our stumblings direction, give our
    visions wider view,
an offering of ashes, an offering to you.

Then rise again from ashes, let healing come
    to pain,
though spring has turned to winter, and
    sunshine turned to rain.
The rain we'll use for growing, and create the
    world anew
from an offering of ashes, an offering to you.

Thanks be to the Father, who made us like
    himself.
Thanks be to his Son, who saved us by his
    death.
Thanks be to the Spirit who creates the world
    anew
from an offering of ashes, an offering to you.

abstaining—eating no meat those two days plus all Fridays in Lent. These practices are required on those particular days, but various forms of fasting are also encouraged throughout Lent.
- **being more self-disciplined**—cutting back on some of the usual distractions and pleasures that keep people from being attentive to deeper things
- **praying** more frequently and being more reflective
- **giving alms**—giving to those in need, whether it is material help, service, or companionship

Lent had its origins in the early centuries of the church, when many adults were converting to Christianity. They

8
Describe one way you could be more self-disciplined.

Easter: Alleluia! Christ Is Risen!

The **Easter Vigil** is the climax of the entire liturgical year. Among its features are the lighting of the Easter fire; the lighting of the Paschal Candle and the congregation's many small candles; the singing of the Easter Proclamation, an extended Liturgy of the Word; and the Baptism, Confirmation, and first Eucharist for adults who have chosen to become Catholic. Here is how theologian Sandra DeGidio describes the Easter Vigil experience:

> In the early hours of the final night of our Easter journey—*the Roman Easter Vigil*—we pause to keep watch. A fire begins to flicker. The Easter (Paschal) Candle is lit from the new fire, carried prominently into the midst of

The Easter Proclamation

DURING the Easter Vigil, in the darkened church—with light coming only from the Paschal Candle and the people's small candles lit from that great one—a strong, clear voice sings out the mighty **Easter Proclamation**, also called the *Exsultet,* in Gregorian chant. Here are some passages from this ancient prayer:

Rejoice, heavenly powers! Sing, choirs of
   angels!
Exult, all creation around God's throne!
Jesus Christ, our King, is risen!
Sound the trumpet of salvation!

Rejoice, O earth, in shining splendor,
radiant in the brightness of your King!
Christ has conquered! Glory fills you!
Darkness vanishes for ever!

. . . .

This is our passover feast,
when Christ, the true Lamb, is slain,
whose blood consecrates the homes of
   all believers.

This is the night when first you saved our
   fathers:
you freed the people of Israel from their
   slavery
and led them dry-shod through the sea.

This is the night when Christians everywhere,
washed clean of sin
and freed from all defilement,
are restored to grace and grow together
   in holiness.

This is the night when Jesus Christ
broke the chains of death
and rose triumphant from the grave.

Father, how wonderful your care for us!
How boundless your merciful love!

. . . .

The power of this holy night
dispels all evil, washes guilt away,
restores lost innocence, brings mourners joy.

Night truly blessed when heaven is wedded
   to earth
and man is reconciled with God! 🖾

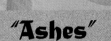

"Ashes"

SOME Catholic churches across North America sing the contemporary hymn "Ashes," by Tom Conry, every Ash Wednesday as people come forward to receive the sign of the cross in ashes on their forehead. The ashes remind them that the journey to new life travels right through the ashes of failure, weakness, and suffering.

> We rise again from ashes, from the good we've failed to do.
> We rise again from ashes, to create ourselves anew.
> If all our world is ashes, then must our lives be true,
> an offering of ashes, an offering to you.
>
> We offer you our failures, we offer you attempts,
> the gifts not fully given, the dreams not fully dreamt.

> Give our stumblings direction, give our visions wider view,
> an offering of ashes, an offering to you.
>
> Then rise again from ashes, let healing come to pain,
> though spring has turned to winter, and sunshine turned to rain.
> The rain we'll use for growing, and create the world anew
> from an offering of ashes, an offering to you.
>
> Thanks be to the Father, who made us like himself.
> Thanks be to his Son, who saved us by his death.
> Thanks be to the Spirit who creates the world anew
> from an offering of ashes, an offering to you.

abstaining—eating no meat those two days plus all Fridays in Lent. These practices are required on those particular days, but various forms of fasting are also encouraged throughout Lent.

- **being more self-disciplined**—cutting back on some of the usual distractions and pleasures that keep people from being attentive to deeper things
- **praying** more frequently and being more reflective
- **giving alms**—giving to those in need, whether it is material help, service, or companionship

Lent had its origins in the early centuries of the church, when many adults were converting to Christianity. They

8
Describe one way you could be more self-disciplined.

were baptized at the Easter Vigil and taken into full membership in the church. But the catechumens needed a time of intense preparation, like a forty-day retreat, to get ready for this big step. The rest of the church joined them in their practices of prayer, fasting, and almsgiving. This time period before Easter became known as Lent.

Today the spirit of the catechumens' preparation is still part of Lent. In parishes where the RCIA (Rite of Christian Initiation of Adults) is practiced, members of the community reach out to support the adult catechumens as they journey toward full initiation into the church. And the catechumens inspire the whole community to take seriously their own baptism and membership in the Body of Christ, to renew their own life.

Thus Lent is about renewal, about preparing our heart to be transformed. The word *lent* is even from a French word meaning "springtime," a time of renewal.

Holy Week

You may find it useful to refer back to events described in chapter 5, "Jesus and the Paschal Mystery," as you read about **Holy Week**, the last week of Lent. Holy Week begins with Palm Sunday, also called Passion Sunday, the day that recalls Jesus' entry into Jerusalem to the praises of an enthusiastic crowd that placed palm branches in his path (a cus-

Top left: The washing of the feet at the Holy Thursday service reminds Catholics that they are called to serve one another.
Top right: Good Friday solemnly recalls the Passion and death of Jesus.
Bottom: At the Easter Vigil on Holy Saturday, the Paschal Candle symbolizes Christ our Light, who overcomes the darkness of sin and death.

Triduum

tom of the time used to welcome visiting kings). The joyous opening of the Palm Sunday celebration is short lived, though, and those who participate in Mass on Palm Sunday realize that Jesus' Passion and death are close at hand. A Gospel account of the Passion is read during the Mass, with the priest, other readers, and the entire congregation taking part.

The last three days of Holy Week, which link together Lent and Easter, are called the **Triduum** (meaning "three days"): Holy Thursday, Good Friday, and Holy Saturday, with the Easter Vigil beginning the new season of Easter on Saturday night.

Holy Thursday. A special Mass commemorates the Last Supper and Jesus' gift of himself in the Eucharist just before he was betrayed by one of his followers. During the Mass, Jesus' call to service and ministry is also emphasized with a rite in which the priest or others wash the feet of representatives of the congregation, recalling Jesus' washing the feet of his disciples (John 13:3–20). Despite the awareness that Jesus' suffering and death follow soon after the Last Supper, Catholics celebrate the feast of Holy Thursday joyfully, for the Eucharist is so great a gift.

Good Friday. The remembrance of Jesus' death is quiet, solemn, and prayerful. For many Catholics it is a day to stop their usual activities and let the meaning of Jesus' death sink in. Good Friday is the only day of the year that Mass is not celebrated. Instead, a three-part liturgy takes place. In this liturgy the story of Jesus' Passion and death is proclaimed, followed by an extensive offering of prayers for the church and all people in the world. In addition, everyone in the congregation approaches a wooden cross with a reverent gesture. The congregation receives Communion, using the Eucharist that was consecrated at Mass on Holy Thursday. From the close of the Good Friday service until the Easter Vigil the next night, an attitude of reflection and quiet vigil is called for.

Holy Saturday. Throughout Holy Saturday, the spirit of prayer and penance continues. All this solemnity is leading up to the greatest celebration of the church year, the Easter Vigil, on Holy Saturday night.

Holy Thursday

Good Friday

Holy Saturday

Easter: Alleluia! Christ Is Risen!

The **Easter Vigil** is the climax of the entire liturgical year. Among its features are the lighting of the Easter fire; the lighting of the Paschal Candle and the congregation's many small candles; the singing of the Easter Proclamation, an extended Liturgy of the Word; and the Baptism, Confirmation, and first Eucharist for adults who have chosen to become Catholic. Here is how theologian Sandra DeGidio describes the Easter Vigil experience:

> In the early hours of the final night of our Easter journey—*the Roman Easter Vigil*—we pause to keep watch. A fire begins to flicker. The Easter (Paschal) Candle is lit from the new fire, carried prominently into the midst of

The Easter Proclamation

DURING the Easter Vigil, in the darkened church—with light coming only from the Paschal Candle and the people's small candles lit from that great one—a strong, clear voice sings out the mighty **Easter Proclamation**, also called the *Exsultet,* in Gregorian chant. Here are some passages from this ancient prayer:

Rejoice, heavenly powers! Sing, choirs of
   angels!
Exult, all creation around God's throne!
Jesus Christ, our King, is risen!
Sound the trumpet of salvation!

Rejoice, O earth, in shining splendor,
radiant in the brightness of your King!
Christ has conquered! Glory fills you!
Darkness vanishes for ever!

. . . .

This is our passover feast,
when Christ, the true Lamb, is slain,
whose blood consecrates the homes of
   all believers.

This is the night when first you saved our
   fathers:
you freed the people of Israel from their
   slavery
and led them dry-shod through the sea.

This is the night when Christians everywhere,
washed clean of sin
and freed from all defilement,
are restored to grace and grow together
   in holiness.

This is the night when Jesus Christ
broke the chains of death
and rose triumphant from the grave.

Father, how wonderful your care for us!
How boundless your merciful love!

. . . .

The power of this holy night
dispels all evil, washes guilt away,
restores lost innocence, brings mourners joy.

Night truly blessed when heaven is wedded
   to earth
and man is reconciled with God!

the assembly, and we begin to tell the story of who we have been and are becoming.

The Easter Vigil is comparable to sitting around a campfire listening to the stories of generations past. The story we hear is long, permeated with powerful symbols of water and new life. It is the story of how we were made, chosen, liberated from bondage and planted in the promised land. Then the story is retold with a new twist in the life, death, and resurrection of Jesus. This is not a night to be hasty.

The Easter water is blessed. Catechumens approach the water, pronounce their baptismal vows and are baptized. With them we renew our baptismal identity.

Bells ring out; flowers and bright, joyful banners replace the more sober environment of Lent. Alleluias and Glorias are sung for the first time in six weeks. It is *the night of all nights*. It is the heart of Christianity. It is Easter!

Easter celebrates our liberation from bondage.
Student art: "Reaching the Top," color photo by Brian N. Smasal, Saint Anthony Catholic High School, San Antonio, Texas

Easter Season and Pentecost: Alive in Christ Jesus

The Easter celebration continues into Easter Sunday and goes on for fifty days, until the feast of Pentecost (you may want to refer back to events described in the first part of chapter 6, "The Church"). During the Easter Season, accounts of the appearances of the Risen Jesus are read at Sunday Eucharists, along with accounts from the Acts of the Apostles of the new community, the early church that experienced Jesus' risen life so powerfully. It is a time of great hope, for death has been overcome by God's power and grace. God has made this great promise to all of us by raising

9
Write one suggestion for making Easter feel as important as Christmas to people your age.

Jesus from the dead: Life, not death, will have the final say. Love is stronger than hate. Hope is stronger than despair. God's peace is stronger than our fears.

Forty days after Easter, on Ascension Thursday, we remember how Jesus said farewell to the Apostles, promising to send the Holy Spirit to them. Then he went to live forever in glory with his Father.

Ten days afterward comes Pentecost Sunday, the feast that recalls the sending of the Holy Spirit to the Apostles, firing up their faith and courage, and filling them with the power of God. In one sense Pentecost is an end—the end of the Easter Season. But in a greater sense it is a beginning—the beginning of the Spirit's work through the church in every age to the present, and beyond that to the end of time.

Sacred Days Throughout the Year

Besides the sacred times of Advent-Christmas and Lent-Easter, many other special feast days are celebrated during the liturgical year:

- Every Sunday is a celebration of the Resurrection, and Catholics are required to attend Mass each Sunday (or Saturday evening) to keep that day holy and affirm their belonging to the Body of Christ.

- Certain holy days are designated by the bishops of each country as feast days when Catholics are obliged to attend Mass. For instance, in the United States the **holy days of obligation** are 1 January, Mary, the Mother of God; forty days after Easter, Ascension Thursday; 15 August, the Assumption of Mary; 1 November, All Saints' Day; 8 December, the Immaculate Conception; and 25 December, Christmas.

- Feasts of the saints, which are usually celebrated on the anniversary date of the death of the saint (which marks his or her birth into eternal life), are generously sprinkled throughout the year. For instance, Saint Elizabeth Ann Seton's feast day is 4 January, and Saint Augustine's feast day is 28 August. To honor their life of holiness, many of the

10
Discuss with a teacher, campus minister, pastor, or youth minister why the Catholic church requires attendance at Mass on Sundays (or Saturday evenings). Write up a report of your discussion.

saints are remembered with special readings or prayers in the Mass of the day.

Entering into the seasons and feasts of the liturgical year is like plunging into a great drama. The overall theme for the drama is the same each year: the life, death, and Resurrection of Jesus as celebrated in the seasons and feasts. But every year the drama gets played out a little differently because *we* are different every year. We are growing in ways we may never have expected. The script is not fixed and unchanging; it is played out and worked on in our own life every year.

For Review

- Explain this statement: *In Advent, Christians reflect on Jesus' coming in the past, in the present, and in the future.*
- On what day do Christians celebrate the Incarnation?
- How long does the Christmas Season last?
- What does the church focus on in Ordinary Time?
- What practices are Catholics challenged to do during Lent?
- What were the origins of Lent in the early church?
- What is the Triduum?
- What features are part of the Easter Vigil?
- What is celebrated on Ascension Thursday?
- In what sense is Pentecost both an end and a beginning?
- Why are Catholics required to attend Mass on Saturday nights or Sundays?
- What are the holy days of obligation in the United States?
- What is the overall theme for the drama of the liturgical year? Why is the drama played out a little differently for us every year?

Living in Tune with God

Catholics who are attentive to the seasons and feasts of the liturgical year have a chance to appreciate the rhythms of life—the high times, the low times, the times of renewal and change, and the ordinary times. Most of all, walking through and participating in the liturgical year enables them to enter into the mystery of salvation again and again, as each year brings them farther along in the journey of life to God. In the next chapter we will explore how we can grow closer to God through prayer and spirituality.

God promised that the Spirit will work through the church in every age, for all time.
Student art: "Promise of God," color photo by Brant Roshau, Trinity High School, Dickinson, North Dakota

11
Give an example in writing of a way you have personally changed this year that one or two years ago you did not expect would happen.

11

Spirituality and Prayer: Growing in Life with God

Spirituality: Toward a Full Life with God

We are meant to be with God now and forever. Our whole life is meant to be a journey of growing closer and closer to God as we become the full person God intends us to be. That journey is what **spirituality** means—becoming a fully alive, whole human being as we grow in our relationship with God. In Christian terms, spirituality is the way we grow in the life of God, the loving life of the Trinity. It is the process of becoming more and more like Jesus Christ, as God's love flows into our actions, our worship and prayer, and our relationships with others.

Being Loved Without Limits

God loves us, each person individually, no matter who we are or what we have done. God reaches out to each person with **unconditional love**, a love that has no conditions or limits placed on it. God's love is not the kind that says, "I'll love you if you're good, and I'll love you even more if you're better"; or "I'll love you if you prove what a great person you are"; or "I'll love you as long as you don't disappoint me." God may not like something a person does, but that does not stop God from loving him or her in the deepest, most tender way—even when the person has committed an awful sin.

We can experience something of God's love through the love of other people for us—our family, our friends, and trusted adults. When someone loves us for *who we are,* not *what we do,* we get a hint of how God loves us. We feel accepted, secure, peaceful, unthreatened. We feel we can really be ourselves without fear—that we don't have to pretend to be someone we're not. Have you ever been forgiven by someone for something bad you did that was tying you in knots of guilt? If so, you know what it feels like to be loved for who you are, not what you do. That kind of love brings healing and makes a person want to change for the better. To receive such love from others is a great and precious gift. But even the most compassionate, accepting human being in the world cannot love us in the unbounded way God does—with no limits at all. God's love is grace at work in us, renewing us and transforming us if we are open to it.

Knowing we are so loved by God is the beginning of wanting to grow close to God. In God's presence we can be ourselves without fear.

Student art: **Untitled, painting by Nate Scatena, University of San Diego High School, San Diego, California**

Being Ourselves with God

Alinda slumped into the chair in her bedroom. It was late already, and she had homework to do, but she felt so dragged down she didn't want to start it. It wasn't sickness, actually, just kind of a "sickness at heart." Another lame day. Her life seemed so pointless. It wasn't that she had such huge problems. Afterall, Alinda's mom wasn't an alcoholic like Cindy's mom. Alinda wasn't pregnant or anything ("Yeah, sure, like I'd even have a chance," she thought). She wasn't flunking out of school. Her parents didn't abuse her. She wasn't homeless, starving, or living through a war like those kids in a refugee camp she saw on the TV news the other night. She didn't have any interesting, dramatic problems. So why did she feel so unhappy most of the time?

Rather than tackle *that* nauseating question, Alinda flipped open her assignment pad. "May as well do religion first—easier than algebra." But the assignment was to respond to the statement that appeared at the end of the chapter in her religion book: "Write a letter to God about whatever is going through your mind and heart right now. Don't worry. No one will see it but you and God."

"Well, that's weird," pondered Alinda. "If no one else sees it, how will Mr. Connor know I did the homework?" It was kind of a "free" assignment. The only person who would ever know about it was herself, so she really did not have to do it!

However, the idea behind the assignment intrigued Alinda, and because she didn't really want to do algebra,

The Armor of Saint Patrick: "Christ with Me"

SAINT **Patrick**, the great missionary to Ireland in the fifth century, composed a prayer that was later called the "Breastplate of Saint Patrick" (a breastplate was a metal piece of defensive armor worn over the chest). When Patrick and his fellow missionaries faced dire situations in which they could be killed by hostile non-Christians, they carried no weapons or defensive shields. Instead they chanted their "breastplate," which reminded them of God's total and constant love for them. This is an excerpt from the prayer:

Christ with me,
Christ before me,
Christ after me,
Christ within me,
Christ beneath me,
Christ above me,
Christ at my right hand,
Christ at my left hand,
Christ in my breadth,
Christ in my length,
Christ in my height,
Christ in the heart of everyone who thinks of me,
Christ in the mouth of everyone who speaks to me,
Christ in every eye that sees me,
Christ in every ear that hears me. . . .

1
Have you been loved by someone whose love for you was close to unconditional? Write about the effect that kind of love had or continues to have on you.

she decided to do the religion project that would never
have to be turned in. It was her little way of declaring,
"I'm doing this because I *want* to, not because I *have* to."

Alinda was surprised at how easily the letter flowed
out of her pen:

> Dear God,
> Hi. What's up? How are you
> doing? I am feeling pretty inse-
> cure. My name is Alinda, and I
> am 15. I think I am fat. That is
> my biggest hang-up. I really
> wish I would become anorexic
> or bulimic. I would stop
> when I reached 125. (I am
> 5'6" and weigh 143.) I al-
> ways look gross! I do soccer,
> swimming, and track, and I
> am bad at all of them. I am
> mediocre at swimming, but no
> matter how much I try I never
> excel.
> I am also not very
> smart. I have a brother
> who's a lawyer and a sister
> at Harvard. I feel only a *little*

pressure (hah!). They are naturally
smart and didn't have to work hard
for A's. Okay, so I don't try extremely hard.

   And I don't have a boyfriend. It
seems as if I'll never get one! What
am I doing WRONG? The worst is I
   always hang out with friends
      who make me jealous. Jeanette,
         my friend, excels at all the things
            I'm bad at. She's an awesome soc-
               cer player, basketball player, and
                  track star. She gets good grades, is
                  pretty, skinny, and has a ton of
                  friends without trying. I really like
                  her but hate this feeling of jeal-
                  ousy. I feel like she is going to
               ditch me any minute. She ap-
            pears anyplace and has no
         problems whatsoever. Makes
      me ill.

   Okay. I just recently found
out that my mother, who I truly
respect and love, had an abortion before she married my
      dad. FREAKED me out total-
         ly! I wasn't supposed to
            know, and I wish I didn't. It
            would be so much easier not
               knowing, being ignorant. I am
                  so ashamed of her. And my dad,
                  before he met Mom, got a girl
                  knocked up and she got an abor-
                  tion. So here's my parents who
                  always preach pro-life and no
                  premarital sex—how can they
               be so hypocritical? How can I
         obey liars!

   Okay, no big deal. I am just a
regular screwed up girl, no big problems, nothing much to say except I
wish I accepted myself, or turned skinny really QUICK.

                     Alinda

   Alinda stared at what she had written. "Oh, my God!
That's the first time I've said any of that stuff to anyone!

2

If you were going to share one important thing about yourself with God in a letter, what would it be? Write it down and explain how easy or difficult it would be to share with God or someone else.

A Prayer of "Being Yourself"

Dear God,
I don't know who my friends are. I don't know who to trust. I've been betrayed by so many. Yet, you want me to forgive. If you love me, why would you want to hurt me? Do believe me when I say I want to believe in you. But how can I believe in something that I don't even know is there? Will you help me to understand and help me to believe in you?

(Megan O'Malley,
Saint Teresa's
Academy,
Kansas City,
Missouri)

Not even to Jeanette—*especially* not to Jeanette!" Then she realized, "Oh, my God, it's because it *is* God! God's the only one I can be totally myself with." Then she almost tore the letter up, but stopped at the last second. "There must be *some* other person I can talk to about this stuff," she thought. She hid the letter under her sweaters in the farthest corner of her bottom drawer, saving it for a time she might be able to share it with someone.

Alinda didn't do her algebra that night. She decided to go to bed and get a good night's sleep, setting the alarm for 6:00 a.m. to finish her homework. And she slept that night—a deep, peaceful sleep.

Alinda didn't immediately solve her problems of insecurity and feeling terribly let down by her parents. She didn't wake up skinny. And she didn't get a boyfriend right away. But she did discover something wonderful—that she could be herself with God, and God would not reject her. Perhaps over time, by sharing herself often with God and knowing God's unconditional love for her, Alinda will come to accept and like herself. Maybe, too, she will eventually feel more comfortable sharing her real self with others and will develop deep friendships of give-and-take, where she does not feel inferior. Alinda may someday be able to forgive her parents because she is able to forgive herself for being less than perfect.

We don't know just how Alinda's story will end. But it has a good beginning. (You might be interested to know that the letter in this story is an actual letter to God written by a teenager on a retreat.)

Growing in Trust

Like Alinda, we all have so many fears— of failure, rejection, lack of popularity, physical or emotional violence, pressures to do things that are harmful and wrong, not meeting others' expectations, being used or taken advantage of, poverty, disaster. Perhaps our fear is not of anything specific—just an overall dread, a feeling that life could fall apart on us and we would not be able to cope.

Jesus' Response to Fears

When Jesus, God's Son, lived on earth as a human being, he felt the same fears we feel. He responded to his fears by trusting more deeply in his beloved Father. Even as Jesus prayed in great anguish over the terrible death that awaited him, he trusted himself into his Father's hands: "'Father, if you are willing, remove this cup from me; yet, not my will but yours be done'" (Luke 22:42). Later, as Jesus hung on the cross, he cried out to God just before his death, "'Father, into your hands I commend my spirit'" (Luke 23:46). Jesus feared, but he also trusted.

Fear Loses Its Power

People who grow closer to God come to trust more deeply over time—trust in God, in themselves, in life itself. Little by little the fear that gripped their heart loses much of its power over them. This does not mean they become naive or let everyone walk all over them. They take precautions; they act reasonably; they get help when they need it. But they do not allow fear to rule them; they do not let their fears overtake them and crush them. Why? Because they know they are in God's hands. They are loved totally by God, and God is with them everywhere, in all ways, even in the worst situation. Recall these words of Psalm 23, "The Lord Is My Shepherd":

> Even though I walk through the valley
> of the shadow of death,
> I fear no evil;
> for you are with me;
> your rod and your staff—
> they comfort me.
>
> (23:4)

Christian belief is that not even suffering and death can destroy us. The example of Jesus shows us not that we *must* suffer, but that when we do suffer we can suffer redemptively; suffering can be transformed into new life. Christians believe in the Resurrection, that God raised Jesus from the dead. This is the foundation of Christian trust and hope in God. And if we are open to the Spirit's work, God will raise us up, too, turning our "little deaths" (rejections, failures, losses) into new life within us and around us. When physical death comes, God will give us new life, life in union with God, beyond anything we could ever dream of.

3
List your top ten fears, the things you are most afraid of or worried about.

4
Imagine yourself in a situation where you are threatened by one of the fears you listed in activity 3. In writing, describe ways that God might walk along with you "through the valley of the shadow of death." That is, what kinds of things might happen to help you deal with the situation?

"Please God, Help Me!"

Here is an example of a teenager who was struggling with fear but also reaching out to God in trust. Like Alinda, this young person addressed God in a letter:

Dear God,
I'm the kind of person who is always happy and trying to solve my friends' problems, but when it comes to me having a problem, I always find myself alone with no one to talk to.
I also have this fear of being put down. I usually don't ask people for favors or help because I'm afraid they might say no. I usually solve my problems by turning to drugs or alcohol. I know that doesn't solve much, but right now I don't know what else to do. I usually do acid.
I really want to stop, but I don't know how I can face my problems without acid or alcohol. Too many people have let me down before. Please, God, help me!

This young person desperately needs to get help from a caring adult. But reaching out to God in trust may be the crucial first step before being able to reach out in trust to a human being who can help. On the other hand, for some people, taking the step of trusting a human being can enable them to trust God for the first time. Trust opens up possibilities for people that they did not even know were there, because they were too afraid to look beyond their fear. Sometimes trust just gives us the courage to hang on and keep going through tough times. Trust in God helps us see ourselves and the world with hope instead of despair.

Let Go . . . Let God

Saint Paul's words to the church at Philippi encourage us to trust in God always:

Do not worry about anything, but in everything by prayer and supplication with thanksgiving let your requests be made known to God. And the peace of God, which surpasses all understanding, will guard your hearts and your minds in Christ Jesus. (Philippians 4:6–7)

Trusting in God does not mean we feel assured that our problems will necessarily be resolved the way we want them to. Trusting in God is not the same as expecting that God will do our will. Instead, it is a gradual "letting go . . . and letting God." We become open to what God is doing in our life, and we respond to it with trust. Over time this trust brings peace and joy, even if not in the way we expected.

Spirituality and the Good Times

In this chapter we have seen examples of people turning to God in times of trouble—when self-esteem is weak or fear is strong. During such times, our spirituality can bring comfort and transform our life in remarkable and dramatic ways. But what about the good times—when we feel confident and strong, untroubled by fear? Do we need spirituality when everything seems just right?

The answer, of course, is yes. Spirituality means becoming fully alive and growing toward God, and this kind of growth happens in all of life's stages and moods. Spirituality may not seem as valuable in the good times as it does in the hard times, but it is

5

If you had a friend who contacted you only when in a panic or crisis, never when things were just fine, what would you think about that friend? Write up a conversation you might have with that friend about how your friend treats you.

still an important part of living. Consider the following prayer, written by a high school student. This young woman's words describe a desire to grow closer to God and others when life is going well:

God,
Thank you for the life I live. Please help me to live this life with a positive outlook each day. Help me to develop into the person I'd like to be: an honest, giving, and healthy individual. To find this me, please grant me the courage to stand up against society and peer pressure as I draw up my own set of values. As I grow through my teenage years, help me to form a special relationship with you that I will be able to build on. Teach me to respect myself, as well as others, and to treat them in a way I would like to be treated. Most of all, help me to develop your gift of love so that it may affect others in a special way—just like the way your love for me has had a great impact in my life.
(Kaitlyn Pratt, Archbishop Williams High School, Braintree, Massachusetts)

When Spirituality Is Genuine

To grow spiritually is to become who we are meant to be as a free and joyful person. Avoiding the world or having a distaste for ordinary life is not part of healthy spirituality. With genuine spirituality, we open our heart to let God into the midst of our everyday life and world. We welcome God as the One who loves us without any limits; the One with whom we are able to be completely, honestly ourselves; the One who helps us live more and more in trust and less and less in fear.

Jesus Christ is at the center of Christian spirituality. As a fully human and divine person, he taught us how to grow spiritually in the midst of everyday joys and sorrows. He showed us, too, that spirituality touches all parts of human life, that God does not want to be confined to one corner of our life— a "religion" or "piety" section. God wants to flow into our work, our dreams, our struggles, our relationships with others. God wants to bring self-respect, love, honesty, strength, healing, and trust into every area of our life. That is what happens, little by little, as a person grows in genuine spirituality.

6
Draw a room as it would appear from above (basically, a square). If that room was your life, where would God be? Draw an *X* in the spot where God would be.

For Review

- What is spirituality?
- With what kind of love does God love each person? How does that kind of love affect a person who is open to it?
- How did Jesus respond to his fears?
- What Christian belief is the foundation of trust and hope in God?
- Describe how genuine spirituality can affect a person's whole life.

Saints Teresa and Ignatius: Total Trust in God

SPANISH saints Teresa of Ávila and Ignatius of Loyola lived in the 1500s, an era when the church was going through tremendous turmoil. They each founded a religious order that brought renewal and hope to a church that was greatly in need of reform—the Discalced Carmelites by Teresa and the Society of Jesus, or Jesuits, by Ignatius.

In the midst of their heroic and intensely active lives, Teresa and Ignatius held a deep, abiding trust in God. Both saints have passed on prayers of trust and surrender to God that have become favorites in the Catholic heritage of spirituality.

Let nothing trouble you,
Let nothing scare you,
All is fleeting,
God alone is unchanging.
Patience
Everything obtains.
Who possesses God
Nothing wants.
God alone suffices.
Saint Teresa of Ávila

Take, Lord, and receive
all my liberty,
my memory, my understanding,
and my entire will,
all that I have and possess.
You have given all to me.
To you, Lord, I return it.
All is yours.
Dispose of it
wholly according to your will.
Give me your love and your grace.
That is enough for me.
Saint Ignatius of Loyola

Prayer: Nourishing Our Relationship with God

Relationships Take Time and Energy

Suppose you have a friendship with someone you care a lot about. You discover that with this person you feel accepted and loved for who you are; you can truly be yourself without fear of being rejected. You trust this person.

What would happen if you never tried to get together with your friend, if you never spent any time talking, having fun, just being with each other? You know your friend cares about you, so you put the person out of your mind. Sounds like a pretty strange friendship, right? Sounds like it may gradually dry up and wither away.

Yet that is the kind of "friendship" many people have with God. They know God loves them. They may have even felt God's love for them at some point. But they never spend any time with God. They take their relationship with God for granted. God does not enter their awareness, except maybe once in a while during a church service.

A friendship takes time and energy. A personal relationship with God is similar. It needs time, attention, and care if it is to survive and grow.

Lifting Our Heart to God

Prayer is the awareness of God and the response of our heart to God in all areas of life. It is *paying attention* to God. Prayer nourishes our relationship with God, like the time and energy we give to someone whose friendship we treasure. Spirituality, the process of becoming a fully alive person as we grow closer to God, depends on prayer.

One saint, **Thérèse of Lisieux**, a young Carmelite nun who lived about a hundred years ago, described prayer this way:

> For me, prayer means launching out of the heart towards God; it means lifting up one's eyes, quite simply, to heaven, a cry of grateful love, from the crest of joy or the trough of despair.

Thérèse emphasized the simplicity of prayer, that it is more a matter of lifting up the heart to God than of using fancy words or saying just the right thing. And we can pray out of joy or out of discouragement. What matters is that we turn to God.

7
Saint Thérèse's way of trying to become holy is known as the Little Way. She did the little everyday activities of life with a spirit of love and a desire to please God, not out of a hope that people would notice or praise her. Agree or disagree with this statement in a paragraph: *The Little Way is the best way to live.*

Different Forms of Prayer

Think of all the different ways we relate to our friends: We share whatever is happening in our life. We talk over problems and ask for help and advice. We *do* fun things together—listen to music, go walking, go to the beach, shop, go dancing. If a friend is away for a few months, we might write letters to each other. If a friend did something nice or helpful for us, we usually say thanks. We let friends know when we think they're great, and also when we're mad at them or disappointed in them.

Like the different ways we relate to our friends, prayer can take a variety of forms:

- *Prayers of conversation.* Sharing with God whatever is happening in our life, our thoughts, and our feelings
- *Prayers of petition.* Asking God for help for ourselves or others
- *Prayers of thanks and praise.* Expressing gratitude for God's gifts to us and telling God how wonderful God is
- *Prayers of meditation.* Focusing our attention on God and the mysteries of God with our thoughts, feelings, and imagination
- *Formal prayers.* Praying in the special words provided by a particular religious tradition

Prayers of Conversation

Perhaps the most ordinary, familiar way people pray is by "talking to God"—usually in the quiet of their own mind and heart. They say whatever is going on inside them—such as the details of their day; their worries; the things they are happy, sad, or angry about; or their concerns about the future. Such talks with God are **prayers of conversation.**

Getting out of bed in the morning or going to sleep at night are typical times when a person might talk to God. For instance:

- Oh, God, I wish I didn't have to get up today. I'm so tired of school. I can't wait for summer. And I've got two tests today. Help!
- Things turned out sort of mixed today, God. The biology test wasn't too bad. History was kind of hard, though—wish I'd studied more. . . . Oh, I found out I made the softball team! That'll be cool to travel with the team. . . .

8
On a typical morning, what do you think about when you first wake up? Write it out in the form of a prayer to God.

Such prayers are like the typical stream of thoughts and reactions a person has in a day, but they are shared with God. God is invited into the person's life, and the person becomes aware that the ordinary activities of life are blessed by the presence and concern of God.

Conversational prayer can also be about deeper feelings and problems—like the prayers by teenagers quoted on pages 272–273, 274, and 276. In those instances the prayers were not just inner thoughts; they were written down, as letters to God. Expressing things in writing to God helps many people because their thoughts and feelings get out on the page instead of just rumbling around inside them and making them anxious. Keeping a journal, a book for recording one's private thoughts, feelings, and experiences, can be a way of conversing with God.

Prayers of Petition

In Matthew's Gospel, Jesus says this about asking God for help: "'Ask, and it will be given you; search, and you will find; knock, and the door will be opened for you'" (7:7).

God wants to hear our every concern and need. These pleas for God's help are called **prayers of petition**; they express how much we depend on God for everything in our life. At times prayers of petition can be part of a conversa-

9
Think of one big concern you have and write it down as a prayer of petition to God to help you with it. Carry around the prayer and read it every time this concern is weighing you down.

tional prayer, as in some of the previous examples.

What do people pray for? Just about anything. For instance:

- Please help me pass the test, God.
- I'm in bad shape with drugs, God. I need your help.
- God, forgive me for being mean to my mom tonight. Help us understand each other so we don't fight so much.
- God, my grandma's sick again. Help her to feel better.
- Please, God, bless all the homeless people, and make our society more compassionate to them.
- God, help me understand your will in my life. I want to serve you better. Please show me how.

From the relatively small concerns to the huge ones, from our personal needs to the needs of the whole world, God wants us to ask for help. This should not be surprising, because in every prayer of petition we recognize that God is there and that we have a relationship with God—and God desires this relationship, too.

That does not mean we will always, or even usually, get exactly what we ask for in prayer. How God answers our prayers is mysterious, not obvious. But Jesus tells us to go ahead and ask, trusting that God will care for us and those we are praying for, often in ways we do not expect or imagine. Praying petitions for ourselves, for people we love, and for people we do not even know, can deepen our trust in God. By asking God for help with all our needs, we place our life in God's hands. When we truly trust God, our prayers of petition are prayers for God's will— the coming of God's Reign on earth.

Asking God for Help

Dear God,

Be with me when my parents are pushing me to go so far.

Be with me when school has me stressed out.

Be with me when my team is losing.

Be with me when a family member is this close to death.

Be with me when the troubles of the world all seem to be on my back.

Through all the times of my life, O God, please be with me.

(Anonymous,
Saint Edmond High School,
Fort Dodge, Iowa)

A Simple Thanks

For all the times
    you
      sent
        a perfect light
          a perfect note
          a perfect word
            a perfect look
              thank you.
                Your simple gifts
                  make me
                    happy.
                      (Anonymous,
            Academy of the Holy Names,
                      Tampa, Florida)

Student art: "Snow Angel,"
color photo by Brant Roshau,
Trinity High School, Dickinson, North Dakota

Prayer of Thanks and Praise

We have so much to be thankful for—our life, our family, our friends, the opportunities we have, the beauties of creation. The Psalms in the Hebrew Scriptures are full of **prayers of thanks and praise** for all God's wonderful gifts and deeds. Here, for instance, is Psalm 100:

Make a joyful noise to the LORD, all the earth.
    Worship the LORD with gladness;
    come into his presence with singing.

Know that the LORD is God.
    It is he that made us, and we are his;
    we are his people, and the sheep of his pasture.

Enter his gates with thanksgiving,
    and his courts with praise.
    Give thanks to him, bless his name.

For the LORD is good;
    his steadfast love endures forever,
    and his faithfulness to all generations.

You could probably make a list of all the things you are grateful for. Constantly finding something to be thankful for is the sign of a heart that is close to God. Writing to one of the early Christian communities, Saint Paul urged them to pour out their gratitude for everything in life: "Rejoice always, pray without ceasing, give thanks in all circumstances; for this is the will of God in Christ Jesus for you" (1 Thessalonians 5:16–18).

You may wonder: Be thankful "in *all* circumstances," even when things go badly for us? even when we are sad or lonely or defeated? Yes, there is something to thank God for even in a situation of suffering. For instance:

> Lord, you know how bad I'm hurting. I've cried myself to sleep every night since Dad died. When will I ever feel normal again?
>
> I don't know why this happened to us, God, and I don't know how we'll make it without Dad. But I know you are with us, Lord, even in this terrible time. You've even made some good things come out of this, like all the support from our family and friends. Thank you for loving us.

This kind of prayer of gratitude does not come easily; it comes through deep, patient trust in God, which develops slowly in a person. The ability to thank and praise God from the heart even in times of trouble characterizes those who have drawn very close to God.

10
Make a list of what you are thankful for. Do you ever thank God or anyone else for all your blessings?

Below: **Make a joyful noise to the Lord!**

Meditation

Most of us in our contemporary, fast-paced society are restless human beings. When faced with a chance to just be quiet for a while, we typically fidget or jump up to do something like turn on the television or play a computer game. We let thoughts race through our head like cars on a speedway. We prefer noise over silence, motion over stillness, being scattered over being focused. We desperately need to calm down and get ourselves together.

Meditation is an inner quieting so that a person can come together within and focus attention on something. You may have heard of meditation as a way for athletes to boost their performance, or for business executives to refresh their mind in the midst of a hectic workday. Doctors even recommend meditation to patients as a way to reduce stress and lower their blood pressure.

Those are all good uses of meditation. However, as a form of prayer, **Christian meditation** has a different purpose. Its goal is to focus on God and the mystery of God's love given to us in Jesus, using thoughts, feelings, and imagination. That kind of focus requires inner quieting, much like the calming and centering techniques people might do to reduce stress and improve their work performance. But Christian meditation aims to clear "inner space" for us *to make room for God in our heart.* It is not about achieving something like health or success but about consciously being with God.

A passage in the Hebrew Scriptures describes well what it means to meditate, "'Be still, and know that I am God!'" (Psalm 46:10). If you have ever tried to empty your mind of thoughts, you know how difficult being still can be. It takes self-discipline, practice, and patience to learn how to meditate.

The first step is to calm the body by consciously relaxing the muscles and breathing deeply and rhythmically. The next step is to introduce some way of focusing attention. A method might be as simple as the slow mental repetition of a sacred word, like *Jesus* or *love.* Or one might read a Bible passage and reflect on it, or zero in on just one line in a passage, or put oneself into a Gospel story as one of the characters, imagining one's feelings and reactions toward Jesus. Books or articles on spirituality, the Scriptures, and the lives of the saints can provide material for meditation as well. Your teacher can probably direct you to some good sources of spiritual reading.

In another method, called guided meditation, a leader reads a script that takes participants through an imaginary event in which they encounter Jesus or a symbol of God or

11
Of the different meditation methods described, which one appeals to you most? Try it out and write a one-page essay describing what it was like.

Facing page: Baila! Baila! by Nicaraguan artist Edda Maria Bird. Dancing can be a way to put your body and soul into prayer.

Putting Body and Soul into Prayer

GOD created each of us as a wonderful, complicated being—body and soul. Each of us is physically, emotionally, intellectually, and spiritually all wrapped up in one whole person. When we pray, we need to bring our whole self to God, not just our mind or our spiritual dimension. We can learn to pray with our body as well as our soul. Here are some possibilities:

A walking prayer. Take a walk in nature and notice everything you see—colorful leaves, spiderwebs, frost-covered bushes, puddles—as a gift from God. Offer thanks for each thing you see. Or walk in your neighborhood past houses and stores where you know some of the people and what they are going through in life. As you walk, say a prayer for each of those persons and their needs.

A musical prayer. Listen to a song that expresses what you are feeling or thinking, and offer the experience to God as a prayer of "being yourself." If you play an instrument, play your favorite piece of music with all your heart and skill. Sing a much-loved song. Music is a good way to praise God.

An artistic prayer. Use your head, hands, and senses to create a drawing, a painting, a mobile, a sculpture, a collage, or a photo. As you work at it, be aware that God's creative energy is within you.

A moving prayer. Pray with gestures. Open your arms up wide to say with your whole being, "God, I'm open to you in my life." Join hands with others when you pray the Lord's Prayer to convey, "We are not alone; we are all in this together with you, Lord." If you like to dance, your dancing can be a prayer of joy, like King David's, who "danced before the LORD with all his might" (2 Samuel 6:14). Or if you are holding on to a lot of anger about something, try punching a pillow while asking for God's help: "Please, God, let me get rid of all this anger." Don't just think it; *move* it.

A writing prayer. Write a letter to God, or keep a journal in which you write your experiences and reflections, offering them to God. In the journal, try writing an imaginary conversation between you and Jesus about an issue you need help with.

12
Focus on one phrase from the Lord's Prayer that has meaning in your life. Reflect in writing on why that phrase is especially important to you.

the sacred. During the process, the participants mentally fill in their own reactions and responses to what the leader is reading. The purpose of such an exercise, of course, is not for the person to create a fabulous imaginary drama but simply to be with God and experience whatever it is that the person needs from the encounter—love, healing, strength, wisdom, challenge, or courage.

Sometimes meditation is so deep that it is purely an experience of the heart—no thoughts or words at all, just the sense of being in union with God. This type of meditation is called **contemplation.**

Formal Prayers

The types of prayer discussed so far involve relating to God with *our own* words or thoughts—"making up" our prayers as we go along. Perhaps you are more familiar with what are called **formal prayers.** These are the special wordings and formulas provided by a religious tradition to help its members express their relationship to God. Formal prayers include prayers of petition, thanks, and praise, as well as statements of belief like the Apostles' Creed.

Why use formal prayers? Because they say just what we need to say on many occasions when we may not be able to think of our own words. Also, these prayers unify people from all over the world who belong to the same religion and pray the same prayers in their own language. Catholicism has many such formal prayers that unite Catholics everywhere.

The Lord's Prayer. For Christians, the most important formal prayer is the Lord's Prayer, or the Our Father:

Our Father who art in heaven,
hallowed be thy name.
Thy kingdom come.
Thy will be done on earth, as it is in heaven.
Give us this day our daily bread,
and forgive us our trespasses,
    as we forgive those who trespass against us,
and lead us not into temptation,
but deliver us from evil.
For the kingdom, the power, and the glory are yours,
now and forever.
Amen.

Taught by Jesus as the best way for his followers to pray, the Lord's Prayer is rich with meaning in every line. It is derived from the Gospels, where there is a short version in Luke and a longer one in Matthew. The longer version is used most often.

Student art: "Marian Devotion," color photo by Martin Rodriguez, Saint Anthony Catholic High School, San Antonio, Texas

The Hail Mary. A formal prayer especially loved by many Catholics is the Hail Mary (known also by its Latin name, *Ave Maria*). It is addressed to Mary as Mother of God.

Hail, Mary, full of grace, the Lord is with you.
Blessed are you among women,
and blessed is the fruit of your womb, Jesus.
Holy Mary, Mother of God, pray for us sinners,
   now and at the hour of our death.
Amen.

The first three lines of this prayer are from Luke's Gospel account of events in Mary's life at the time she learned she was pregnant with Jesus. The Hail Mary is the basic prayer recited many times in the Catholic devotion called the **Rosary.**

The Liturgy. The entire liturgy of the church—its sacraments and rituals, including the Mass and the church's official prayer for each day called the **Liturgy of the Hours**—is formal prayer. Many prayers in the Scriptures, like the Psalms, are formal prayers as well, intended to be prayed in union with others in the church.

The eucharistic celebration, or Mass, deserves special attention. The Mass is a formal prayer, but it is also much more than that. It is the center of the life of the church. As a community celebration, the Mass consists of common elements throughout the world. The Word of God is always proclaimed through readings from the Scriptures. Petitions are offered by members of the community for the needs of the church and the whole world. God is thanked and praised in the "Glory to God" and in the eucharistic prayer, in which the bread and wine are consecrated, becoming the body and blood of Jesus Christ. Members of the congregation receive the body and blood of Christ by eating and drinking the consecrated bread and wine. These elements add up to an act of worship that is at the core of Catholic life.

Memorizing certain formal prayers is a helpful practice because then these prayers will always be there for us when we need them—when our own words are not enough, or when we want to pray in unity with other believers who pray the same thoughts and words.

For Review

• What is prayer? How is it related to spirituality?
• Briefly describe five different forms of prayer.
• Write the Lord's Prayer and the Hail Mary.
• What act of worship is at the core of Catholic life?

Prayer and Community

Prayer Unites People

All genuine prayer unites us with one another as well as with God. If we are truly drawing closer to God, we will be drawing closer to other people, even when we are praying privately. For Christians, this is the reality of the Body of Christ: What one person does affects all the rest because all are united in Christ.

Genuine prayer helps us love others because we are dwelling in God's love. The First Letter of John makes this point strongly:

> We love because he first loved us. Those who say, "I love God," and hate their brothers or sisters, are liars; for those who do not love a brother or sister whom they have seen, cannot love God whom they have not seen. The commandment we have from him is this: those who love God must love their brothers and sisters also. (1 John 4:19–21)

So even **private prayer**, done in the solitude of one's heart, connects the praying person with other people. Likewise, other people are connected to the person through *their own* prayer. Whenever prayer seems impossible because we are too low or drained or discouraged, it helps to know that the whole Body of Christ is supporting us, holding us up. Prayers of others, even those we do not know or have never seen, can make up for our own lack by carrying us through times of weakness and doubt. And we, too, can offer prayers when others cannot, making up for whatever is lacking in them. The Communion of Saints, living and dead, is always there to support one another.

Prayer of Saint Francis: Creating Bonds of Peace

SAINT Francis of Assisi, known as a peacemaker, understood that prayer was a way to let God's love flow through us to create bonds of peace with others:

Lord, make me an instrument of your peace;
Where there is hatred, let me sow love;
Where there is injury, pardon;
Where there is doubt, faith;
Where there is despair, hope;
Where there is darkness, light;
Where there is sadness, joy.

O Divine Master,
grant that I may not so much seek
to be consoled, as to console;
to be understood, as to understand;
to be loved, as to love;
for it is in giving that we receive,
it is in pardoning that we are pardoned,
it is in dying that we are born
to eternal life.

Praying Together

All the prayer forms discussed in this chapter can be prayed in private, but they can also be prayed together with others. Besides private prayer, we need such **community prayer**, occasions when we express our connections with others by praying with a group or faith community. Celebrations of

Praying for a World Without Prejudice

God,
Why do some people
see others through hateful eyes,
see only the color of skin, the texture
of hair, or the sound of accent instead of
trying to see beyond that? Sometimes I feel
like I'm the only one who feels that prejudice is
wrong, not only against Blacks, Hispanics, or
Jews, but what about gays, Christians, Muslims,
women, children, Asians, and every other race,
religion, or creed. God, please help people realize that these prejudgments are wrong. Let
them learn to love, no matter what's on the
outside.

(Grecia Mercedes,
Saint Michael Academy,
New York, New York)

13
In what ways are you involved in community prayer—at home, at school, or at church? In writing, describe your reactions to these occasions of prayer.

Mass and the other sacraments are times of community prayer. They always involve at least two people, and typically many more than that.

We have many opportunities to join with others for prayer—a family grace or blessing before meals, a prayer at the beginning of a class period, a prayer service for a school or youth group.

Community prayer can take some surprising forms. For example, in a suburb of Chicago, every year hundreds of youth group members from several parishes participate in "Harvest Sunday." They do a door-to-door collection of groceries for food pantries that serve poor people. After a day of high spirits and hard work collecting about twenty-five large truckloads of food, the young people deliver the food items to inner-city Chicago and then have a huge celebration: a festive Mass and grand pizza party, followed by a dance. Harvest Sunday is really a daylong community prayer, a powerful celebration of shared service and having fun together.

Some people join a prayer group specifically to share their prayers with others. As Saint Paul encouraged the community of Christians at Ephesus:

Be filled with the Spirit, as you sing psalms and hymns and spiritual songs among yourselves, singing and making melody to the Lord in your hearts, giving thanks to God the Father at all times and for everything in the name of our Lord Jesus Christ. (Ephesians 5:18–20)

Members of a prayer group may build a strong bond of caring because they have shared their concerns and their reliance on God with one another. They understand part of what is in one another's hearts.

For Review

- How does all prayer, even private prayer, unite us with others?
- Why do we need community prayer? Give three examples of this kind of prayer.

The Fruits of Spirituality and Prayer

How do we know we are growing in life with God? How do we know that our spirituality is genuine and not off-base or distorted, as some spiritualities can be?

We certainly cannot evaluate our spirituality by how well spoken our prayers are. That is the last thing God is interested in from us. God looks at our heart, and a prayer we cannot even find words for may be more real and true than anything we could articulate. Even when we are unable to pray, as Saint Paul tells us, the Holy Spirit prays within us:

> The Spirit helps us in our weakness; for we do not know how to pray as we ought, but that very Spirit intercedes with sighs too deep for words. And God, who searches the heart, knows what is the mind of the Spirit, because the Spirit intercedes for the saints according to the will of God. (Romans 8:26–27)

Instead of looking for great prayers or awesome spiritual experiences as a sign of growing toward God, we need to look at the fruits of spirituality and prayer in our life. Saint Paul can help us understand these **fruits of the Holy Spirit:**

> The fruit of the Spirit is love, joy, peace, patience, kindness, generosity, faithfulness, gentleness, and self-control. . . . If we live by the Spirit, let us also be guided by the Spirit. (Galatians 5:22–25)

In our own life, we can ask ourselves:
- Are we trusting our life more fully into God's hands?
- Are we more loving toward others?
- Are we more honest and peaceful with ourselves?
- Do we have a grateful heart?
- Are our moral behaviors and actions rooted in the Gospel of Jesus?

The way to know if we are really growing closer to God is to look for the fruits of our relationship with God. In the next chapter, on morality, we will look at what it means to live in the Spirit of Jesus.

14
Write a character sketch of someone you know who has many of the fruits of the Holy Spirit.

12

Christian Morality: Living in the Spirit of Jesus

God's Love for Us: The *Why* of Christian Morality

Chapter 11 described spirituality as the process of becoming a fully alive, whole person as we grow in our relationship with God. Prayer was presented as a way to nourish that relationship with God.

Consider the Fruits

Keeping the meaning of spirituality and prayer in mind, reflect on this story:

> There was a woman who was filled with love for God. She was known to be religious and devout, and every morning she walked along the city streets on her way to church. As she walked, children called to her for a kind word, and hungry and homeless people pleaded for help. But the woman was so immersed in the love of God that she did not see or hear them.
>
> One day she approached the church just as the service was scheduled to begin. It was early morning. She climbed the steps, passing the homeless men, women, and children gathered there. Some were sleeping; others were just waking up. She opened the church door and walked in, expecting to see the long, narrow aisle and endless rows of pews. But instead, she was amazed that the inside of the church seemed to be a mirror image of

the outside world she had just left behind. She stood at the top of the steps, looking down at the same needy children and homeless people she had passed by moments before. Why, she wondered, were they here to greet her?

A child spoke, "Every day, God has been waiting for you—not just in the church but in all of us who need you."

- The story says the woman was "filled with love for God." Do you think that was true?
- What was missing in the woman's life of prayer and devotion to God?

Recall from chapter 11 that the genuineness of one's prayer and spirituality can be seen in the fruit that comes about in the person's life: "The fruit of the Spirit is love, joy, peace, patience, kindness, generosity, faithfulness, gentleness, and self-control" (Galatians 5:22–23). How we live our life is the real test of how close we are to God.

Morality has to do with the way we live our life. The principles of morality help us define right and wrong behavior. For example, one kind of morality instructs us to "Do good and avoid evil." Everyone—Christian or non-Christian, believer in God or nonbeliever—has a morality, even if they do not realize it or call it by that name. Whether it leads them to good or to evil, some kind of morality is part of everyone's life.

The Commandment of Love

Christian morality, the ideal that Jesus presents, is summed up in the word *love*. Remember when someone once asked Jesus which commandment of the Law was the greatest? He answered with the **Great Commandment**, rooted in the Jewish tradition—a twofold yet single commandment of love:

"'You shall love the Lord your God with all your heart, and with all your soul, and with all your mind.' This is the greatest and first commandment. And a second is

Volunteers with Habitat for Humanity give their time, energy, and skills to help build a home for a family in need of housing.

like it: 'You shall love your neighbor as yourself.' On these two commandments hang all the Law and the prophets." (Matthew 22:37–40)

On another occasion, Jesus said to his disciples, "'This is my commandment, that you love one another as I have loved you'" (John 15:12). Love—freely given and for the good of others—is the core of the morality that Jesus taught.

God's Love: Open or Closed to It?

Why should we love? Because God loves us. The Christian Testament expresses this truth in a well-known passage:

> Beloved, let us love one another, because love is from God; everyone who loves is born of God and knows God. Whoever does not love does not know God, for God is love. God's love was revealed among us in this way: God sent his only Son into the world so that we might live through him. . . . Beloved, since God loved us so much, we also ought to love one another. No one has ever seen God; if we love one another, God lives in us, and his love is perfected in us. (1 John 4:7–12)

1

From your experience, describe an incident in which someone was open to goodness, truth, or beauty. Do you believe the person was really being open to God? Why or why not? Explain your answer in writing.

Christian morality means living out the love God has already given us human beings. The Christian vision is that we lead a moral life of love not to gain God's love or favor; rather, we love because God loved us first. God created us in the divine image as God's beloved ones, and sent the Son of God, Jesus, to be one of us and to give his life for us. Each of us is precious to God. Realizing that gives us the true basis for self-esteem: we can believe in ourselves because Someone already believes in us.

God loves us first; that is for sure. However, we may be open to divine love or closed to it. If we are open—like a cup that has a wide mouth—God's love fills us up and spills over into our thoughts, words, and actions. We may not even be conscious that God is the One we are opening ourselves to. We may only be aware of opening our heart to goodness, truth, or beauty. But God is the source of all those good fruits, even when we do not realize it.

On the other hand, if we are always closed to God's love—like a cup with a tightly fastened lid—we end up living a self-centered, small, and empty life, never experiencing the great joy for which we were destined.

Most of us are somewhere in between—neither completely closed nor completely open to God's love. It takes a lifetime for most of us to become totally open to God.

For Review

- What is the general definition of morality?
- What is the ideal of Christian morality?
- Why do human beings love?
- What is the effect on a person of being open to God's love? closed to God's love?

We are free to be open to divine love or closed to it.
Student art: **"Study of a Hand," pencil drawing by Jessica Wagner, Chaminade Julienne High School, Dayton, Ohio**

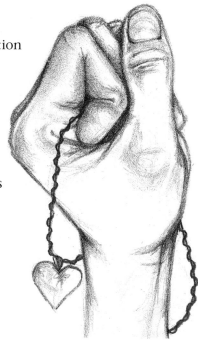

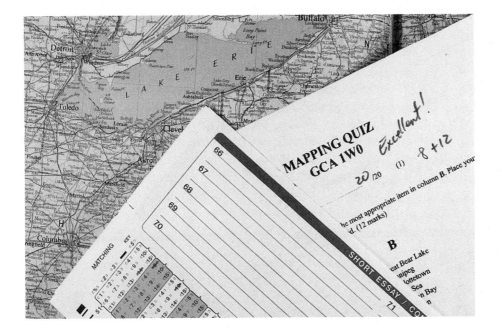

We can easily fool ourselves into thinking we would score an A+ on the Great Commandment.

The Law of Love:
The *What* of Christian Morality

The Great Commandment—to love God with our whole being and to love our neighbor as we love ourselves—is the foundation and summary of Christian morality.

Is that it—end of chapter, end of discussion? Imagine someone doing a quick self-check on keeping the Great Commandment of love:

> Well, sure, I really do love God. After all, I go to church on Sundays, and I often ask God for help. As for loving my neighbor as myself, of course I do that. I'm really good to my friends, and lots of people like me because I'm so nice. So I guess I score an A+ on the Great Commandment!

This self-talk illustrates that we can fool ourselves into believing that love is a rather simple matter. We may believe that if we think we are loving, then we really are. Recall the woman in the opening story. She probably convinced herself that she was very loving, but apparently she didn't quite get what love is all about.

The Ten Commandments: Love Spelled Out

How do we know what love really asks of us? The requirements of loving God and neighbor are contained in the Ten Commandments, revealed by God to Moses (recall the story on pages 68–69). These Ten Commandments—also called the **Decalogue**, meaning "ten words"—were what God expected of the Israelites if they were to be faithful to God's Covenant with them.

When Jesus stated that the Great Commandment is to love God and neighbor, he was summing up the Ten Commandments.

The Decalogue

The Ten Commandments are given with somewhat different wording in two places in the Hebrew Scriptures— Exodus 20:2–17 and Deuteronomy 5:6–21. Here is the wording that has become customary for many Christians:

1. I am the LORD your God: you shall not have strange gods before me.
2. You shall not take the name of the LORD your God in vain.
3. Remember to keep holy the LORD's Day.
4. Honor your father and your mother.
5. You shall not kill.
6. You shall not commit adultery.
7. You shall not steal.
8. You shall not bear false witness against your neighbor.
9. You shall not covet your neighbor's wife.
10. You shall not covet your neighbor's goods.

You may already have noticed that the first three commandments refer to love of God, and the next seven refer to love of neighbor. All the Commandments together spell out the meaning of the Great Commandment.

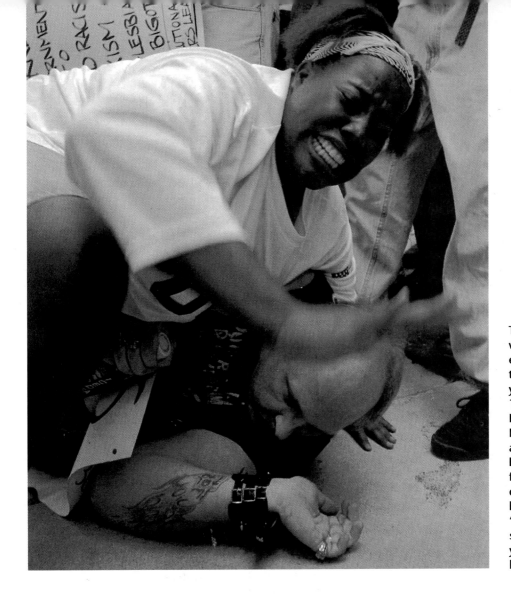

The meaning of Jesus' words, "'Love your enemies and pray for those who persecute you,'" was shown at a 1996 rally of the Ku Klux Klan in Ann Arbor, Michigan. Keisha Thomas, age eighteen, used her body to shield a Klansman from a crowd of anti-Klan demonstrators who were beating him with sticks. "Just because you beat somebody doesn't mean you're going to change his mind," she said.

The Letter and the Spirit of the Law

When Jesus preached that we should follow the Commandments, summed up in the Great Commandment, he did not mean that we should follow only the bare minimum of each commandment. He told people that they must go beyond just the **letter of the Law**—its literal, obvious meaning—to embrace the **spirit of the Law**—its deeper meaning of love. As an example, consider something Jesus taught in the Sermon on the Mount:

> "You have heard that it was said to your ancestors, 'You shall not kill; and whoever kills will be liable to judgment.' But I say to you, whoever is angry with his brother will be liable to judgment, and whoever says to his brother . . . 'You fool,' will be liable. . . ." (Matthew 5:21–22, NAB)

Jesus understood that we can "kill" someone with attitudes and words, not just by literally killing the person. So the fifth commandment, "You shall not kill," is about two

2
Focus on one of the Ten Commandments that seems especially hard for teenagers today to follow. Use the reflection questions about that commandment on pages 302–303. Write a reflection on how you or people you know struggle with keeping the spirit of that commandment.

Keeping the Spirit of the

1 I am the Lord your God: you shall not have strange gods before me.

- Do I acknowledge God as the center of my life?
- Do I treat anything or anyone with the honor and reverence that belong only to God? In other words, do I give my whole heart, soul, and mind to other "gods"— like popularity, boyfriends or girlfriends, money, clothes, power, pleasure, good grades, or winning at sports?
- Do I nourish my faith in God by turning to God in prayer?
- Do I refuse to place my trust in superstitious practices, magic, or evil powers?

2 You shall not take the name of the Lord your God in vain.

- Do I have an attitude of reverence to God?
- Do I treat God's name with respect?
- Do I avoid using God's name casually or offensively?

3 Remember to keep holy the Lord's Day.

- Do I reserve space in my life for rest and relaxation, especially on Sunday (or another day that is sacred in my religion if I am not Christian)?
- Do I worship God with others on that sacred day, participating in the Eucharist on Sunday or Saturday evening if I am Catholic?

4 Honor your father and your mother.

- As a young person, am I obedient to my parents or those who have raised me? And am I respectful toward them always?
- Do I treat my parents with gratitude?
- Do I try to act with love in my family, with brothers and sisters as well as parents and grandparents?
- Do I treat those in positions of authority with respect?
- Do I obey government laws that are in accordance with God's Law?

5 You shall not kill.

- Do I treat all human life, my own and others', as a precious gift to be nurtured? Do I recognize the dignity and worth of every human being?
- Do I avoid harming others by violent, hateful, or prejudiced words and attitudes, as well as by physical violence?
- Do I reject abortion, which is the killing of the unborn?
- Do I refrain from driving a car or operating machinery in a way that could harm others?
- Do I try to foster peace by helping people reconcile their differences without violence?

Ten Commandments

6 You shall not commit adultery.

- Do I treat sexuality, my own and others', with respect and care?
- Do I develop healthy friendships with others, whether of the same sex or of the other sex?
- Do I refrain from genital sexual expression outside the committed union of marriage?
- Do I keep the desire for sexual enjoyment from ruling me, my behavior, and my relationships?

7 You shall not steal.

- Do I refrain from taking what does not belong to me?
- Do I refuse to engage in cheating—trying to gain something for myself by manipulation or dishonesty?
- Am I up front and honest in my dealings with others?
- Do I treat others with justice, allowing them to meet their own material needs and not being selfish with what I have?
- Do I treat the earth as a gift from God for everyone's benefit, not as a possession to be exploited for my own convenience or profit?
- Do I support efforts toward the just distribution of goods and resources in society and the whole world?

8 You shall not bear false witness against your neighbor.

- Do I uphold the truth in my relations with myself and others? Am I honest?
- Do I avoid lying—intentionally telling a falsehood?
- Do I refrain from harming the reputation of others by spreading rumors and gossip about them?
- Do I respect my own and others' privacy by keeping confidential what other people have no right to know?

9 You shall not covet your neighbor's wife.

- Do I try to see others as precious in God's eyes, not as sexual objects to be used for my entertainment?
- Do I try to be modest in my appearance and actions, protecting the mystery of my own intimate self?

10 You shall not covet your neighbor's goods.

- Do I try to banish greed, envy, and jealousy from my heart?
- Do I try to practice goodwill toward those who have better fortune than I do?
- Do I try to find happiness in things of the spirit, rather than assuming that wealth, material goods, pleasure, and power will make me happy?

things. It is certainly about the wrongful taking of another's life. But it is also about dispelling hatred and vengeance from our heart and respecting the dignity of every human being. It does more than forbid us from committing murder. It also calls us to be peacemakers. As Jesus taught, "'Love your enemies and pray for those who persecute you'" (Matthew 5:44).

To reflect on the "spirit" of the Ten Commandments as well as their "letter," consider the questions for each commandment on pages 302–303.

Themes in Catholic Moral Teaching

All the Christian churches find the basis for their moral teachings in the Great Commandment, the law of love, which Jesus taught and which sums up the Ten Commandments. The Jewish faith as well sees love of God and love of neighbor as central to morality, and it follows the Ten Commandments. So Christians—Catholic, Protestant, and Orthodox—and Jews have much in common in their teachings about morality. In fact, most of the world's religions hold similar principles about what is right and wrong. For instance, all major religious traditions hold that it is wrong to murder and wrong to steal, although they may define those general principles in varying ways.

The Catholic church, through its official teaching voice, the Magisterium, has spoken out strongly on issues that especially challenge the society and world of this era. Catholicism is not alone in its teaching on these issues; many of its concerns are shared with other Christians, Jews, members of other religions, and nonbelievers. But in response to these issues, the Catholic voice has been particularly clear and strong.

These issues come under three themes emphasized in Catholic moral teaching in the last few decades:
- the dignity and worth of all human life
- the necessity of social justice
- the sacredness of human sexuality and its expression

The Dignity and Worth of All Human Life

The Catholic church has spoken out repeatedly and passionately about the need to protect human life at every stage of existence—from the fetus growing in its mother's womb to the old person dying in a nursing home bed. Every human being, "from womb to tomb," has dignity and worth because every human is created by God in God's image.

This theme is at the heart of Catholic teaching on issues that involve direct killing: murder, abortion, euthanasia, capital punishment, war. You are likely to study these issues later in a course on morality.

Many other threats to human life exist today besides direct killing—among them are racism, discrimination, terrible living conditions, malnutrition and hunger, domestic violence and abuse, reckless driving, alcohol and other drug abuse, the drug trade, torture, the military arms trade, and the exploitation of people for economic gain. All these issues are matters of the dignity and worth of all human life, and thus they fall within the realm of the fifth commandment, "You shall not kill." The Catholic church consistently communicates to the world the importance of human dignity. In Pope John Paul II's 1995 encyclical, *The Gospel of Life,* he appealed to every person to reject killing and other forms of violence and to "build a new culture of life" that will welcome and cherish human life in all its conditions (number 95).

Facing page: **Pope John Paul II is a prophetic voice of Catholic moral teaching.**
Above: **A beggar woman sits forlornly near the ruins of war-torn Grozny, Russia, waiting for passersby to give her a few coins to support her life.**

The Necessity of Social Justice

Catholic teaching on social justice builds on the theme of the dignity and worth of every human being. It affirms that everyone's needs in society should be provided for, not just the needs of a few or even of the majority. A world in which some people and nations have most of the wealth and resources while others have almost none is an unjust system. Immense human misery due to poverty cries out for justice around the world. We must work to reverse injustice

3
What do you think is the most serious threat to human life in today's world? Explain your answer in a paragraph.

In a refugee camp in Somalia, a country in Africa that has suffered from drought and civil war, a starving Somali boy receives a bowl of beans and rice.

so that everyone can share in the goods of the world, which are a gift from God to us all. The theme of social justice is related to the seventh commandment, "You shall not steal."

Catholic social teaching stresses that we must foster the **common good**—the well-being of all in society—in contrast to pursuing our own individual good without concern for others.

The Catholic church has always spoken out on behalf of poor and powerless people, especially in the last century, through numerous documents by popes and bishops. Catholic popes and bishops have addressed issues such as work and employment, poverty and global economics, war and nuclear weapons, national health care, education, racism, the development of the world's poor nations, the environment, the problems of farmers and people in rural areas, and homelessness.

Besides the official documents, the example of modern-day Catholics who have given themselves in service to poor people has modeled Catholic social teaching perhaps better than words could ever do.

4
Do some research on one of the models of social justice pictured below. Write an imaginary dialog between you and that person on why he or she lived such a life.

Modern-day Saints, Models of Social Justice

Some "teachers" of social justice include the following modern-day saints, whose heroic lives of service to poor people have inspired countless others:

• **Dorothy Day.** As cofounder of the Catholic Worker Movement, Dorothy Day started houses of hospitality for the hungry and homeless, beginning in New York City in 1933. And throughout her life, she protested war and injustice.

• **Oscar Romero.** As archbishop of San Salvador, in El Salvador, Oscar Romero stood up to his country's oppressive government and wealthy elite on behalf of poor peasants and workers. He was assassinated in 1980.

• *Mother Teresa of Calcutta.* Herself a worldwide symbol of charity in our time, Mother Teresa founded the Missionaries of Charity, who minister to desperately poor, sick, and dying people who have no one else to care for them.

The Sacredness of Human Sexuality and Its Expression

Catholic moral teaching stands for the sacredness of sexuality in an age when sexuality has been terribly misunderstood and abused. In our society, sex is often used to sell products and make money, to manipulate persons, to exert power over another, or to express a temporary attraction. Many people regard sexuality as an idol, the answer to all human needs, but that does not mean they respect sexuality. Sex is often treated with little respect, as simply a means to get something desired.

Although societal norms in recent decades have gone in the direction of treating genital sexual expression more casually than before, Catholicism continues to voice its conviction loud and clear: Human sexuality and its genital expression are sacred; they are gifts from God that are to be treated with love and care.

Sexual intercourse is God's way of enabling a man and a woman to express their love for each other and bring forth the new life of children in a family. That is why intercourse is meant to be part of the permanent commitment of marriage. In an age when one out of every two marriages ends in divorce, the Catholic church continues to assert that the sacred union of a couple in marriage is not broken by divorce. The sixth commandment, "You shall not commit adultery," and the ninth commandment, "You shall not covet your neighbor's wife," are the bases for Catholic teaching on the sacredness of sexuality and its expression in sexual relations.

The Catholic church speaks out against premarital and nonmarital sex, adultery, and homosexual activity. It also condemns exploitative uses of human sexuality, which have nothing to do with expressing love—rape, sexual harassment, pornography, prostitution, advertising, and the abuse of children and other vulnerable people. In all these teach-

ings runs the theme that as a gift from God, sexual expression is not to be engaged in casually, selfishly, or harmfully.

The law of love is spelled out in the Ten Commandments, and these are further expressed by the tradition of the Catholic church's moral teaching. The law of love is the *what* of Christian morality. Let's now turn to the *how*, that is, how persons decide about their own moral behavior.

For Review

- What spells out the requirements of loving God and loving neighbor?
- List the Ten Commandments, with one example from the questions given on pages 302–303 of how to practice each commandment.
- What is meant by keeping the spirit of the Law, not just the letter of the Law?
- Give brief summaries of the three themes the Catholic church has emphasized in its moral teaching in recent decades.

5
Select one of the issues in this paragraph and express your views about it in an essay.

Freedom and Grace: The *How* of Christian Morality

We are faced with situations every day in which we need to make choices, many of them having to do with morality. Think of the possible moral choices we may have to make:

- whether to join in on gossiping about another person
- whether to copy another student's answers on a test
- whether to have sexual intercourse before marriage
- whether to deceive parents to avoid getting in trouble
- whether to be silent when others are hurting someone in word or actions
- whether to let a friend drive a car while drunk

Some or all of these issues may seem like common sense to you. "Of course," you may say, "they are all wrong." But another person might not be so sure about the rightness or wrongness of any one of them, claiming, "It all depends." Someone else might think, "Such-and-such action is wrong, but I'm going to do it anyway." Still another might wrestle inside about whether something is right or wrong, or be torn about whether to commit an act that he or she knows to be wrong, and finally refuse to do it. In all these cases, Christian morality offers guidelines to help us make wise moral choices.

We Are Responsible

Conscience: Deep in the Human Heart

The Catholic church teaches that all human beings have a **conscience**, the ability to recognize the difference between good and evil. Although people do not always make properly informed judgments of conscience (that is, they may make mistakes in judging about good and evil), a person's conscience must always be respected. That is, no one should ever be forced to do something that is against the judgment of her or his conscience.

Free Will: The Ability to Choose Right or Wrong

Furthermore, God created humans with **free will**, as creatures able to choose freely between moral good and evil, right and wrong. However, the freedom of a person's decisions may be limited by such factors as ignorance, strong emotions like fear, or psychological problems.

Responsibility: Owning Our Actions

Because we can recognize the difference between good and evil (conscience), and we are able to choose between right and wrong (free will), we are **responsible** for our moral actions, both the good and the bad. We own them; we have to answer to God for them. If we perform a deed that is

6
Imagine two cases involving a similar moral dilemma—one case in which the person can be considered fully responsible for her or his choice, and another case in which the person can be considered much less responsible for her or his choice. Write a comparison of the two cases.

Right: We are responsible for forming our conscience correctly, like the potter shapes and molds a piece of earthenware.

wrong, we cannot simply deny our responsibility, nor can we blame anyone else for our mistakes.

However, our responsibility for an action is lessened if our conscience is incorrectly formed through no fault of our own. For example, a woman who steals may have been taught in childhood that stealing is okay, and she carries that attitude with her.

Responsibility is also lessened if our free will is threatened or reduced through no fault of our own. For instance, a terrified man who tells a lie to protect his life cannot fully exercise his free will. Fear is making him less free and therefore less responsible. So we are responsible for our actions, even though because of circumstances our responsibility might be less than it would otherwise have been.

Mature persons are honest persons, and honest persons take responsibility for their actions. To grow in maturity we must increasingly take responsibility for what we do. An example that involves a simple mistake, not a moral choice, can illustrate this growth in responsibility:

A one-year-old who spills a cup of milk cannot take responsibility for the spill; an adult will clean up the mess and give the child another drink. A twelve-year-old, however, is mature enough to take responsibility for such an action. He or she would be expected to clean up the mess and refill the cup.

In the same way, people who are growing in maturity take more and more responsibility for their moral actions. And when they have done something morally wrong, taking responsibility is the first step toward forgiveness.

Forming a Conscience

We should always follow our conscience in moral matters, doing what we believe to be right. But we are also responsible for forming our conscience correctly, leading to an **informed conscience**. In other words, we must try sincerely to seek out the best knowledge and help we can get to shape our conscience toward the truth and not simply toward what we want to think. We cannot just plead ignorance about right and wrong, if the ignorance is our own fault.

The Catholic church teaches that deep within the human conscience is a law "written" by God that calls us to love, to do good, and to avoid evil. All people are called to listen for the truth of that law within. For Catholics, the process of forming one's conscience correctly also includes searching out the meaning of the church's teachings on moral issues and letting those insights guide one's thinking.

Parents have the duty and privilege of helping their children form their growing conscience through example, teaching, correction, and the love that is present in their home.

7
Answer in a paragraph: *What obligation, if any, do teenagers have to help their friends form a correct conscience?*

A Story of Conscience

A group of boys has gone into a video store. Two of them, Pharoah, age ten, and Lafeyette, who is almost fourteen, are brothers. Rickey is one of the guys they hang around with.

As Pharoah admired the wrestling movies, Lafeyette and Rickey looked at the new releases, which included various Ninja and horror films. "Hey, Lafie," Rickey whispered, "let's take us some." Pharoah, who was standing nearby, overheard him. Before Lafeyette had a chance to respond, Pharoah sidled up to his brother.

"Lafie, let's go leave them," he pleaded. Lafeyette hesitated. "Let's go home, Lafie."

"I'm still looking 'round, man. If you wanna go, go!" Lafeyette said in a loud whisper.

Pharoah and the others left. Pharoah was disappointed in Rickey, but even more so in Lafeyette, who seemed to bow to the pressure of his friend. Maybe they wouldn't get caught, he hoped. (Kotlowitz, *There Are No Children Here*, pages 151–152)

In the story, Lafeyette and Rickey are caught in the act of shoplifting, but the store owner decides not to press charges. The boys get a lecture and a ride home in a police car.

Reflect on the following questions, and relate the experience of Pharoah, Lafeyette, and Rickey to your own struggles to listen more closely to your conscience.

- Which person in the story is best at listening to his conscience?
- What might be some reasons behind the different reactions of the brothers, Lafeyette and Pharoah, to Rickey's suggestion to steal?
- Knowing what his brother and friend plan to do, what, if anything, should Pharoah do about it?
- If you were in Lafeyette's or Pharoah's position, what might you have done? What reasons would you have had for your choice?
- Having been caught, what might the experience teach Lafeyette and Rickey about conscience? ▣

Sin Can Be Overcome by Grace

The Attraction of Sin

Sin is the act of knowingly and willingly choosing evil. Evil is the opposite of God, who is the source of all goodness and love. So to sin is to turn away from God in favor of other things that seem, at the time, more attractive—popularity, thrills, pleasure, safety, convenience, power, money or possessions, a boost to the ego, even the approval of some authority. Not many people sin out of a love for evil itself. Most don't love lying, cheating, or harming life. Rather, they are drawn to the benefits of doing evil. For example:

- Tell a lie to your parents about where you are going with friends, and you'll be able to go where you want.
- Cheat on a test, and you'll get a good grade.
- Have an abortion, and you won't have to deal with the difficulty and suffering the baby would have caused you.

These benefits appear to the person as good, not evil:

- Of course I want to be able to go where my friends are going, and I'll feel more comfortable with them if I can just go without my parents making a big deal of it.
- Naturally I want to get a good grade, which will pull up my grade point average and get me into college.
- It makes sense not to mess up my life and abandon all my dreams for my future—not to mention the grief it would cause my parents if I had a baby.

The apparent benefits of doing evil are really hooks that pull us into committing sin—the **temptations** of evil. They put a disguise on evil and make it look good, so that we deceive ourselves into thinking that doing evil is justified. Unfortunately many people live in a state of almost constant self-deception, convincing themselves that the wrong they do is really right—according to their needs and wants.

The Degrees of Sin

Catholic moral teaching describes two categories of sin based on how serious the evil caused is and how much the sin damages the person's relationship with God. **Mortal sin** involves a serious or grave offense, done with full knowledge and freedom, which turns the person completely away from God. **Venial sin** involves a lesser offense that weakens the person's relationship with God but does not turn him or her completely away from God.

Every human being comes into a world where human weakness and sin are already present. Thus the tendency to sin goes along with being human. This condition of humanity is called **Original Sin**, a term that recalls the Genesis story of the first sin by Adam and Eve in the Garden. God's grace has the power to overcome even this weakened condition of humanity, saving each person from the tendency to sin.

The Victory of Grace

Sometimes when we look at the world around us, it may seem that evil is winning in the struggle with goodness. Wars go on; violence increases; poverty and injustice abound; human life appears more threatened than ever. You may be wondering where the good news is in all this talk of sin.

Christianity puts hope in the promise that God's grace is stronger than all the sin in the world. The power of love, peace, joy, forgiveness, reconciliation—God's power—can transform even the worst situations of sin and suffering into new life. We know this through the Resurrection of Jesus and the Paschal Mystery. But God needs human beings to cooperate with grace. God never forces us to be good. God invites, and human beings can respond in freedom to God's grace.

In the end, Christian faith tells us, God's grace will be victorious over all sin, suffering, and death. And if our eyes are open, even today we can see God's grace triumphing over evil in a world that is burdened with sin and suffering.

8
Give an example from your own life of how a temptation presents a moral evil to you as if it is actually justified.

9
Reflect in writing on whether you have seen a victory, small or great, of God's grace over sin in the last week, and if so, where.

For Review

- What does the Catholic church teach about following one's conscience and responsibility for moral actions?
- What is sin?
- How does temptation lure us into committing sin?
- Define mortal sin, venial sin, and Original Sin?
- What do Christians believe about the power of God's grace in the struggle with sin?

Grace: Victorious over Sin

This account of a real incident, written by a high school student in Baltimore, Maryland, expresses the victory of grace over sin.

Well, it all started a little bit before now on the west side of town. Off and on I was selling drugs, not because there was no money, but my father only gave me what he thought would satisfy me.

So about ten o'clock one night, I called up one of my friends and said, "Like man, this is not cutting it. I need more clothes and more money." I started to get upset. There was a hustler that my buddies and myself knew from a while back. In school his girlfriend gave me his pager number. That next night I was basically doing the same thing and watched some videos.

Later that evening I called his pager, and he called me back. When I picked up the phone, I told him it was me. He said he would pick me up at the Mondawmin Mall.

The next day I saw him, and we greeted each other. He was driving a Mercedes Benz. We got in the car and picked up the boy Little Black from my old neighborhood and another boy named Wayne. The hustler kept the gun while we rode behind them in a hack, and Black had the drugs. We got up to Pimlico Road where the stash house was. We had to make about $1,000, and we weren't even out there all day.

Then I thought about it, "Why am I here? I have two parents that love me and I'm out here doing this." After that I was talking to Black, telling him, but he was just a back stabber because he was in charge of us. He left when the hustler arrived and told him about my idea. Well, when he approached me, he had a gun. But the police came. I was dirty, which means I had drugs on me. I threw them down and walked down this alley. I never came back after that.

The good thing that came out of this whole ordeal is that I know that I don't belong selling drugs, but I do need to get an education in school. This is true, especially here at my school now, because without teachers telling you they believe in you and people telling you when you are in the wrong it could cause a person who is not that strong to be drawn into doing other things. This is one of the very reasons I try so hard in school, because this is the only way I can make it positive.

Virtue and Character:
The *Who* of Christian Morality

This chapter has examined these aspects of Christian morality, which is the law of love:

- the *why* behind the law of love (God loves us first)
- the *what* of the law of love (the Ten Commandments and some themes of Catholic moral teaching)
- the *how* of following the law of love (the dynamics of conscience, free will, responsibility, and sin and grace)

A picture of Christian morality would be incomplete without considering the *who*—the person choosing and doing the moral activity.

What Kind of Person?

Perhaps the most important question you will ever have the chance to answer is the one you are answering with your actions every day of your life:

- What kind of person are you, and what kind of person do you want to become?

This question is not about specific moral issues or decision-making dilemmas. It is about *you*—about what kind of person you are as you consider the issues and decisions you face. The question is about your character.

Character consists of the **virtues**, or good habits, and the **vices**, or bad habits, that a person has developed by repetition of moral acts (each one of us is a mixed bag of virtues and vices). Moral **acts**, large and small, good and bad, are the stuff of which character is ultimately made. And the moral acts you do tomorrow will be shaped by your character, what you have become as of today. You bring your character to every moral decision and act. In turn, every moral decision and act shapes your character. Here is the way the cycle looks in a simple diagram:

The Character Cycle

Let's say that one day a ninth grader is faced with a choice in school: she can join in on making fun of somebody with classmates, she can walk away from the situation, or she can speak up in defense of the person being ridiculed. Suppose she joins in with the others and gets a lot of laughs for her clever, sarcastic comments. The next day a similar situation comes up. She will probably find it a little easier to join in on being sarcastic than on the day before.

Habits you form
(virtues and vices)

What you do
(acts)

Who you are
(character)

If a whole week goes by, and she ridicules somebody every day, she is certainly developing a habit—in this case a vice, not a virtue. She not only pokes fun at others once in a while; she is becoming mean. Meanness is getting to be part of her character!

Now every time she is faced with a decision to be hurtful or not, the meanness in her character influences her decision. In fact, she is so used to ridiculing others that it doesn't even feel like she's deciding. It seems to come automatically. Her character is shaping her actions.

The previous example illustrates a character cycle in which a vice, meanness, is involved. But we could just as easily (and more happily!) give an example of a virtue, like compassion, being developed, becoming part of a person's character, and shaping the person's later actions. You can probably think of an example yourself.

Once a person has developed a persistent vice that has become part of that person's character, it is not impossible to change, but it can be difficult. The place to begin changing is in the little actions of everyday life. Becoming aware that one is making choices in those actions may be the first challenge. Once aware, a person has a chance to try to make changes.

Christian Virtues: Habits for Living Out the Law of Love

In his life on earth, Jesus showed by his example and teaching the virtues that enable a person to faithfully keep the law of love. No full and comprehensive list of Christian virtues exists. We could probably come up with dozens of virtues that help us lead a Christian life. But here are some key ones, which you may consider in depth in a later course on morality:

Theological virtues. The virtues of **faith**, **hope**, and **charity** are called theological (from *theos* meaning "God") because they are given to us by God, who is their source, and are directly concerned with our relationship with God and our participation in God's divine life.

Cardinal virtues. Four moral virtues are called cardinal (from a word meaning "hinge") because all other moral virtues hinge, or depend, on them. These are **prudence**, **justice**, **fortitude**, and **temperance.** Names for these virtues that may sound more familiar to you are wise judgment, justice, courage, and wholeness.

Other virtues. Among many possible virtues can be listed honesty, respect for persons, compassion, reverence for human life, respect for creation, and peacemaking.

10
How would you answer this question: *What kind of person are you, and what kind of person do you want to become?*

The virtues and vices we develop through our lifetime will be part of our character. And our character will influence our destiny—what finally becomes of us.

For Review

- What is character? What are virtues and vices? Diagram the character cycle and describe how it works.
- Name the theological virtues and the cardinal virtues.

Our Final Destiny

What finally becomes of us? How does it all end? What kind of existence or nonexistence are we meant for after we die? These are questions about our final destiny as human beings.

The Christian answer to these questions is this: In the end we are meant to be united with God in perfect joy and happiness. All those united with God will also be united with one another in a great eternal celebration (the eternal banquet, as it has been called).

Will we *all* end up with God and one another? We do not know. God, who loves us all, would want us all to be united in joy. But human beings, remember, are free. In their lifetime, they can choose to turn away from God and close themselves off from God. Or they can choose to draw closer to God and open up more and more to God's love.

On the day we die, all opportunities to become the person we were meant to be will be over. At death we will at last have completed the character we have been developing for all the years we have lived. We will be who we are, no more and no less. Our character, with all its virtues and vices, is what we will be able to present to God as the sum of our life.

The Last Things

Catholic teaching speaks of four "last things": death, judgment, heaven, and hell. Catholic belief is that every human being at **death** faces God as the person he or she has finally become. This facing God is called **judgment** (in this life we cannot understand what this facing God will be like).

If the person has been closed from God during life and has chosen to turn away from God's love, that person's destiny will presumably be to remain eternally closed off and turned away from God, losing the perfect happiness for

In a page, describe your imaginings of heaven and hell.

which human beings were created. We cannot imagine what that condition is like, but Catholic Tradition calls the experience of the eternal absence of God **hell**. Hell is not a place that God condemns a person to but is a condition that the person has basically chosen as a consequence of her or his own life choices.

If the person chose during life to become open to God's love, and has drawn near to God, then at death that person will be united with God and enjoy perfect happiness eternally. This is **heaven**, and we cannot possibly imagine what it will be like. In Saint Paul's words,

"No eye has seen, nor ear heard,
 nor the human heart conceived,
what God has prepared for those who love him."

(1 Corinthians 2:9)

We are not "sent" to heaven or hell by God, but we "arrive" in heaven or hell as a consequence of how we live our life.

Catholic Tradition holds that some condition of purifying must happen for those who are turned toward God at death but are not yet ready for total union with God because of obstacles they carry from life. This purification is called **purgatory**. We do not know how this purifying takes place; in faith, we trust in God's providential care. But Catholic teaching holds that our prayers for people who have died can help those who at death were not yet ready for union with God.

A Parable of Heaven and Hell

A man spoke with the Lord about heaven and hell. "I will show you hell," said the Lord, and they went into a room which had a large pot of stew in the middle. The smell was delicious, but around the pot sat desperate people who were starving. All were holding spoons with very long handles which reached into the pot, but because the handle of the spoon was longer than their arm, it was impossible to get the stew into their mouths. Their suffering was terrible.

"Now I will show you heaven," said the Lord, and they went into another room identical to the first one. There was a similar pot of delicious stew and the people had the same long-handled spoons, but they were well-nourished, talking and happy. At first the man did not understand. "It is simple," said the Lord. "You see, they have learned to feed each other." (Anonymous, in Cavanaugh, *The Sower's Seeds*, pages 33–34) 📖

The Last Judgment

How will the "whole thing" end—not just our own individual life but the life of all creation? What is the final destiny of the whole world?

The Book of Revelation offers a beautiful, poetic vision of how everything will be transformed when Jesus comes again in glory at the end of time for the Last Judgment. In this passage the "new Jerusalem" is an image of the Reign of God, at last come to fulfillment:

Then I saw a new heaven and a new earth; for the first heaven and the first earth had passed away, and the sea was no more. And I saw the holy city, the new Jerusalem, coming down out of heaven from God, prepared as a bride adorned for her husband. And I heard a loud voice from the throne saying,

"See, the home of God is among mortals.
He will dwell with them as their God;
they will be his peoples,
and God himself will be with them;
he will wipe every tear from their eyes.
Death will be no more;
mourning and crying and pain will be no more,
for the first things have passed away."

(21:1–4)

For Review

- What are the four last things? What is the Catholic understanding of them?
- What is purgatory?
- What is the Catholic belief about what will happen at the end of time?

Be Not Afraid

It is not easy to live out Christian morality in today's world, but then it has never been easy. The law of love requires sacrifice. It goes against the grain of so many of the dominant values of society—and it always has.

We can take heart from some words of a contemporary hymn, "Be Not Afraid." Based on biblical passages from the prophet Isaiah and the Gospel of Luke, the song speaks the sentiments of the ancient Jews and Christians who faced great challenges in living the law of love. Through it all, they knew that God was with them:

If you pass through raging waters in the sea,
you shall not drown.
If you walk amid the burning flames,
you shall not be harmed.
If you stand before the pow'r of hell
and death is at your side,
know that I am with you through it all.

(Chorus)
Be not afraid.
I go before you always.
Come follow me, and I will give you rest.

12
Do you think that eventually everyone will be with God in perfect happiness? Describe in writing why you think as you do.

Epilogue:
A Journey of Discovery

This course has come to an end. You have traveled through the core beliefs, stories, values, and practices of Catholic Christianity. Now what comes after this?

In the next few years of high school, you will have the opportunity to learn in greater depth about many of the subjects covered in this course, which has given you only an overview of Catholicism. The meaning of Catholic Christianity will be fleshed out in your other high school religion courses on the sacraments, morality, social justice, the Bible, prayer, and so on.

It is hoped that you will not only study the Christian faith but also experience it in these next years—in the everyday life of your school as a faith community, in the life of whatever parish or congregation you may belong to, in your family, and with your friends. Faith is not just a matter of the head but of the heart, and the heart is touched by the movement of the Holy Spirit in the happenings of our life.

The Spirit may be at work in a revealing or encouraging conversation with a friend, a teacher, or a parent; in sharing a crushing defeat or a glorious victory with your teammates; in a classroom activity or discussion in which a realization hits home for you. The wind of the Spirit might be rustling through a prayer service or schoolwide liturgy that pulls everyone together in a time of great sorrow or celebration. The Spirit's warmth may be felt in the day-in, day-out friendliness of a school secretary or the wise humor of a custodian.

The Spirit's transforming power might be experienced in a retreat where you are challenged to grow in compassion for others, or in a time of being wonderfully forgiven after making a serious mistake. The Spirit may touch you in a service project in which you discover the ways poor and vulnerable people can show us what is really important in life. The Spirit moves within us as we discover more and more about who we are and what the purpose of our life is.

So this introduction to Catholic Christianity is meant to launch you into a much wider and deeper search for what is true and good and beautiful in life. That search will not end with high school; it will last your whole life. And your search is crucial not only for you but for the whole world.

In a message to the youth of the world, Pope John Paul II called young people the "builders of the twenty-first century." He saw them as longing for a world at peace—not just a world without war but a world of justice and love among persons, communities, and nations. His words can offer encouragement, hope, and challenge as you set off on the journey of finding your own life's meaning:

> Do not be afraid! Do not be afraid of your own youth and of those deep desires you have for happiness, for truth, for beauty and for lasting love! Sometimes people say that society is afraid of these powerful desires of young people and that you yourselves are afraid of them. Do not be afraid! When I look at you, the young people, I feel great gratitude and hope. The future far into the next century lies in your hands. The future of peace lies in your hearts. . . .
>
> For it is true to say that life is a pilgrimage of discovery: the discovery of who you are, the discovery of the values that shape your lives, the discovery of the peoples and nations to which all are bound in solidarity. While this voyage of discovery is most evident in the time of youth, it is a voyage that never ends. . . .
>
> The world needs young people who have drunk deeply at the sources of truth. . . . You must form in yourselves a deep sense of responsibility . . .
>
> So do not be afraid to commit your lives to peace and justice, for you know that the Lord is with you in all your ways.

Index

Italic numbers are references to photos or illustrations.

candles, *257, 262,* 264–265
canonical Scriptures, 182–183, 187
canonized saints. *See* saints
cardinal virtues, 318
Carmelites, 279
Catechism of the Catholic Church, 203
catechumens, 154, 229, 231, 261–262, 264, 265
cathedrals, 215
Catherine of Siena, Saint, *157*
Catholic Worker houses, 232–234, 307
ceremonies. *See* rituals
Chalcedon, Council of, 95
character cycle, 317–318, 319
charity, 318
chastity, 151
cheating, 314
cheerleaders, 43, 221
chief priests, 113, 115, 116
childbirth, 8
children: battered, 223; Bolivian, 114; conscience formation in, 313; dependency of, 21; Jesus and, 104; male, 63; Mexican American, 239–241; poor, *128,* 159, 295–296, *306;* racism of, 29; religion and, 9–10, 56; responsibility of, 312; stories for, 91; time and, 248. *See also* adolescents
choices, 41, 55, 310, 318
Christ. *See* Jesus Christ; Messiah
Christian Brothers, 223
Christian church, 139, 141, 142–144, 145–147, 152–153
Christian denominations, 149, 199, 206, 211, 229, 304
Christian feasts, 251, 266–267
Christian meditation, 281, 286, 288
Christian morality, 85, 295–321
Christian Testament, 169, 172; canon of, 183, 187; contents of, 171, 177–182; first documents of, 141; Tradition and, 200–201; Trinity revealed in, 208. *See also individual books by name;* Gospels
Christmas, 251, 254, 255, 257–259
church councils, 95, 140, 159–160, 203

church images, Body of Christ, 145, 146, 224; People of God, 145, 146; Temple of the Holy Spirit, 145, 146–147, 224
Church of the Annunciation (Nazareth), *97*
circumcision, 63
Clare of Assisi, Saint, 155–157
clergy, 150, *151. See also* Holy Orders, sacrament of; priests
colors, 254
commitment, 27, 28, 126, 214
common good, 26, 306
communal emphasis, 211, 212–214, 215, 236
Communion. *See* Eucharist, sacrament of
Communion of Saints, 162, 163, 215, 291
community life, 20, 26, *148,* 253, 290–291
community prayer, 291–292
conception, 7–8, 11, 13. *See also* Immaculate Conception
confession, *236. See also* Penance, sacrament of
Confirmation, sacrament of, 229–231
Confucian Analects, 169
Conry, Tom, 261
conscience, 311, 312–313
Constantinople, Council of, 95
consumerism, 25–26, 27
contemplation, 288
conversational prayer, 281–282
converts, adult, 154, 229, 231, 261–262, 264, 265
Corinth, 141
Corinthians, First Letter to the, 126, 146, 147, 320
councils, church, 95, 140, 159–160, 203
courage, 318
Covenant, 60, 62, 169; with Abraham, 63; Decalogue and, 300; endurance of, 85; Jesus and, 87; messianic hope and, 79, 82; New, 76; of Sinai, 68, 69, 174; unfaithfulness to, 72, 73, 74
creation, 47
Creation stories, 77, 91, 174, 187, 188
crèches, 257–*258*
creeds, 95, 206–207, 211, 288
criminals, 180
criticism, 29–30. *See also* ridicule

Crucifixion, *115,* 116, *118*–119, 121, 123, 130, 133
Crusades, 155

D

dating, 16
David, King, *71,* 78, 102, 174; dancing by, 287; Joseph of Nazareth and, 97; messianic hope and, 79, 80, 101; successors of, 72
Day, Dorothy, *307*
deacons, 150, 151
Dead Sea Scrolls, *183, 186*
deaf people, 195
death: accidental, 43–44; Christian commitment and, 126; final destiny and, 319; questions raised by, 44–45; Resurrection and, 128, 275; rites for, 239
Decalogue. *See* Ten Commandments
decisions, 41, 55, 310, 318
deicide, 116
democracy, 26
denominations, Christian, 149, 199, 206, 211, 229, 304
Denver, 193–197
destiny, 319–321
Deuteronomy, Book of, 300
developmental tasks, 20–21
devil, 99
Diaspora, 74
Diego, Juan, 216
dignity, 304, 305
disabilities, 18, 237–238
Discalced Carmelites, 279
disease, 28, 81, 104, 157, 185, 238–239
divorce, 129
doctrines, 203–204, 205
dogmas, 203–204, 205
Dome of the Rock (Jerusalem), *150*
Dominicans, 157
Doubting Thomas, 132
drought, 210
drug dealing, 316
drug use, 25, 27, 29, 276

E

Easter: Proclamation, 264; Season, 254, 259, 263, 265–266; Sunday, 122, 251, 254; Vigil, 229, *262, 263,* 264–265

Ecclesiastes, Book of, 249

economic injustice, 25–26, 27, 305–306

ecumenical councils, 95, 140, 159–160, 203

ecumenism, 149

Egypt, 65, 66. *See also* Exodus

Elijah, 73

Elizabeth (mother of John the Baptist), 96

El Salvador, 120, 307

Emmaus, 123, 133

emotions, 19, 23, 35, 52, 53, 54

encyclicals, 203

enemies, 104–105, *301*, 304

Ephesians, Letter to the, 147, 292

Ephesus, 141, *168*; Council of, 95

Epiphany, 257, 259

Epistles, 141, 181, 187. *See also individual Epistles by name*

eternity, 252, 319–321

Eucharist, sacrament of, *9*, 232–234, 290; in Africa, 198; clergy and, *151*, 242; community prayer and, 292; for dying persons, 239; in early church, 140, 148; in Easter Season, 265; at Easter Vigil, 229, 264; Elizabeth Seton and, 158; emotions and, 54; faith and, 133; Hebrew Scriptures and, 169; in Holy Week, 263; Lamb of God and, 130; Last Supper and, *109*, 114; marriage and, 244; martyrs and, 155; Nicene Creed and, 95, 207; requirement of, 213, 266; saints' feasts and, 267; Second Coming and, 143; Seder and, 67; unity through, 146; at World Youth Day, 194, 195

Europe, 157

Evangelists, 178

events. *See* historical events

evil, 49. *See also* sin; suffering

Exile. *See* Babylonian Exile

Exodus, 67, 68, 91; Baptism and, 229; Easter Proclamation on, 264; Eucharist and, 130; forgiven sin as, 172; remembrance of, 111–112, 113, 251; Revelation through, 51, 184; Temptations in the Desert and, 99

Exodus, Book of, 69, 70, 172, 186, 300

Exsultet (Easter Proclamation), 264

Ezekiel, 73, 88

F

faith, 33–57, 323; Eucharist and, 133; in Incarnation, 92; marriage and, 59–60; prayer for, 274; reason and, 211, 214–215; Resurrection and, 125, 131, 132; unity of, 196–197; as virtue, 318. *See also* religion

farmworkers, 239–241

fashion, 26

fasting, 260–261

fear, 274–276, 277, 312

feasts, 251, 266–267

feelings, 19, 23, 35, 52, 53, 54

Felicity (martyr), 154–155

food drives, *139*, 292

foot washing, *262*, 263

forgiveness: in friendship, 23, 172; by Jesus, 105, 119; of parents, 274; through Penance, 235–236; unconditional love and, 270

formal prayers, 281, 288–290

fortitude, 318

Franciscans, 156

Francis of Assisi, Saint, 155–157, 258, 291

Frank, Anne, 56–57

freedom, 23, 55, 69, 190, 315

free will, 311, 312

French kings, 157

friendship: deepening capacity for, 20; disappointments in, 22; discarding of, 27; forgiveness in, 23, 172; lying and, 172; neglect of, 280; qualities of, 23; sacredness of, 242–243, 244; togetherness in, 92, 281; trust in, 23, 39, 274

fruits of the Holy Spirit, 293, 296

Fuller, Buckminster, 18–19

G

Galatians, Letter to the, 293, 296

Galilee, 99, 102, 122

gangs, 223

Garden of Gethsemane, 115

gay people, 185

Genesis, Book of, 19, 77, 315. *See also* Creation stories

Gentiles, 97, 140, 179, 189, 228. *See also* non-Christian religions

Gifts of the Holy Spirit, 231

Gnosticism, 95

God: afterlife and, 319–321; Babylonian Exile and, 74, 75; canon of Scriptures and, 182–183, 187, 190; church beloved by, 146; conflicting worldviews of, 33–34; Covenants with (*see* Covenant); creation by, 77, 91, 174, 187, 188; Crucifixion and, 119, 126; death overcome by, 265–266; evidence for, 46–49; faithfulness of, 243–244; fatherhood of, 102–103; gifts of, 12, 13; grace of (*see* grace); gratitude to, 111–112; human longings and, 24; image of, 19; Israelite worship of, 71; Jeremiah and, 72; love of (*see* love of God); messianic hope and, 79; metaphors for, 36; mystery of (*see* Sacred Mystery); name of, 66–67; prayer to (*see* prayer); prophets and, 73, 88; punishment by, 81; questioning of, 44–45, 129; reconciliation with, 236; reflection on, 30; Reign of (*see* Kingdom of God); Revelation of (*see* Revelation); salvation by (*see* salvation); Samaritan worship of, 81; sexuality and, 308, 309; spirituality and, 279; submission to, 115; Tradition and, 199–200, 201; trust in (*see* trust in God); unfaithfulness to, 70; union with, 31; voice of, 98, 99. *See also* Holy Spirit; Jesus Christ; Messiah; Trinity

godparents, 228, 229

"God question," 46

God's Word. *See* Bible

Golgotha, 118

Good Friday, 119, 260, *262*, 263

good Samaritan parable, 107

Gospel of Life, The (Pope John Paul II), 305

Gospel of the Holy Spirit. *See* Acts of the Apostles

Gospels, 177–180, 186; on behavior, 156; on Crucifixion, 118, 119; on disciples, 101; on miracles, 104; on Passion, 263; on Resurrection, 123–125, 126; on Risen Christ, 122–123, 133; on Temptations in the Desert, 99; on women, 81. *See also* John, Gospel of; Luke, Gospel of; Mark, Gospel of; Matthew, Gospel of

Jesus Christ: Advent of, 254, 255–257, 259; Ascension of, 135–137, 138; Baptism of, 98, 102; belief in, 40; Covenant established by, 169; Creation stories and, 77; Crucifixion of, *115,* 116, *118*–119, 121, 123, 130, 133; decision for, 41; early ministry of, 83, 98–99; on enemies, 304; Francis of Assisi and, 156, 157; Gospel portraits of, 178–180; on Great Commandment, 296–297; Incarnation of, 88–89, 92–94, 95, 203, 219, 257; infallibility of, 205; Jewish heritage of, 57, 61, 87; leper healed by, 185; messianic longing and, 82, 84; mission of, 142, 151, 191; Mosaic Law and, 69, 87, 97, 105; Nativity of, 97, *189;* Ordinary Time teachings on, 254, 259; Paschal Mystery and, 111–133, 224–225, 233; Passion of, 115, 116, *118*–119; on prayer, 102–103, 282, 283, 288; on prodigal son, 165–167; Resurrection of (*see* Resurrection); Revelation through, 51, 55, 87–109, 150, 191; Risen, 135–136, 265; Sabbath and, 76; as sacrament, 224, 233, 234, 290; Second Coming of, 143, 182, 320; Seder and, 67, 113–114; social classes and, 81; on spirit of the Law, 301, 304; spirituality and, 269, 278–279; unity prayer of, 149; virtues and, 318; wilderness period of, 260. *See also* Holy Spirit, Messiah, Trinity

Jewish Dispersion, 74
Jewish Holocaust, 56–57, 84, 85
Jewish Law. *See* Mosaic Law
Jewish Passover. *See* Passover
Jewish Scriptures. *See* Hebrew Scriptures
Jews, 59–85; Catholic Christianity and, 57, 211; Decalogue and, 300, 304; in early church, 139–140, 148, 179; folktale of, 33–34; Gospel of Matthew and, 178, 189; Great Commandment and, 296, 321; Jesus and, 107–108, 112–113, 116, 121; Pentecost and, 138; People of God church image and, 146;

prophets and, 53, 176; restoration hopes of, 101; Revelation to, 51, 150, 259
John, First Letter of, 291, 297
John, Gospel of, 178, 179, 181, 186; on church unity, 149; on Crucifixion, 119; on eternal life, 92; on foot washing, 263; on Holy Spirit, 135; on Last Supper, 109, 114; on love, 297; on Passion, 116; on Risen Christ, 123
John, Saint, 100, 101, 119
John Paul II, Pope, 193–195, 196, *304,* 305, 324
John the Baptist, 98
John XXIII, Pope, *159*–160, 162
Jordan River, *98*
Joseph (husband of Mary), 87, 95, 96–97, 256
Joseph (patriarch), 64–65
Joseph of Arimathea, 119
Joshua, 70
Joshua, Book of, 174
journal writing, 282, 287
Judah (southern kingdom), 72, 74, 78, 79, 174
Judaism. *See* Jews
Judas Iscariot, 100, 115
judges (Israelite leaders), 70–71
Judges, Book of, 174
Judgment Day, 143, 180, 319, 320
justice, 318. *See also* social justice

K

killing. *See* abortion; murder
King, Martin Luther, Jr., *88*
Kingdom of God: apostolic responsibility for, 136; Communion of Saints and, 163; Crucifixion and, 121; future of, 252, 255, 320–321; Holy Spirit and, 191; laity and, 150; Last Supper and, 109; ordained clergy and, 241; parables of, 106–107; People of God church image and, 146; prayer for, 283; proclamation of, 101, 138, 142, 190; Second Coming and, 143; signs of, 104–106
Koran, 51, *169*
Ku Klux Klan, *301*

L

laity, 150
Lamb of God, 130
Last Judgment, 143, 180, 319, 320
Last Supper, 109; betrayal in, 115; Crucifixion and, 119; Holy Thursday and, 251, 263; Paschal Mystery and, 128, 130; Seder and, 111, 112, 113–114
last things, 319–321
Latin America, *198*
Latin language, 258
Law of Moses. *See* Mosaic Law
laypeople, 150
Lazarus, *124*
learning disabilities, 237–238
lectionary, 254
legalism, 105, 108, 301
Lent, 254, 259, 260–262, 265
leprosy, 81, 104
letter of the Law, 105, 108, 301
life experience, 50
life seasons, 249, 267, 277
life states, 150–151
"little deaths." *See* suffering
Little Way, 280
liturgical year, 212, 247–267
Liturgy of the Eucharist. *See* Eucharist, sacrament of
Liturgy of the Hours, 290
Liturgy of the Word, 75, 234, 264
loneliness, 26, 27, 29, 48
longings: of adolescence, 21–22; of Augustine, 31; for God, 40, 208; reflection on, 30; society's "answers" to, 24–29
Lord's Prayer, 103, 288
lost sheep parable, 107
love: centrality of, 190; of enemies, 104–105, *301,* 304; expression of, 53; "God question" and, 48; Great Commandment of, 291, 296–297, 299, 300, 321; hunger for, 108; of Jesus, 109, 114; in Kingdom of God, 101; mystery of, 128; for saints, 215–216; togetherness in, 92

love of God: human existence and, 11; Incarnation and, 92; Jesus on, 103; John Paul II on, 195; marriage and, 244; morality and, 297–298; neglected need and, 295–296; prayer and, 291; rejection of, 91, 319; reminders of, 271; Revelation and, 50; trust in, 39, 115, 119; unconditionality of, 269–270, 274; yearning for, 208

Luke, Gospel of, *178*, 179, 186, 289, 321; on Annunciation, 95–96; on fulfilled prophecy, 83, 87–88; on leprosy, 185; on Nativity, 97, 189; on prayer, 288; on prodigal son, 165–167; on Risen Christ, 133; on trust, 275

Luke, Saint, 135, 181

lying, 172, 314

M

magi, 97, 189, 257, 259

Magisterium, 202–203, 304, 306

Magnificat, 96

Mandela, Nelson, 210

marginalized people: Jesus and, 104, 106; John Paul II on, 195; in Kingdom of God, 105; modern-day saints and, 307; in Nativity story, 189; social teaching on, 213, 306; Virgin Mary and, 96. *See also* homeless people; poverty

Mark, Gospel of, *178*, 179, 186; on Apostles, 100–101; on Crucifixion, 119; on Gethsemane, 115; on Temple cleansing, 112–113

marriage: friendship in, 20, 244; moral teachings on, 308; mutual responsibilities in, 69; promises of, 59–60; sacrament of, 242–245

martyrs, 125, 141, 154–155, 179

Maryknoll order, 201

Mary, Virgin, 87; Annunciation to, 95–96; Assumption of, 144, 204; Crucifixion of Jesus and, 119; devotion to, 215; of Guadalupe, 216; Immaculate Conception of, 96, 204; marriage of, 97; as Model and Mother of Church, 143–*144*; Pentecost and, 137;

Posadas representation of, 256; prayer to, 289

Mary Magdalene, 121–122, 123

Masada, 82

Mass. *See* Eucharist, sacrament of

mass media, 27, 29–30

matriarchs, 64

Matthew, Gospel of, *178*, 179, 186; on anger, 301; on Baptism of Jesus, 98; on Beatitudes, 106; on Great Commandment, 296–297; on Last Judgment, 180; on Last Supper, 113; on Nativity, 95, 97, 189; on Peter, 88; on prayer, 103, 282, 288; on Resurrection, 121–122; on Sabbath, 105

meanness, 318

meditation, 281, 286, 288

memory loss, 61–62

Messiah, 79–80, 101, 107. *See also* Jesus Christ

metaphors, 36, 209

Mexican Americans, 15–16, 239–241

Mexico, 163, 216

Micah, 73

Middle Ages, 215, 257, 258

migrant workers, 239–241

miracles, 104, 121

Miriam, Song of, 172, 186

Missionaries of Charity, 307

missions, 158, 160, 271

Model of the Church (Mary), 143–*144*

monarch butterflies, *163*

monasticism, *52*, 155

monotheism, 64, 150

morality, 85, 295–321

mortal sin, 315

Mosaic Law: Gentile Christians and, 140, 141; giving of, 68–69, 174; Jesus and, 69, 87, 97, 105; Pharisees and, 81, 113; in post-exilic era, 78; Sadducees and, 80. *See also* legalism

Moses, 102, 174; concrete experience of, 184; Israelite idolatry and, 69–70; Revelation to, 50, 66–67, 300

Mother of God and the Church. *See* Mary, Virgin

Mount of Olives, 115

Mount Sinai, *68*

moving (relocation), 14

moving prayers, 287

Muhammad, *169*

murder, 301, 304, 305

music, 30, 287, 292

Muslims. *See* Islam

mystery, 11, 45, 47, 286. *See also* Paschal Mystery; Sacred Mystery

N

National Conference of Catholic Bishops, *202*, 203

Nativity, 97, *189*, 257–258. *See also* Christmas

natural world, 47

nature miracles, 104

Nazareth, 83, 87–88, 95, *97*, 98, 99

Nazism, 49, 56–57, 84, 85

New Jerusalem, 320

New Testament. *See* Christian Testament

New York City, 307

Nicaea, Council of, 95

Nicene Creed, 95, 207

non-Christian religions, 55–56, 64, 149–150, 250–251, 304

North Africa, 154

Northern Hemisphere, 251, 255–256

northern kingdom (Israel), 72, 74, 81, 174

North Vietnam, 201

Nostra Aetate (Vatican Council II), 55–56

O

obedience, 151

Odyssey, The (Homer), *167*, 168

old age, 238

Old Testament. *See* Hebrew Scriptures

oral tradition, 184, 186, 187, 200

ordained clergy, 150, *151*. *See also* bishops; Holy Orders, sacrament of; priests

Ordinary Time, 254, 259

Original Sin, 96, 203, 204, 315

Orthodox Christians, 149, 183, 304

Our Father (Lord's Prayer), 103, 288

P

pain. *See* suffering

Palestine: crucifixions in, 116; Crusades in, 155; early churches in, 140; promise of, 63, 67; struggle for, 70–71

Palm Sunday, *112,* 262–263

papacy, 149; of Avignon, 157; dogmas of, 204; ill behavior of, 217; infallibility and, 205; Magisterium and, 202; social teaching of, 214, 306

papal encyclicals, 203

parables, 89, 106–107, 120, 165–167, 320

parents: conscience formation by, 313; disagreements with, 15–16, 22; divorce of, 129; family planning by, 11, 13; forgiveness for, 274; hypocrisy of, 273; lying to, 314; relationships with, 8, 20, 21–22; separated, 230

parochial schools, 159

Paschal Candle, *262,* 264–265

Paschal Mystery, 111–133; Easter and, 254, 260; Eucharist and, 233; sacraments and, 224–225; time and, 252–253; victory through, 315

Passion of Christ, 115, 116, *118*–119

Passion Sunday, *112,* 262–263

Passover: ancient spring festivals and, 251; camping place for, 115; Easter Proclamation on, 264; history recalled by, 67, 111–112; Paschal Mystery and, 128, 130; Roman rulers and, 113

pastoral letters, 203

patience, 27

patriarchs, 64, 102

Patrick, Saint, 271

Paul, Saint: on baptism, 229; on Body of Christ, 146; conversion of, 140, *181;* epistles of, 141, 181, 187; on gratitude, 285; on heaven, 320; on Holy Spirit, 147, 293; on home worship, 148; on humility, 94; on Jesus, 93; martyrdom of, 141, 179; on Resurrection, 126, 128; Revelation to, 50; on salvation, 150; on song, 292; on trust, 276–277; on Word of God, 168

peasants, 258, 307

Penance, sacrament of, 194, 235–236. *See also* repentance

Pentateuch, 173–174

Pentecost, 137–138, 139, 265–266

"people of the Book," 77

Perpetua (martyr), 154–155

persecution, 125, 141, 154–155, 179

Persian Empire, 78, 79

personal experience, 50. *See also* individualism

personal faith. *See* faith

personal God, 208

Peter, First Letter of, 146

Peter, Saint: in Acts, 181; calling of, 100–101; confession by, 88, 94; martyrdom of, 141, 179; papacy and, 149, 157, 202; Risen Jesus and, 122, 123, 133; sermon by, 138, 139

Peter, Second Letter of, 92

petitions, 281, 282–283

pharaohs, 65, 66, 67, 111

Pharisees, 81, 82, 105, 113, 165

Philippi, 141

Philippians, Letter to the, 94, 188, 276–277

Pilate, Pontius, 115–116

pilgrims, 193–197, 205, 216, *256*

plague, 157

play, 248

pollution, 29

polytheism, 64

Poor Clares, 156

popes. *See individual popes by name;* papacy

popularity, 25, 27, 93

Posadas, Los, 256

poverty: in Americas, 216; in divided kingdom, 72, 78, 176; in Guatemala, 161; of migrant workers, 240; modern-day saints and, 307; of prodigal son, 165–166; relief of, *139,* 140, 292; in Roman era, 81; social teaching on, 213, 306; vow of, 151

praise, 281, 284–285

prayer, 280–293; "Breastplate of Saint Patrick," 271; conversational, 281; for the dead, 320; formal, 281, 288–290; on Good Friday, 263; at Guadalupe shrine, 216, *217;* Hail Mary, 289; for healing, 238–239; Jesus on, 102–103, 282, 283, 288; in

Lenten season, 261; Lord's, 103, 288; meditation, 281, 286, 288; of Muslims, *150;* as Penance, 236; petitional, 281, 282–283; Rosary, 194, 215, 289; Serenity, 13; of Spanish saints, 279; of teenagers, 53, 230, 231, 272–274, 276, 278, 283; of thanksgiving, 281, 284–285

pregnancy, 28

prehistoric humans, 48

prejudice, 29, 292

priests: baptism by, 229; confession to, *236;* Eucharist served by, 233, 234; foot washing by, 263; Jewish, 113, 115, 116; ordination of, 241–242; sick anointed by, 238; vestments of, 254

prisoners, 180

private prayer, 290, 291

prodigal son parable, 165–167

Promised Land. *See* Palestine

prophetic books, 176

prophets, 53, 91; divided kingdom and, 72–73; Jesus as, 88; on Messiah, 79; warnings by, 74

Protestant Christians, 95, 149, 183, 254, 304

Protestant Reformation, 158, 159

prudence, 318

Psalms, Book of, 175; Psalm 22, 119; Psalm 23, 275; Psalm 46, 286; Psalm 100, 284; Psalm 137, 75

puberty, 14, 17

purgatory, 320

pyramids (Giza, Egypt), *66*

Q

Qumran (Jordan), *183*

Qur'an, 51, *169*

R

racism, 29, 292

reason, 47, 200, 208, 211, 214–215

Rebekah, 64

Reconciliation, sacrament of, 194, 235–236. *See also* repentance

reflection, 30

Reformation, 158, 159

Reign of God. *See* Kingdom of God

relaxation, 286

Acknowledgments (continued)

The scriptural quote on page 301 is from the New American Bible with revised New Testament. Copyright © 1986, 1991 by the Confraternity of Christian Doctrine, 3211 Fourth Street NE, Washington, DC 20017. All rights reserved.

All other scriptural quotations in this book are from the New Revised Standard Version of the Bible. Copyright © 1989 by the Division of Christian Education of the National Council of the Churches of Christ in the United States of America. All rights reserved.

The facts about the population of the earth on page 7 are reprinted from *Reader's Digest 1982 Almanac and Yearbook,* by the Reader's Digest Association (Pleasantville, NY: Reader's Digest Association, 1982), page 200. Copyright © 1982 by the Reader's Digest Association.

The excerpt by John Hockenberry on page 18 is from *Moving Violations: War Zones, Wheelchairs, and Declarations of Independence* (New York: Hyperion, 1995), page 69. Copyright © 1995 by John Hockenberry. Reprinted with permission by Hyperion.

The statistic on page 28 about the teen pregnancy rate in the United States is from "Teen Sex," by Douglas Besharov with Karen Gardiner, *American Enterprise,* January-February 1993, no page.

The quote by Augustine on page 31 is reprinted from *The Confessions,* Book I, 1.

The Jewish folktale on pages 33–34 is adapted from *Storytelling: Imagination and Faith,* by William J. Bausch (Mystic, CT: Twenty-Third Publications, 1984), page 72. Copyright © 1984 by William J. Bausch.

The excerpt on page 40 is from *Taking Flight: A Book of Story Meditations,* by Anthony de Mello, SJ (New York: Doubleday, 1988), pages 62–63. Copyright © 1988 by Gujarat Sahitya Prakash. Used by permission of Doubleday, a division of Bantam Doubleday Dell Publishing Group.

The prayers by Alaine Gherardi on page 50, by Michael Elmer Bulleri on page 221, by Megan O'Malley on page 274, by Kaitlyn Pratt on page 278, by an anonymous student on page 283, by an anonymous student on page 284, and by Grecia Mercedes on page 292 are from *More Dreams Alive: Prayers by Teenagers,* edited by Carl Koch (Winona, MN: Saint Mary's Press, 1995), pages 80, 86, 75, 59, 30, 89, and 50, respectively. Copyright © 1995 by Saint Mary's Press. All rights reserved.

The facts on page 53 about young people's religious life are from *The Religious Life of Young Americans: A Compendium of Surveys on the Spiritual Beliefs and Practices of Teen-agers and Young Adults,* by the George H. Gallup Institute (Princeton, NJ: George H. Gallup International Institute, 1992), pages 23, 39. Copyright © 1992 by the George H. Gallup International Institute.

The excerpt by Dag Hammarskjöld on page 54 is from *Markings,* translated by Leif Sjöberg and W. H. Auden (New York: Alfred A. Knopf, 1976), page 205. Translation copyright © 1976 by Alfred A. Knopf and Faber and Faber.

The quotes on pages 55–56 from the *Declaration on the Relation of the Church to Non-Christian Religions (Nostra Aetate)* are from *Vatican Council II: The Conciliar and Post Conciliar Documents,* revised edition, edited by Austin Flannery, OP (Northport, NY: Costello Publishing Company, 1988), page 739, number 2. Copyright © 1975, 1984, 1987 by Harry J. Costello and Rev. Austin Flannery.

The quote by Anne Frank on pages 56–57 is from *The Diary of a Young Girl: The Definitive Edition,* edited by Otto H. Frank and Mirjam Pressler, translated by Susan Massotty (New York: Doubleday, 1995), pages 261–262. Translation copyright © 1995 by Doubleday, a division of Bantam Doubleday Dell Publishing Group. Used by permission of Doubleday, a division of Bantam Doubleday Dell Publishing Group.

The excerpts from the Rite of Marriage on page 59, from the Rite of Baptism on page 229, and from the Rite of Confirmation on page 231 are from *The Rites of the Catholic Church,* volume 1, study edition, by the International Commission on English in the Liturgy (ICEL) (New York: Pueblo Publishing Company, 1990), pages 727, 100, and 330, respectively. The English translation of the Rite of Marriage is copyright © 1969 by the ICEL. The English translation of the Rite of Christian Initiation of Adults is copyright © 1974 by the ICEL. The second edition of the English translation of the Rite of Confirmation is copyright © 1975 by the ICEL.

The excerpt by Marian Dolores Schumacher, MM, on page 114 is reprinted from "Missioner Tales," *Maryknoll,* July 1992, page 25.

The excerpt by Tara Coohill on page 117 is from "Different but the Same," *Maryknoll,* June 1994, pages 37–38. Used with permission.

The quote by Oscar Romero on page 120 is reprinted from "Remembering Romero," *Maryknoll,* March 1995, page 59.

The excerpt on page 129 by a student from La Salle High School, Pasadena, California, and the excerpt on page 316 by a student from Saint Frances Academy, Baltimore, Maryland, are from *I Know Things Now: Stories by Teenagers 1,* edited by Carl Koch (Winona, MN: Saint Mary's Press, 1996), pages 94–95 and 46–47. Copyright © 1996 by Saint Mary's Press. All rights reserved.

The excerpts from the Mass on pages 130, 233, and from the Easter Proclamation on page 264 are from the English translation of the Roman Missal, copyright © 1973 by the ICEL, and from the English translation of the Rite of Holy Week, copyright © 1972 by the ICEL. Used with permission. All rights reserved.

The population statistics on page 142 are from the *1995 Catholic Almanac* (Huntington, IN: Our Sunday Visitor, 1995), page 368. Copyright © 1995 by Our Sunday Visitor.

The excerpts on page 148 are from "Good Faith Comes in Small Communities," by Carol Schuck Scheiber, *U.S. Catholic,* April 1991, pages 32 and 34–35, 33–34, 36, 38. Reprinted by permission from U.S. Catholic, published by Claretian Publications, 205 West Monroe Street, Chicago, IL 60606.

The excerpts by Jerry Daoust on pages 193–195 and the excerpts by youth and by John Paul II on page 195 are from "World Youth Day Demonstrated the Unity of Youth," *The Courier* (Diocese of Winona, MN), September 1993, pages 11–12, 13; and 10. Used with permission.

The quote by Mev Puleo on page 196 is from "Denver's Divine Olympics," by Charles Dittmeier, *Maryknoll,* December 1993, page 8.

The excerpt about Catholic Tradition on page 199 is from *The Emergence of the Catholic Tradition (100–600),* volume 1 of *The Christian Tradition: A History of the Development of Doctrine,* by Jaroslav Pelikan (Chicago: University of Chicago Press, 1971), page 9. Copyright © 1971 by the University of Chicago Press.

The excerpt by Nhuan Nguyen on page 201 is quoted from "Bread upon the Waters," by Margaret Gaughan, *Maryknoll,* October 1993, page 16.

The Apostles' Creed on page 207 and the Ten Commandments on pages 300 and 302–303 are reprinted from the *Catechism of the Catholic Church,* by the Libreria Editrice Vaticana, translated by the United States Catholic Conference (USCC) (Washington, DC: USCC, 1994), pages 49–50 and 496–497. English translation copyright © 1994 by the USCC—Libreria Editrice Vaticana.

The excerpt by Kevin LaNave on page 213 is from "Nurturing Prophets: Educating Youth in Social Justice," *Today's Catholic Teacher,* August–September 1995, page 36. Used with permission.

The excerpts on page 216 are from "Pilgrims to Guadalupe," by Kevin Thomas, MM, *Maryknoll,* January 1994, pages 51, 52, 53. Used by permission.

The excerpt on page 223 is adapted from *The San Miguel Messenger,* volume 1, issue 5, November 1995.

The excerpt from *Los Posadas* on page 256 is from "Celebrating Advent in Your Home," by Kathryn A. Schneider and Robert M. Hamma, *Catholic Update,* November 1991.

The excerpt on page 261 is from the hymn "Ashes," by Tom Conry. Copyright © 1978 by New Dawn Music, 5536 NE Hassalo, Portland, OR 97213. Used with permission. All rights reserved.

The excerpt on pages 264–265 by Sandra DeGidio is from "The Liturgical Year: How Christians Celebrate Time," *Catholic Update,* November 1995. Used with permission.

The quote by Saint Patrick on page 271 is from *The Saint Book: For Parents, Teachers, Homilists, Storytellers and Children,* by Mary Reed Newland (New York: Seabury Press, 1979), page 49. Copyright © 1979 by Seabury Press.

The letters to God by young people on pages 272–273 and 276 are used with permission of Michael Dowd, who does youth retreat ministry, 34 Winsor Way, Weston, MA 02193.

The poem by Teresa of Ávila on page 279 is from volume 3 of *The Collected Works of St. Teresa of Ávila,* translated by Kieran Kavanaugh and Otilio Rodriguez (Washington, DC: ICS Publications, 1985), page 386.

Copyright © 1985 by the Washington Province of Discalced Carmelites, ICS Publications, 2131 Lincoln Road NE, Washington, DC 20002.

The prayer by Ignatius of Loyola on page 279 is from *The Spiritual Exercises of Saint Ignatious Loyola,* translated by Elisabeth Meier Tetlow (Lanham, MD: University Press of America, 1987), page 79. Copyright © 1987 by the College Theology Society, University Press of America.

The excerpt by Thérèse of Lisieux on page 280 is from the *Autobiography of St. Thérèse of Lisieux,* translated by Ronald Knox (New York: P. J. Kenedy and Sons, 1958), page 289. Copyright © 1958 by P. J. Kenedy and Sons; copyright renewed.

The Prayer of Saint Francis on page 291 is quoted from *The Fire of Peace: A Prayer Book,* compiled and edited by Mary Lou Kownacki, OSB (Erie, PA: Pax Christi USA, 1992), page 8. Copyright © 1992 by Pax Christi USA.

The excerpt by Pope John Paul II on page 305 is from *The Gospel of Life (Evangelium Vitae),* number 95, as quoted in *Origins,* 6 April 1995, page 721.

The excerpt on page 313 is from *There Are No Children Here: The Story of Two Boys Growing Up in the Other America,* by Alex Kotlowitz (New York: Doubleday, 1991), pages 151–152. Copyright © 1991 by Alex Kotlowitz. Used by permission of Doubleday, a division of Bantam Doubleday Dell Publishing Group.

The parable on page 320 is quoted from *The Sower's Seeds: One Hundred Inspiring Stories for Preaching, Teaching, and Public Speaking,* by Brian Cavanaugh, TOR (Mahwah, NJ: Paulist Press, 1990), pages 33–34. Copyright © 1990 by Brian Cavanaugh. Used by permission of Paulist Press.

The excerpt from the song "Be Not Afraid," by Robert J. Dufford, SJ, on page 321 is copyright © 1975, 1978 by Robert J. Dufford and New Dawn Music, 5536 NE Hassalo, Portland, OR 97213. Used with permission. All rights reserved.

The excerpt from Pope John Paul II's 1985 World Day of Peace message, quoted on page 324 and the back cover, is reprinted from "Youth, Builders of the Twenty-first Century," *Origins,* 10 January 1985, pages 493, 495, 496. Used with permission.

Photo Credits

We appreciate the hundreds of students from Catholic high schools around the United States who submitted their artworks and photography for possible use in this text. Unfortunately we could not use all the submitted works. The following students' works appear on the pages indicated: Lane Barham, page 21; Brandon Canepa, page 128; Michael Caudill, page 228; David Christianson, page 8; Amy Cooper, page 214; Saribel Daza, pages 74, 115; Holly Esposito, page 76; Sean Finley, page 84; Mary Gattas, page 45; Christine Grier, page 149; Lisa Huebner, page 144; Sarah Johnstone, page 105; Regina Kwan, page 131;

Jaime Maiorano, page 29; T. J. Meeks, pages 93, 108, 224; Carina Mo, page 174; Lisa Munzenrider, pages 161, 199; Emmy Murray, page 16; Sara Nicol, page 100; Julie Oattis, page 67; Rita O'Donnell, page 42; Mikki Parker, page 196; Stephanie Przedwiecki, page 47; Martin Rodriguez, pages 14, 288, 289; Brant Roshau, pages 152, 250, 267, 284; Nate Scatena, pages 91, 119, 270; Brian N. Smasal, page 265; Kelly Snook, page 38; Lainie Tiscia, page 146; Jessica Wagner, page 298; Melanie Weickel, page 57; Amy Westerman, pages 44, 48; Eleanor White, page 235; Lisa Wojtowicz, page 243; Anthoney Woodard, page 78; Beth Zunkiewicz, page 80

Front cover photos: © 1997 PhotoDisc, Inc.

Back cover photo of door: © 1997 PhotoDisc, Inc.

Back cover photo of night sky: © Photosynthesis, International Stock Photo

Mike Agliolo, International Stock Photo: pages 142, 197

Wayne Aldridge, International Stock Photo: page 137

George Ancona, International Stock Photo: page 77

APF, Bettmann: page 305

Associated Press, Wide World Photos: page 301

James Baca, *Denver Catholic Register:* page 304

Scott Barrow, International Stock Photo: pages 187, 220

Laurie Bayer, International Stock Photo: page 92

Sr. Margaret Beaudette, SC: page 158

The Bettmann Archive: page 88

Bridge Building Images, P.O. Box 1048, Burlington, VT 05402: page 156

Cleo Freelance Photography: pages 102, 154

James David, International Stock Photo: page 127

Gail Deham: page 130

Editorial Development Associates: pages 98, 122

Chad Ehlers, International Stock Photo: pages 52, 318

Bob Firth, International Stock Photo: pages 129, 184

Giraudon, Art Resource, New York: page 182

Vincent Graziani, International Stock Photo: pages 27, 141

Anne Hamersky: pages 145 (left), 147, 238, 262 (bottom)

Jack Hamilton: pages 24, 25, 60 (top)

Scott Hanrahan, International Stock Photo: page 176 (right)

C. M. Hardt: page 18

Hollenbeck Photography, International Stock Photo: page 99

© 1991 by Marion C. Honors: page 166

Michael Howell, International Stock Photo: page 209

ITP, International Stock Photo: page 150

Sharon Jacobs, International Stock Photo: page 249 (foreground)

Ted Kean, *Denver Catholic Register:* page 194 (bottom)

Shirley Kelter: page 160

Ward Klesenski, International Stock Photo: page 253

Peter Langone, International Stock Photo: page 26

Jean-Claude Lejeune: page 226

Erich Lessing, Art Resource, New York: pages 31, 63, 68, 69, 70, 83, 124, 133, 167, 168

Ken Levinson, International Stock Photo: pages 89, 249 (background)

Ryan Lew, International Stock Photo: page 248

Michael Philip Manheim, International Stock Photo: page 61

Lou Manna, International Stock Photo: page 232

Roger Markham-Smith, International Stock Photo: page 136

Marquette University: page 307 (top)

Buddy Mays, International Stock Photo: page 97

John Michael, International Stock Photo: page 230

Sr. Ramona Miller, OSF: page 211

Nicaraguan Cultural Alliance: pages 189, 287

© 1997 PhotoDisc, Inc.: pages 4–5, 28, 49, 60 (bottom), 65, 66, 106, 113, 123, 126, 212, 221, 240, 310, 314, 315, 316, 324

© Photosynthesis, International Stock Photo: pages 10, 321

Gene Plaisted, The Crosiers: pages 23, 37, 51, 108–109, 143, 145 (right), 148, 151, 178, 227, 229, 234, 236, 242, 254, 258, 262 (left), 264

Barry Pribula, International Stock Photo: page 173

Z. Radovan, Jerusalem: pages 170–171, 183, 186

Reuters, Corbis-Bettmann: page 306

Reuters, Gary Caskey, Archive Photos: page 194 (top)

Rae Russel, International Stock Photo: page 222

Ron Sanford, International Stock Photo: pages 163, 176 (left)

San Miguel Center, Chicago: page 223

Gian Luigi Scafriotti, International Stock Photo: page 293

Scala, Art Resource, New York: pages 71, 95, 181

James L. Shaffer: pages 9, 17, 20, 43, 50, 72, 109, 112, 118, 140, 206, 233, 244, 252, 256, 260, 276 (left), 290, 291, 296

Vernon Sigl: pages 40–41, 56, 251

Skjold Photographs: pages 121, 190, 191, 237, 278, 283, 300

Suzanne Smith, Liaison International: page 30

Sonia Halliday Photographs: page 169

Wayne Sproul, International Stock Photo: page 231

Bill Stanton, International Stock Photo: pages 46, 198, 204, 205

Stockman, International Stock Photo: page 82

Johnny Stockshooter, International Stock Photo: pages 36, 64

Robert J. Stottlemyer, International Stock Photo: page 104

Scott Thode, International Stock Photo: page 297

Jay Thomas, International Stock Photo: pages 280, 292–293

Kevin Thomas, MM, Maryknoll: page 217

Bill Tucker, International Stock Photo: page 35

UPI, Bettmann Newsphotos: page 307 (left)

UPI, Corbis-Bettmann: pages 159, 307 (right)

Michael Ventura, International Stock Photo: page 200

Visual Reporter, International Stock Photo: page 55

Suzanne Vlamis, International Stock Photo: page 261

Bill Wittman: pages 125, 139, 162, 203, 208, 239, 257, 262 (right), 272, 275, 276–277, 281, 285, 299, 309, 311, 312–313, 319

Bobbe Wolf, International Stock Photo: page 202